A
Rowman and Littlefield
Library Edition

GREAT ECONOMISTS IN THEIR TIMES

By Broadus Mitchell

About the Editor

Broadus Mitchell is Visiting Professor of Social Science in Hofstra University, assigned to New College of Hofstra. He is Emeritus Professor of Economics in Rutgers University, and previously taught economics in Johns Hopkins University, Occidental College, and New York University. Of the several volumes of which he is author or co-author the latest are *Alexander Hamilton* (Macmillan, 2 vols., 1957, 1962) and (with Louise P. Mitchell) *A Biography of the Constitution of the United States* (Oxford University Press, 1964).

About the Book

It treats selected economic thinkers, from the mercantilist era to the present, in relation to their environment. An introductory chapter supplies links between them.

GREAT ECONOMISTS IN THEIR TIMES

By
BROADUS MITCHELL
New College, Hofstra University

1966

LITTLEFIELD, ADAMS & CO.
Totowa, New Jersey

CONTENTS

CONTENTS

FOREWORD

The aim of this book is to present significant economic thinkers, each in the context of his environment, on which he gave a report. Ideas are inseparable from lives; principles and policies belong, after all, to persons. It is hoped that the doctrines reviewed will be readily understandable when we see how they sprang from prevailing circumstances. This slant allows us to appreciate progress. We are less apt to condemn shortcomings of analysis in, for example, the seventeenth century, when we keep in mind the stage of economic development which provoked what then seemed to be appropriate beliefs. "Other men, other minds" is an accepted saying, but changed notions were linked to the passing scene.

Any acquainted reader may prefer that different writers had been chosen. Doubtless most will agree that those included made memorable contributions, but should not this or that one have been substituted, or the list been extended? Given the plan of the book, it was necessary to limit the selection. Some not separately treated are briefly described incidentally. While this cannot pretend to be a history of economic thought, the personalities and periods discussed are connected in the summary offered in the Introduction.

B.M.

Hempstead, New York
February, 1966

INTRODUCTION

A Summary View

We say that one thinker or reformer was "ahead of his time," or that another writer or ruler was "behind the times." We mean that ideas about conduct are acceptable at particular periods. Truth or what is useful in human relations is time-bound. It is also place-bound. Few guides for people in their dealings with others are permanent or universal. In society the only certainty is change. Dogma, hard and fast maxims, yield to development or degeneration. Such and such a proposition "is no longer valid," or "may one day be the case."

This is an uncomfortable notion. We should like to arrive at a conviction and expect to preserve it. Weak, buffeted mortals on the sea of life, we want to cling to a rock of ages. We crave a creed. Maybe our principles are more honored in the breach than in the observance, but, inconstant ourselves, we treasure the constant ideal. If we lapse, we may repent. Faith is our consolation.

Alas, in our yearning for fixity—in economics, government, and social ethics anyhow—we are doomed to disappointment. Eternal verities are few. Rather, we are confronted by choices, better or worse. Principles give way to policies. "Right" is a relative term. The good becomes the expedient. Not that we may manufacture excuses at every turn, or continually embrace what is easiest; we must conform our behavior to the "foreseeable future." We follow our noses, but noses should not be so stubby as not to be able to sniff the wind.

The pages that follow explore the history of economic ideas. The emphasis is on alteration, progression. Lest we be accused of denying dogma only to make of that a new dogma, we hasten to agree to a number of conclusions which appear to be enduring. One is that we set less value on a single unit of what is abundant compared to our wants than on the same unit of a smaller total stock. This is the principle, the reliable principle, of diminishing utility. When we have satisfied our more insistent needs, or desires, or fancies, continued indulgence pleases us less and less.

Also in the realm of valuation, one is apt to prize the present, or present goods, more highly than the future or goods to be obtained in the future. Numbers of reasons for this may be cited, principally the uncertainties of life. This preference for the present explains the phenomenon of interest. "Gresham's law" is familiar: it is that "bad money drives out good money." We thrust into circulation media of exchange which are inferior or suspect, and keep or hoard coins or paper currency which is genuine or superior.

Production, and hence enjoyment in consumption, is aided by specialization. This is simply to say that skill is preferable to bungling. Division of labor, or assigning parts of a task to different workers who learn to be swift and accurate in their separate functions, makes for efficiency in the whole operation. Of course their distinct efforts must be organized and combined. A connected observation is that the economy of specialization is limited by the extent of the market, or of the demand for the product. It would be foolish for editors, reporters, correspondents, printers, stereotypers, pressmen to turn out newspapers for ten readers; tens of thousands are required to justify the trouble and expense.

Another dependable observation is that a peculiar advantage in production furnishes a non-competitive or differential return. Land or other natural resource limited in supply, if of superior fertility or location, yields a rent. Other monopolies or near-monopolies do the same.

If these may be called rules or invariable results, they are by the same token virtually self-evident, or truisms. When we go beyond these axioms, and perhaps a few more, generalization becomes dangerous. It is risky to attribute kinds of behavior to "human nature" and assume that it is dependable. Self-interest is not the mainspring of economic activity among all peoples or under all circumstances. Peace is not necessarily the best means to prosperity or social progress. The benefits of free trade are contingent on circumstances. The wisdom of minimal governmental intervention in the economy is subject to contradiction. The desirability of taxation according to capacity to pay encounters dispute. More broad canons might be named, only to provoke exceptions.

Economic thought is therefore a stream, meandering, doubling back upon itself, now widening, now narrowing. What is the secret of its course? The most revealing answer lies in experience. It consists in a succession of prescriptions considered to be serviceable for the time and place. It cannot be a theology, but is a teleology, a description of aims. It is not a foreordained system, but a shifting scene.

If what we have said meets approval, then we must know something of the lives of those who have contributed to economic understanding and direction. The environment and experiences of a thinker go far to explain his teachings. The most abstract speculation or analysis is inseparable from the man in his time. The history of economic thought—or philosophy generally—has not always been treated in this fashion. Rather, doctrines were recounted, with authors' names appended. The exposition was hollow. True, one surmise or contention followed another, as expansion, correction, or refutation. But why? Serious writers were not consulting their immortal minds, each in a vacuum. What he had to say was prompted by what he saw, or what he was a part of. Many who contributed significantly began with little or no knowledge of what others had written, and only after they became involved did they acquaint themselves with the literature. Each was making a report and comment on the environment in which he moved. Often, to be sure, he put his observations in general terms, rationalized his impressions, spoke in the large. But the impetus was apt to come from his situation, his own and that of the community.

This is illustrated by a few striking examples among many that might be given. Adam Smith, the Scots philosopher, saw a society irked by mercantilist and indeed feudal restrictions. Regulation had become frustrating. Like the

> . . . monk of Siberia,
> Whose existence grew drearier and drearier,
> He burst forth from his cell, with a hell of a yell . . .

declaring for freedom, a fair field for individual initiative. Smith repulsed government, celebrated business enterprise. He carried a crusade which went far.

Seventy-five years later industrial capitalism, with splendid accomplishments, was also guilty of cruel oppressions. The workers, indeed much of society, demanded reform, and not a few cried for revolution. The result was a resort to a degree of government regulation of hours and wages of workers, industrial combinations, and commercial practices. These mild correctives did not touch the causes of the evil of economic instability which became acute following World War I. The war itself precipitated the Russian Revolution. The Great Depression of the nineteen-thirties produced unexpected public intervention in the economy of the United States, and Britain emerged from World War II a semi-socialist society.

We offer here a brief running account of developments in practice which prompted changes in economic doctrine. Schools of thought amount really to a succession of interpretations of what was happening in each period. Of course, also, ideas and advocacy of what seemed appropriate influenced events. History has been a combination of matter and mind. Nor are stages of social evolution, both in action and in explanation, to be sharply defined. They blend into one another, with a shadow land of old and new marking the transition. A certain type of behavior in commerce and industry continued to recede while novel modes were emerging. Similarly, some observers clung to former impressions, while others ran forward to urge views that they believed must fit the future. So we get a rainbow, the vivid bands joined by vaguer, mixed colors.

The mercantilists (mostly from the sixteenth to the eighteenth centuries) made up, loosely, the first school of economic opinion. They were spokesmen of the national states which superseded the local rule of manorial lords, merchant and craft guilds of the towns, and petty political and military chieftains. The national states required unity and power, which meant liquidating the internal dissensions of feudalism. Capitalism, in finance and commerce far more than in manufactures, appeared. Trade centers clustered on the western seaboard of Europe. Geographic discovery invited to wider markets and colonization. The national states—Spain, Portugal, Holland, France, England—would promote larger-scale economic operations. Their object was the prosperity and strength, not of municipalities and predatory potentates, but of the whole kingdom. The mercantilists used many of the methods of those they worked to supplant. They were exclusive and selfish, but now the monopolies were fostered by national governments, not by competing groups within the country. The process was one of forced coalescence, building on ampler credit, navigation, and internal communications.

At first the idea was to enrich the monarch by drawing precious metals into his coffers, or at least into the country. Exploiting mines at home or finding them in the colonies were the simplest means. If these sources of gold were lacking, then a favorable balance of trade would compel foreign countries to pay precious metals for the excess of goods which they took. To restrict imports and conserve money, duties were levied at the national frontiers. These unified tariffs were to replace the multiplicity of internal tolls of towns and "robber barons" that victimized merchants on roads and rivers.

This mercantilist identification of wealth with gold and silver, never as crude as here suggested, gradually gave way, in different countries at different periods, to wiser policies for insuring the state a commanding position among its neighbors. A large, healthy, industrious, thrifty population, engaged in a variety of forms of production—agriculture, commerce, and manufactures—would render the kingdom self-sustaining. Men for armies and navies could be readily recruited for the wars always in the background, often in the foreground, or mercantilists' methods.

We must not suppose that these aims were prosecuted to completion. France, under Colbert, the persevering minister of Louis XIV, weakened the local guilds, promoted shipping, fisheries, and national industries, and made a beginning on a single tariff frontier. Queen Elizabeth I of England, in the Statute of Apprentices and Artificers, 1562–3, standardized and made compulsory the most useful regulations of labor. She chartered trading companies to extend England's commercial and political ambitions. But the national states were feeble in administration, a function of central government that had only begun to develop. The central authority had to rely for enforcement of its decrees on the very local antagonistic monopolists it was trying to discipline. Wars squandered the substance so anxiously mustered.

Mercantilist aims were not realized before the system developed its own abuses. Spain, depending on her golden galleons, was the most naïve offender. France long persisted in controls which hampered more than they helped, so that she was not ready for the breakthrough of private initiative which brought the Industrial Revolution first to Britain. But in Britain too the fetish of a favorable trade balance, with a variety of auxiliary restraints, lingered to invite Adam Smith's historic attack in his *Wealth of Nations* of 1776.

Individualism, private profit-seeking enterprise rebelled against governmental hobbles. Capital was accumulating in the hands of merchants, money-lenders, even of manufacturers. They were restless to be free of official curbs, felt they could go it alone without public protections. French philosophers (the physiocrats) were among the first, in the middle of the eighteenth century, to proclaim a new gospel of no controls over economic life. The law of nature, "let things take their own course," or *laissez faire*, was cried up to displace the interfering maneuvers of royal ministers. Public solicitude would find its aims best served by trusting to the selfish prompting of every man seeking his own interest. Private vices (as the mercantilist anxious mamas saw them) were in fact public virtues.

The Scots scholar, Adam Smith, previously converted to the new spirit, improved on his friends, the physiocrats. Dealing Samson blows against the mercantilists, he came down to cases, citing chapter and verse in his indictment. Years were needed for the preachment of *The Wealth of Nations* to be adopted in practice, but he had substantially discredited the creed of governmental oversight of economic activity. Thenceforth mercantilism was progressively eroded.

Adam Smith proved himself a prophet. No thinker has held such sway in the economic realm for so long. After forces issuing from the Industrial Revolution rendered his tenets inapplicable in this and that and another area, he continued to be the generally accepted authority. His major premise lives in more than name in the western world to this day. Others whom we call the classical economists, French and English (represented in these pages by Malthus and Ricardo), followed in his train. They gave further amplitude and precision to the natural principles of production, exchange, and division of wealth.

But, as we have said, no projection for economic conduct, however timely, but later meets amendment and then refutation, partial or complete. The apostles of let-alone became, in their turn, too dogmatic. They "planted a terrible fixed foot"

against changes in policy demanded by unexpected developments. The theory of individual incentive, declaring itself
universal and absolute, had taken in too much territory. True,
Britain flourished as the mistress of industry and trade, but
new countries in an earlier stage of progress, notably the United
States and Germany, could not profit by Smith's prescription.
In America, hardly was Smith in his grave when the Secretary
of the Treasury, Alexander Hamilton, was urging for his young
nation a selective return to governmental aids and controls in
commerce, manufactures, and credit. Collective wisdom and
resources were necessary to promote private opportunity, and
through private advantage the public benefit. He put forward
protective tariffs, a national bank, and assumption of the
debts of the states by the central government.

These policies of a government-assisted economy were
elaborated by followers of Hamilton, especially by Friedrich
List, a German sojourning in America, and by Henry C.
Carey. They corrected *laissez faire* theory in the light of actual
historical experience. Adam Smith had held that the freedom
and competition which he advised for individuals within a
country was applicable to all men everywhere. Not so, said
these realists. The nation comes between the individual and
the world of individuals. Nations are in different stages of
development, and hence require different economic policies.
What suited Britain, far advanced in industry and commerce,
would retard the progress of more backward economies. The
wealth of a nation consisted not in commodities, as Smith had
taught, but in capacity for rounded production. This demanded
the positive encouragement by government of agriculture, industry, trade, and finance. Lively exchanges between a variety
of producers within a country were preferable, at one stage, to
obtaining goods from outside. Economic principles were not
permanent and universal, but were relative to time and place.
This doctrine, characteristic of the historical school, emphasized,
in place of revealed truth, expedient policies.

Meanwhile, the same idea that economic activity could and
should be deliberately molded was fortified by social reformers.
The first and one of the most influential treated in these pages
was Robert Owen. In the midst of the Industrial Revolution
he was shocked by the human oppression which resulted from
ruthless pursuit of private profit. He strove for a "new moral

world" substituting cooperation for competition, salvation through mutual aid rather than from selfish gain. He boldly threw over the major premise of the classical economists by whom he was surrounded, most of all Malthus, who taught that human misery was well-nigh inescapable.

Other reformers in England and France, whom we may group as Utopian socialists, followed. Their earnest challenge to the existing order was more important than their overidealistic dreams and their impractical experimental communities. They helped prepare the way for a different scrutiny of society by the self-styled "scientific socialists," Marx and Engels. The analysis and advocacy of the latter used the historical approach. They did not cultivate the historical method for its own sake— as did the Italian-Swiss Sismondi and the Germans, Roscher and Hildebrand—but relied on history to enforce their ardent urging of a classless workers' society. They depicted a long development in economic structure which had reached the point where mere owners of the means of production would be dispossessed by the true producers whom they had exploited. In harmony with Darwin's principle of evolution in the world of animate nature, but a decade before Darwin published his *Origin of Species,* Marx and Engels rehearsed alterations in social physiology. The next stage, in their view, was not to be ushered in by wishing and exhortation, but must ensue inevitably from what had gone before. In spite of the certainty, as they contended, of the new order which impended, they sought to forward it by every means of argument. Though their position was inconsistent—denying the function of volition, but appealing to the workers of the world to unite for revolution—their great thesis was historical social change.

In spite of the thunderings of Marx and Engels in the *Communist Manifesto* and *Das Kapital,* and the quieter criticisms of others of the historical persuasion, the classical preoccupation with abstractions rather than institutions did not expire. Instead, the principles which Ricardo, especially, had espoused were liberalized by John Stuart Mill and later were amended by Jevons and a group of Austrian economists. Mill was sincerely alert to the need for deliberate efforts at social betterment. As we shall see, he worked for land reforms congenial to the American advocate, Henry George. At length Mill recanted from the time-honored wage-fund doctrine which had seemed to limit workers' prospects, and his disciples in academic posts in England echoed his concessions.

Jevons and the Austrians, in half-conscious rebuttal of Ricardo's labor theory of value which had been turned to such alarming uses by Marx, gave a new twist to classical doctrine. Value, they contended, instead of depending on cost of production, was mainly fixed by demand. The critical determinant was the subjective estimate of utility at the margin of demand. To pinpoint it, the purchaser who was barely persuaded to buy set the price and, within limits, the supply. This seemed to detour the labor theory of value and consequently the claim for the workers to the whole produce.

The neo-classical school, whose home was England, is represented in the present series of sketches by the Cambridge economist, Alfred Marshall. He may be considered the scientific and spiritual son of John Stuart Mill. He was a perceptive, careful, sympathetic amender of previously received doctrine. His patient review, with needed corrections in the light of later developments in action and thought, made his basic book the staple of instruction for a full generation. He elaborated the economics of equilibrium, or balance of forces; he extended the differential feature of land rent to other elements in distribution of income; and he thoroughly applied the marginal utility exposition of value. Unobtrusively, Marshall used mathematical analysis and graphic representation of economic phenomena. His alterations and additions did more than tidy up the body of classical *laissez faire* explanation, but his changes were on the whole deferential.

The marginal notion was increasingly adopted by American writers at the close of the nineteenth century and far into the twentieth. A notable example was John Bates Clark's treatment of the distribution of wealth. Many of this country's economists, however, were actively concerned with exploring current practices and problems, such as public and corporate finance, business consolidation, transportation, the policy of protection to industry, and developments in labor unionism. Their emphasis on theory, while apt to be conformist, was secondary. Some, though, while perfectly aware of confronting practical problems, were also critical of accepted doctrine. Indeed, trends in practice stimulated them to indict individualist enterprise and to recommend collectivist reforms. Most of these dissenters were not professional economists—for instance, Edward Bellamy with his *Looking Backward* and *Equality*. Others, journalists, disparagingly called "muckrakers," added to the social discontent: especially Henry Demarest Lloyd in *Wealth* vs. *Commonwealth* recounted evidence before public commissions of high-handed destruction of competition by industrial and financial tycoons.

The academic economist who pointed to antisocial conduct in half-serious, half-amused vein was Thorstein Veblen. Instead of tomes of which colleagues were delivering themselves, Veblen ridiculed follies in satirical essays. Sans footnotes, bibliographies, and the rest of customary scholarly apparatus, he vexed the satisfied with his spirited sallies. Beneath his raillery ran a solemn protest against waste in the economy. Earlier than others he separated goats from sheep, pecuniary manipulators from efficient contributors to production. Toward the end of his career he dropped banter and frankly recommended that engineers and technicians, who alone understood and could operate industry, should take over from mere owners, strategists of price and profit whom he considered expendible. He shared many of the ideas of the contemporary English Fabians, but doubtless increased his influence by never accepting the socialist label.

Veblen died on the eve of the Great Depression of the nineteen-thirties which manifested, for all to see, evils Veblen had defined. The masters of business, who had ridden so high, were brought low with everybody else. The money changers were not driven from the temple; they abdicated. The "acquisitive society," as R. H. Tawney had termed it, was in dire distress. Government, most emphatically in America, was obliged to accept unwonted responsibility both for salvage and for fresh enterprise. The "New Deal" of President Franklin Roosevelt, under press of necessity, pushed aside reliance on individual competitive initiative and provided collective means of relief and rescue.

The economist who rationalized intervention of government was the Englishman John Maynard Keynes. Though he had been a favorite pupil of Alfred Marshall, he recognized, and said, that the faith in profit-seeking enterprise to bring about full employment of material and human resources was too optimistic. A capitalist economy, left to traditional autonomous forces, might sink to and remain indefinitely in a dreadful equilibrium at far less than capacity. Unless millions were to starve or be driven to revolt, the organized community—government—must step in to move the wheels of industry and commerce off dead center. Keynes shifted attention from accumulation of the means of production to insuring means of steady, robust consumption. Instead of consumption being limited by production, it was the other way around; production responded to dependable demand. Keynes influenced American antidepression domestic policies, but his contribution was wider. Prevailing economic theory is Keynesian, or, with amendments, post-Keynesian. He was the principal figure in devising world organizations for regulating money and credit.

Keynes was prone to clothe his reasoning in an intricacy of mathematical formulas and graphic representations which make reading him difficult. Many have been so taken with the outward dress of Keynes's propositions that, in their own work, they pursue the shadow for the substance, substitute the method for the genuine matter. But, shorn of its trappings, the moral of Keynes's tale is plain enough, namely, that if human values are to be preserved and promoted in a predominantly capitalist society, there must be a generous participation and oversight by government. Keynes's expedients for capitalist countries in depression owed much to contrast of haphazard reliance with the totally planned economy of the Soviet Union.

1

RICH PEASANT, RICH PRINCE

Jean Baptiste Colbert

To appreciate the career of Jean Baptiste Colbert (1619–1683) we must recall the main changes in Europe during the centuries that preceded him. The story is one of breakdown and rebuilding. The forms, or maybe we should say the images, of union had been two—the Holy Roman Empire, primarily political, and the Roman Catholic Church, mainly religious and cultural. These blended into each other at many points. Always shadowy, each lost influence by degrees. The Holy Roman Empire, successor to Charlemagne's tighter territorial control, dissolved in the rise of national monarchies (for example France, Prussia, the Netherlands) but lingered on to find its finish in the conquests of Napoleon. The Roman Catholic Church received body blows in the Protestant Reformation of the sixteenth century, associated with the names of Luther, Calvin, Zwingli.

As these bonds were weakened, smaller social units were formed. Feudalism parceled out authority to local chieftains. These were originally military lieutenants, owing service to higher lords who in turn were subordinate to a prince holding sway over a larger area. This loose organization invited jealousies and dissensions which resulted in magnifying the powers of nobles and diminishing the sovereignty of kings except in name.

At first the typical agricultural community was the manor. A petty lord might possess a single manor embracing a few hundred acres. He lived in a castle or more modest semi-fortified manor house which was the dominant feature of the rural village. He was supported by serfs who spent about half their time working their little fields and on other days cultivated the lord's farm or "demesne." This was in return for their small holdings of land and for their lord's protection. The manorial landlord was by the same token military leader, governor, judge, alms-giver, and patron of the village priest. The immediate lord might own several manors, and he might be not a lay functionary but an abbot or a bishop.

Besides the agricultural villages there were towns inhabited by merchants and craftsmen. Here life was regulated by guilds, which were economic, fraternal, and religious associations of the different occupations. As the town was a market center, so the tradesmen managed not only their shops, but the public affairs of the place as well. The guildsmen composed both the chamber of commerce, as we should say today, and the town council. Typically the towns were enclosed by walls; these defenses were also symbolic of the exclusiveness of the urban community. The towns were hostile to each other, and toward the surrounding countryside they maintained a mixture of dominance and jealousy. The rural people nearby must bring their produce—food and raw materials—to the town for sale. Here they must buy their manufactured goods. To the extent that townsmen could prevent, peasants were not permitted to make any wares beyond the crudest—say meal, yarns, and beer.

Toward the end of the middle ages these distinct units, rural manors and market towns, little by little lost their separate qualities. The Black Death (bubonic plague) which swept over Europe in the middle of the fourteenth century was a formidable cause of change. With a third to half of the population destroyed, old local customs and rules were broken and only half-heartedly enforced. It was as though an earthquake had shaken manor houses and tumbled town walls. The remaining serfs, now that their labor was in sharper demand, rebelled against repression by their lords. When the lords could not prevent the peasants' escape from the manors, they enclosed the previously open fields with hedges and pastured sheep. Thus the former petty cultivators were expelled.

By hundreds of thousands country people sought the towns. Here, if they were not to starve, they must practice their village crafts of blacksmithing, tanning hides, and weaving coarse cloths. But their intrusion was forbidden by guildsmen fearful of losing their monopoly. Rural immigrants had not served the required apprenticeships. If they worked cheap "in chambers," they were excluded or fined. If they settled in cottages outside the walls, they must smuggle their wares into the town. Large numbers "who had been brought up to the spade and the cart," and could neither stay on the manors or find lodgment in the towns, wandered together through the country, begging, stealing, and rioting.

The earlier frozen structures of society were melting. A prime force in their decay was the extension of commerce which in turn resulted from geographical discovery. The sea route to the Orient brought precious spices, silks, incense, jewels. The finding of Central and South America furnished commodities more precious, silver and gold. The sudden amazing flow of money to Europe through Spain was a potent solvent. As long as trade, depending on barter, was local, local habits of life and local authority could persist. But when universally desired media of exchange were increasingly available, the money economy eroded old ways. Gold loosened the ties of guilds; custom yielded to credit. The European world was undergoing a radical social transformation from status to contract. Enterprise was the death of tradition. The peasant need no longer pay his lord in labor. Money offered him the means of freedom. The walls of the tight little town were breached by merchants who came from afar and would bear its goods to mysterious distances. Just as the cannon demolished feudal strongholds, so currency and credit tore at the defenses of local custom. Goldsmiths abandoned fashioning ornaments and became bankers. Private profit scorned collective obedience. The individual was born.

In the sixteenth, seventeenth, and eighteenth centuries generalizing tendencies, principally economic, called for larger units of political organization. Slowly national states arose to absorb the powers previously belonging to privileged towns and provincial rulers. The intermediate stages were all associated with the extension of trade. Money, credit, and better communications were the means; the opening of distant markets and the exploitation of recent colonial possessions were compelling inducements. The progress that centered authority in the national state was marked by both expansion of the private economy and of political responsibility. Signs of the first alteration were several. The Hanse cities, no longer content to control local trade, reached into foreign parts where, in a loose league, they maintained extraterritorial stations. The Hanse at its height was political and military as well as commercial. Another evidence of coalescence was the tendency toward concentration of important industries, such as textiles, leather, and hardware, in favored areas instead of being scattered and conducted on a petty scale.

Of mixed interest, private and public, were the chartered trading and colonizing companies—Muscovy, East India, West India, Levant, etc. However, these corporate bodies had not the resources to reap the rich rewards offered by mines, plantations, and fisheries. Much less could they support the fleets and armies to defend national frontiers and colonies. Only sovereign power and command of taxes were equal to the demands of warfare and the opportunities of far-flung commerce and colonial government.

The nations of Europe came to maturity at different times depending on geographic, historical, political, and economic causes. Insular England reached unity earliest. Spain, Portugal, the Netherlands, Sweden, Denmark, and Germany followed more or less in that order. Since France was the object of Colbert's labors, we shall be concerned mainly with mercantilism in that country. Unlike Germany, which was fragmented into dozens of minor states, the French king, fortunately, presided over a large territorial domain. But the country was not consolidated politically as it was geographically. The problem was to combat local and provincial authorities and enforce throughout certain major national policies.

Schmoller has made clear that the devices of mercantilism (favorable balance of trade, navigation acts, import duties at the frontiers, reduction of internal tariffs, and so forth) all looked to national strength and integration. While the instruments concerned commerce, industry, currency, and labor, these were plied primarily for political and only secondarily for material purposes. The momentous change in process was that from narrow limits of loyalties, controls, production, and exchange of goods to larger areas, both political and economic. But when national regulation superseded that of the locality, the larger community inherited many disabilities of the smaller units. Just as the medieval town had been egoistic, so the new national states were in jealous rivalry with neighbors, held that one could flourish only at the expense of others, and wished each to be as far as possible self-sufficient. Treaties, military and commercial, had selfish motives only. The idea of mutual benefit from trade and diplomatic relations among numerous nations emerged only tardily. Grotius did not publish an outline of international law until the seventeenth century. We must remember that the League of Nations was not formed until three hundred years later, and that it dissolved in a welter of hostilities, financial, commercial, industrial, and military, conducting to a more monstrous world war. It is easy to believe that the supreme task before mankind is to blend the nations in a global unity.

Colbert followed two ministers of centralizing policies. Richelieu (1624–42) had ideas for strengthening France economically, both internally and in opposition to rival powers; he accomplished something through trading companies, industrial enterprises, and fostered the arts by founding the French Academy. But he was content too largely with prudent maxims and paper projects while he devoted the vitality of the country to suppressing Protestants, humbling nobles, and to the dire drain of the Thirty Years' War. His successor, Mazarin, inherited domestic rebellion and foreign conflict, both of which he quieted at heavy cost. It is remarkable that under Mazarin economic development did not positively recede. In any event when Colbert came on the scene, the monarchy of Louis XIV was at peace and ready for the vigorous housekeeping which was the forte of the new chief minister. Available, if perchance Colbert knew them, were numerous writings setting forth means to profit France, the most notable being Antoine de Montcrétien's *Traicté de l'oeconomie Politique* of 1615.

Jean Baptiste Colbert was born at Reims August 29, 1619. It would be appropriate to subscribe to the tale, favored by Colbert, that he was distantly descended from a Scots nobleman. The French are not lacking in realism where money is concerned, but the economy of the Scotch transcends mere parsimony, as witness men living in Colbert's time—William Paterson, founder of the Bank of England and the Darien Scheme, and John Law, whose ambitions for French finance deserved a better fate. Later Alexander Hamilton's administration of the American Treasury owed not a little to Colbert's example. Whether or not the husbandman of French resources had some drops of Caledonian blood, he had more than a little of the touch. His grandfather and father were merchants; the latter salvaged enough from declining ventures in wine and woolens to purchase a routine office at the Paris Hôtel de Ville. An uncle did better as private banker and seems to have aided Colbert's preferment at the beginning.

The brilliance of Colbert's career cast his early life into shadow. Maybe because his scant schooling omitted the classics, he later counseled that Latin was less desirable than knowledge of geography and history, a recommendation which he amply vindicated. He was apprenticed to merchants in Paris and Lyons and worked for a time as a notary. His first public appointment was under Le Tellier, secretary of state for military affairs. Eight years of zeal in this post won him the title of *conseiller d'état* and marriage to an heiress, Marie Charon.

Of most importance, he earned the confidence of Cardinal Mazarin, who found that Colbert "was born for work to an unbelievable degree." When Mazarin was forced to flee Paris by uprisings of nobles and populace, he left his private affairs—household, management of estates, and lucrative financial ventures—in Colbert's hands. During four or five years Colbert was Mazarin's proxy, an introduction to his later service as Joseph to Louis XIV. No detail was too little for Colbert's watchfulness, nor did he scruple to advise the absent chief minister to promote his own and the public prosperity by founding a company to trade in the Levant. Meantime Colbert did not neglect the interests of himself and his relatives. He became rich enough to lend on occasion to his patron, accumulated offices and honors, and secured soft berths in government and church for brothers, cousins, and friends. When so much was being reaped by chicanery and corruption, why should not a competent man, "loving work as if by nature," amass a fortune and enjoy influence? If his noble Scotch ancestor was a myth, he himself became Baron (later Marquis) de Seignelay and counselor of the king in all his councils.

Mazarin died in 1661. In his will he left Colbert a residence and a recommendation to the king "to use him as he is very useful." Mazarin is reputed once to have said to Louis, "Sire, I owe you everything, but I believe that I am acquitting myself of some of that debt to Your Majesty in giving you Colbert."

This sounds like the encomium of a romantic biographer, but the reality of the benefit to the king may not be doubted.

Louis XIV grieved eager candidates to succeed Mazarin by announcing that he would be his own chief minister. Fouquet, who had been Superintendent of Finance, for some months continued to hope he would step into Mazarin's shoes, but Colbert had demonstrated Fouquet's embezzlements and prepared the way for his condemnation to life imprisonment. In all but war and foreign affairs, which the king managed personally, and sometimes in these areas too, Colbert became the most relied upon servant of Louis.

The king, twenty years younger than Colbert, was like his famous minister in energy of body and mind, in frostiness of manner, and in his determination to make France the dominant power in Europe. But there the similarity ceased. Louis was ludicrously pompous, egoistic, warlike, and extravagant. He was one of the last sovereigns to flaunt belief in the divine right to rule. He made himself absolute, though the boast attributed to him (*L'état, c'est moi,* the state, it is I) was a fabrication. Wherever he roamed and looked in his palace of Versailles (a monstrous indulgence against the pleadings of Colbert), he beamed on portraits and sculptures of himself, all in the spirit of praise (*Le Roi Soleil,* the Sun King; *Le Grand Monarque*). Poor Colbert, charged with finding royal revenues, uttered an inevitable remonstrance: "In regard to expenditures, although they are in no way my concern, I beg Your Majesty to permit me only to say to him, that in war and in peace he has never consulted the amount of money available, in determining his expenditures, a thing . . . so extraordinary that assuredly there is no precedent for it." Did Colbert, a man of genius, demean himself by devotion to Louis' authority and glory? When we remember the spirit of the times and what was expected of even the highest courtier, our answer must be, No. On the other hand, much that admiring historians recorded of Louis' reign was made possible by the resourcefulness of Colbert.

We have chosen Colbert as the symbol of mercantilism because he illustrated, more than any other one statesman, the bundle of policies which we call by that name. Basic was the passion for opulence of the nation, for its own sake and in contrast with other countries inferior in population, industriousness, attraction of the precious metals, and military might. The nation must strive to be self-sufficient, while through a surplus of exports it kept others steadily in its debt. Colonies to furnish raw materials and buy finished products, a busy merchant marine and protecting navy, fisheries to bring in cod and herring and breed up a race of seamen, figured prominently. The worship of gold and silver bullion was not as fatuous as has sometimes been said, for abundant sound currency enlivened internal trade, enabled the payment of taxes, and filled the war chest. In the race to keep ahead of rivals it was natural to exclude foreigners from fattening on, and above all taking out, domestic riches. Luxuries, especially if purchased abroad with money, were restricted because they were temptations to idleness where work was the commandment. Hindrances to domestic commerce were condemned, while a tariff wall to encircle the nation was just the thing to discourage imports and favor home manufactures and agriculture.

All of these purposes demanded national, that is to say centralized, management. Local peculiarities and privileges thwarted system and order. Exemptions of certain classes or districts from taxes, disparity in currencies, weights, and measures made against the desired uniformity. Administration of law, oversight of commerce, and collection of revenue so far as possible should be in the hands of national officers or those under national control. In any event taxes should not take out of the pockets of the people, if avoidable, sums much in excess of what was drawn into the public treasury.

Not all of these expedients were used or perfected in any one country at any one time, though they were common aims of the mercantilists for two and a half or three centuries. Taken together, they formed a coherent body of rules. They were practical measures suggested by varying cirmustances, but they were sufficiently distinct from what went before and from what came after to warrant terming them a school of economic policy if not of doctrine. Unless we are to go back to the fragmentary moral-economic code of Thomas Aquinas of the Middle Ages, it is proper to consider mercantilism as the earliest rounded system of economic rules of public conduct.

Colbert became the Pooh-Bah of the court; he held enough offices to make him a one-man administrative staff; if his expansive desk had held a brass plate for every department he conducted, there would have been no room for the piles of reports he examined or for him to pen, mostly in his own hand, his meticulous responses. He was Intendant of Finances, Superintendent-general of Commerce, Secretary of State in charge of navy and galleys, Superintendent of Buildings, of the king's household, of Paris, of merchant marine, fortifications, seaports, clerical affairs, and, for full measure, horse-raising. He had helped prepare for the king's marriage, saw to it that the king's mistresses were presented with jewels, and summoned midwives for the birth of the mistresses' children. Though it must have made him wince to buy foreign fripperies, he got toys for the dauphin from Nürnberg. Between organizing commercial companies and building ships, he ordered fruit and flowers for the king's table and supervised search for swans that had defied the royal authority by flying off like birds instead of remaining ornaments on a garden pool.*

Colbert rejoiced in his heavy and manifold responsibilities as a strong man to run a race. If one were casting his career into the form of a drama, his antagonist would be Louvois, the War Minister. Twenty years younger, Colbert had assisted Louvois' rise, only to see him winning the king's favor by lavishing on military campaigns funds which Colbert would devote to peaceful development. Colbert resisted his rival to the last, and a playwright could show the old minister looking down from the skies when Louvois had succeeded to his influence, not knowing whether to weep at the decline of the kingdom or to chortle at Louvois' misadventures.

Colbert's chief preoccupation was the finances, which at his accession were in a tangle of debt, fraud, gross inequities, and scandalous waste. Colbert at once commenced a grand audit through the specially created *Chambre de Justice*, which, reviewing abuses of a quarter-century previous, compelled grafting officials to disgorge 100,000,000 livres. This recapture amounted to more than three times the royal revenues when Colbert began his inquisition. Chastising other robbers, he used fraud himself by repudiating part of the interest promised on the *rentes*, or government bonds, thereby saving 8,000,000 livres annually.

---

* For such industriously gathered particulars, spice in a complete account of the minister's service, see Charles Woolsey Cole, *Colbert and a Century of French Mercantilism*, (New York: Columbia University Press, 1939, 2 vols.), to which this sketch is chiefly indebted.

His own impulse was to buy up these public obligations at their depreciated value, but the holders would not have it, so he felt forced to the less honorable course. Colbert had no difficulty in hardening his heart against *rentiers*; France had too many mere interest-mongers; they should put their capital into productive enterprises.

The finance minister, besides correcting the past, provided for enlarged public revenues, fairly levied and faithfully collected, for the future. He set up a system of bookkeeping that made income and outgo visible. He spread the tax burden by cutting the *taille* (personal income and land taxes) from which nobles, other favored classes and places had obtained exemption, and raised the *aides* (excises on liquors and other sales, license fees, and stamp duties). He decreased the price of salt while at the same time, through reforms in collection, he got more from the salt taxes—one of his neater tricks. For a decade he made substantial fiscal progress until Louis' expensive seven-years' war against the Dutch (1672–78) deranged his cherished system. Among expedients to meet the emergency were the tobacco monopoly, famously productive and flourishing to this day, and the postal monopoly.

He suppressed private mints, set the silver-to-gold ratio at fifteen-and-a-half to one, and standardized the coinage, though with some debasement during the Dutch war. He repossessed the king's lands, alienated and usurped, and in twenty years increased their yield from 80,000 to more than 5,000,000 livres.

A European visitor in the twentieth century observed to a New York politician that America's material progress surpassed the country's attention to music and art. "True," the city father replied, "but when we turn to culture we'll make it hum." Colbert coerced culture, though, fortunately, his aggressive patronage was not premature or oppressive. He rejuvenated existing academies of letters, painting, and sculpture, founded new ones for architecture, music, and science, subsidized theatrical companies, secured palace lodgings and pensions for men of many talents who designed and adorned famous public buildings under his supervision. He systematically collected manuscripts and books for his library, part of which enriched the Bibliothèque Nationale. He encouraged inventors. Colbert, unlike some mercantilist statesmen, did not neglect agriculture for industry and commerce. His constant concern for farming was reflected in crop experiments on his own estates.

The elegancies of France, artistic and intellectual, like all other proofs of progress which Colbert induced, depended on the comprehensive economic development which was his dearest purpose. Finances, his first care, must be fed by commerce, which in turn rested on industry, agriculture, shipbuilding, and internal transport. He created the Council of Commerce, presided over by the king himself, to forward business in all its aspects. While we praise Colbert for his Argus-eyed solicitude and incessant drive, we must recognize his basic limitation as evangel of prosperity. It was the mercantilist conception, then universal, that any country must progress at the expense of its rivals. There was only so much to be had in the world— in precious metals, in ships, in markets—so the object was "the double elevation" of France, "augmenting the power and greatness of Your Majesty," while "abasing that of his enemies and those who are jealous of him." Again Colbert reminded the king, "This state is flourishing not only in itself, but also by the want which it has inflicted upon all the neighboring states. Extreme poverty appears everywhere. There is only Holland which still resists, and its power in money decreases visibly."

The disability of the mercantilists was their static notion of a closed world economy. The idea of sharing in growth, which now makes notable headway, was not theirs. The astounding release of productivity manifested in the Industrial Revolution was yet a century and more in the future. The gospel of commercial freedom, preached by Adam Smith, would win only slow and partial acceptance. Advanced nations of the mid-twentieth century had to be told, by the International Labor Office, that "poverty anywhere in the world is a threat everywhere." As these lines are written, the American Secretary of State has just said that "The conflict between the Communists and the free world is as fundamental as any conflict can be. . . . Since 1948 we have used export controls to keep strategic commodities from the Soviet Union and its European satellites. Since 1950 we have maintained a total embargo on trade with Communist China and North Korea. . . ." Happily, he went on to explain that "it is our policy to do what we can to encourage evolution in the Communist world toward national independence and open societies," and presumably trade restrictions by the United States will be relaxed when and where this purpose appears to be succeeding. The struggle now is between blocs of countries; it is held to be ideological and only incidentally economic, as was not true in Colbert's time. In effect, however, the correspondence between policies in the two periods is uncomfortably close. We, like Colbert, view the misfortunes of our rivals with satisfaction. Thus "Throughout the Communist world the economic shortcomings of Communism are vividly manifested. Failures in food production have become endemic." Before we throw stones at the mercantilists, we should perhaps remember our own glass house.

In any event, Colbert shaped his plans to aggrandize his own country at the expense of other nations. His method was commercial warfare. "The effort," he declared, "is to prevent money from going out, by means of the establishment of all sorts of manufactures, and of everything necessary for use in life; and to make it come in by all sorts of commerce and by facilitating the export of all our goods and manufactures." Imports from abroad must be thwarted, and what must be brought in should be paid for so far as possible in French goods, not in money. Money, procured by a favorable balance of trade, must be kept within the kingdom. A precious source of money was French trade with Cadiz, siphoning off the precious metals flowing to Spain from America.

The trade of France must be conducted, to the utmost extent he could promote, in French ships with French seamen. New markets must be opened by chartered companies—East India Company, West India Company, Company of the North—with government support. Where private initiative and resources for trade were insufficient or misdirected, government would aid with capital and thorough regulation. Colonies and trading stations in foreign parts also figured prominently in Colbert's program.

Commerce within France must be quickened by improved roads, new canals, and the promotion of manufactures that gave employment to women and children and idlers. Internal customs barriers must be thrown down.

Among numerous internal waterways improved or constructed, the most ambitious was the Languedoc Canal permitting passage of barges from the Bay of Biscay on the Atlantic to the Mediterranean at Cette, thus avoiding the ocean voyage around Spain and through the Straits of Gibraltar. Canal projects, then and later, encountered unexpected problems, engineering and financial, and only the undiscouraged persistence of Colbert and of Riquet, the patriotic enterpriser, pushed this major work to completion in fifteen years. This canal, 175 miles long, with 65 locks surmounting a height of 600 feet, required the expenditure of 17,000,000 livres. The king was the heaviest contributor, the provincial estates (with some reluctance), invested nearly as much, and Riquet exhausted his resources for the remainder. The mercantilist penchant for a combination of public and private promotion was further embodied in a monopoly of management by Riquet's family, under government supervision.

From a poor start, with fewer than 400 vessels of size, Colbert used every endeavor and device to increase and improve the merchant marine. The tax of 50 sous a ton on foreign shipping was an over-all encouragement, and Colbert granted subsidies—the larger the new vessels built, the larger the king's gift—in an effort to compete with lower costs of the Dutch. To protect the merchant ships, especially against pestiferous pirates in the Mediterranean, and for conquest, he built up the navy to ten times its former strength, with more than proportionate betterment in armaments, personnel, and port facilities. Even petty criminals were sent to join Turkish, Russian, Negro, and Iroquois slaves in the terrible toil at the oars of the galleys. He instituted what we should call a selective service system for sailors in the king's ships, replacing the old practice of impressment.

Colbert's colonizing and commercial penetration in the West Indies, Scandinavia, the Levant, and in the East Indies, directed against the prosperity of the Dutch, English, Portuguese, and Spanish in these fields, were not notably successful. Their intention was thoroughly mercantilist. An example of Colbert's care for overseas commerce was the provision for sending young boys from France to be educated in Near East languages in Constantinople and Smyrna. Later they would act as interpreters for French merchants in the Levant, replacing unreliable local go-betweens.

Much as Colbert was devoted to development of commerce as the means of attracting the moneys of other countries, he was equally active in developing varied manufactures. This was in accordance with his policy of promoting every aspect of the economy to be a rounded, integrated whole. Fundamental to mercantilism was the closest approach to complete self-sufficiency of the nation, with a surplus of commodities for export to insure a favorable balance of trade to draw in wealth—hopefully the precious metals—from outside. Manufactured products were most eligible for export, especially manufactures worked up from domestic raw materials. Manufactures, offering employment, helped to sustain a large and industrious population, invigorated trade within, and distributed money to all parts of the kingdom. By many and ingenious means—subsidies, protections, privileges, and inducements to skilled foreigners to settle in France—Colbert revived declining enterprises and supported new undertakings. To this end he bypassed local guild and tariff restrictions wherever possible by exercise of the royal authority. He was assisted by and in turn he furthered large-scale industry under capitalist enterprisers. Some of these, no longer confined to the single master's workshop, put out materials to be made up in scattered cottages. Others progressed to the next stage of genuine factories. Here premises, tools, and materials were owned by the employer, often a company, and hundreds of workers increased efficiency by division of labor.

Textiles, from coarse sail cloth to sophisticated tapestries, commanded Colbert's main efforts, but other wares of utility and ornament were comprehensively fostered. Government—army, navy, and furnishing of public buildings, especially the palaces—offered dependable demand for various articles. We may not even summarize the meticulous regulations which Colbert promulgated for manufactures. Their purpose was to amplify production and insure quality of workmanship. The modern manager of an industrial undertaking would regard Colbert's multifarious directions and exhortations as intolerable interference by government. But it must be remembered that government in Colbert's France was an active participant with private enterprisers large and small. At that time individual proprietors and companies had not developed the techniques and controls which they later practiced.

Our description of Colbert's efforts to raise the competence of France at home and as a competitor among trading nations must not lead us to suppose that he always got the results at which he aimed. Far from it, for he met obstacles in the court and more in the country. Provincial authorities were jealous of his intrusions, traditional guilds were inert, and he was obliged to work through local civil servants who mostly lacked his breadth of view and driving purpose. Colbert's reach exceeded his grasp. Yet at his death in 1783 he, more than any other one man, had erected a national economy.

We close this sketch with comments of Adam Smith, the prime foe of mercantilism, on the character and policies of Colbert, written almost a century after the Frenchman's death. Smith's dissent will serve to introduce us to his own system of no system, or of freedom for the individual.

Colbert, as we have seen, sought to favor French manufactures by restraining the importation of competing foreign goods. ". . . Mr. Colbert," said Smith, "notwithstanding his great abilities, seems in this case to have been imposed upon by the sophistry of merchants and manufacturers, who are always demanding a monopoly against their countrymen. It is at present the opinion of the most intelligent men in France [the physiocrats] that his operations of this kind have not been beneficial to his country." And again: "Mr. Colbert, the famous minister of Louis XIV., was a man of probity, of great industry and knowledge of detail, of great experience and acuteness . . . and of abilities, in short, every way fitted for introducing method and good order into the collection and expenditure of the public revenue. That minister had unfortunately embraced all the prejudices of the mercantile system. . . . The industry and commerce of a great country he endeavoured to regulate upon the same model as the departments of a public office; and instead of allowing every man to pursue his own interest in his own way . . . he bestowed upon certain branches of industry extraordinary privileges, while he laid others under as extraordinary restraints."

For Further Reading

Cole, Charles W., *Colbert and a Century of French Mercantilism* (New York: Columbia University Press, 2 vols., 1939). Has been of principal assistance in the present brief account.

Sargent, Arthur John, *The Economic Policy of Colbert* (New York: Longmans, Green & Co., 1899).

Heckscher, Eli Filip, *Mercantilism*. Translated by Mendel Shapiro (2d. ed., New York: The Macmillan Co., 2 vols., 1955). This is the standard treatment of the subject.

Schmollar, Gustav Friedrich von, *The Mercantile System and its Historical Significance* (New York: The Macmillan Co., 1910).

Horrocks, John Wesley, *A Short History of Mercantilism* (London: Methuen & Co., 1925).

2

INVISIBLE HAND

Adam Smith

In the seventeen-eighties along the High Street in Edinburgh might have been encountered an elderly gentleman marching with his cane carried over his shoulder like a musket. His eyes, though protruding, had an abstracted look, and you would rightly conclude that his mind was not on his walk. He talked to himself as he strode along. His family name was one of the most common and his given name was that of mankind, but Doctor Adam Smith enjoyed unique celebrity throughout the western world. In a field of ever-changing thought, nearly two centuries have served to spread his fame. Rarely has a more modest man exercised such authority.

He was born in nearby Kirkcaldy, the posthumous child of the customs collector of that place. When one visits the town today he finds reminders of Adam Smith—the burgh school which he attended, a tablet at the site of his mother's house, the public hall named in his honor. He studied at Glasgow College, where his instructors are remembered not least because they influenced him. The most important one was Francis Hutcheson, the professor of philosophy, who delivered his free thoughts in eloquent lectures. Adam Smith's optimism and faith in liberty may be accurately traced to Hutcheson, even if we do not take into account other thinkers and observations from which he learned. Not only Smith's mood, moral and social, is in Hutcheson's pattern, but particular expositions in Smith's celebrated works are found earlier in the teachings of his Glasgow mentor.

From Glasgow Adam proceeded on a scholarship to Balliol

College, Oxford. Here he suffered nothing from the prevailing languor. Most of the professors had ceased to lecture, but the young Scotsman sat day after day for six years in his library alcove, exploring the Greek and Latin classics, the Italian poets, and practicing composition by translating from French authors. He stocked his mind with a wealth of reading which enabled him afterward to illumine his thought and writings with knowledge from many quarters. The "darkness then ruling in Oxford" seems to have denied Smith one book, Hume's *Treatise of Human Nature*. When he was found reading it—probably his own copy, too, given him by the author at the suggestion of Smith's Glasgow professor, Hutcheson—the volume was confiscated and the student was severely reprimanded. Though Hume's heresy was snatched from him, Adam Smith was not discouraged from accumulating a private library remarkable for the variety of fields of knowledge and pleasures embraced.

From Oxford he returned to Kirkcaldy for two years of further reading under his mother's roof. Probably at this time he wrote a history of astronomy intended for teen-agers. He liked this, for he wanted it spared from the flames that consumed most of his unpublished manuscripts at the end of his life. We must not be surprised at Smith's versatility, for during the next three years he was lecturing in Edinburgh, to applause and profit, on literature and art as well as on political economy.

His learning and lively presentation commended him for the chair of logic in his old college in Glasgow, to which he was elected in 1750 at the age of 27. This move set him on his career. Glasgow, a commercial town, in contrast to Edinburgh, the old Scottish capital and cultural center, had gladly accepted union with England and was thus in the trade currents of Europe and the American colonies. Glasgow importers of tobacco and grain, and exporters of textiles and hardware, had their agents and warehouses on the American continent and in the Caribbean. The father of Alexander Hamilton was one of numerous young Glasgow merchants who sought their fortunes in the sugar islands. Glasgow was helping to generate the wider market which, Adam Smith showed, was a necessary preliminary to the division of labor and what became in his lifetime the Industrial Revolution.

Glasgow College received from and contributed to this stimulating scene. Its innovating professors drew students from many

quarters. In his opening lectures Adam Smith gave short shrift
to formal logic, then branched into other fields of philosophy.
In the second session he was transferred to the vacant chair
of ethics, where for a dozen years his talents enjoyed free rein.
His students have recorded how, from a hesitant start, he would
launch into "extemporaneous eloquence. . . . As he advanced
. . . the matter seemed to crowd upon him, his manner became
warm and animated. . . . By the fulness and variety of his illustrations the subject gradually swelled in his hands and acquired
a dimension . . . to seize the attention of his audience, and
to afford them pleasure as well as instruction. . . ." His bent
was secular, not devout; took from physics rather than the
"subtleties and sophisms" of abstruse metaphysics; looked to
nature instead of bewildering speculation. He explored "the
happiness . . . of . . . an individual, . . . of a family, of a state,
and of the great society of mankind."

First fruit was Smith's *Theory of Moral Sentiments*, 1759,
which went through six editions before his death. Evidence is
that he misjudged this, and not *The Wealth of Nations*, to be
his principal work. He found the spring of moral responses
in the quality of sympathy. It has required the ingenuity of
critics to reconcile this with his later fixation on selfish advantage
as the motive that makes the economic world go round.

Adam Smith was caught up in the business as well as academic life of Glasgow. He was active in college administration,
inspected accounts, mediated disputes between town and gown.
He was fond of saying that a few spirited merchants were better
for a city than the residence of a court. The leading merchants
of Clyde he met in the Political Economy Club. These worthies
damned import duties on raw materials of Glasgow manufactures of iron and textiles, though it took all of Smith's
persuasion to wean them from protection for their own finished
goods. Smith was a founder of the Literary Society, which
engaged in debates faculty lights, neighboring landed proprietors,
some public officials, Robert Foulis the printer, and, not least,
Smith's young protégé, James Watt, who described himself as
"but a mechanic" among discussants "all my superiors." To the
new location of the University of Glasgow, on a splendid hilltop,
has been brought the old gatehouse, where Adam Smith dined
on Friday nights in a company gathered about Dr. Robin
Simpson, the famous mathematics professor. They adjourned

these campus arguments only to meet on Saturdays at the nearby village of Anderston for chicken broth, claret, punch, and whist.

Smith's conviviality took him often to Edinburgh, where he helped establish the Select Society and the Poker Club. The first rose to importance as promoter of Scottish agriculture, arts, and industries. The second promoted political agitation on the strength of Scottish patriotism and unexcised Burgundy. In both circles Smith ripened his friendship with David Hume, though this distinguished skeptic went unnoticed in the pages of the first, short-lived, *Edinburgh Review* for which Smith wrote.

These social evenings of Smith, with talk and tankards, were more than the diversion of an amiable bachelor. From communicative friends in many walks of life he stocked his mind with particulars which supplied a wealth of illustration for propositions in his books.

Smith's conversations and observations, plus much thought and reading, resulted in *Lectures on Justice, Police, Revenue and Arms*. His notes were destroyed at his own direction, and for nearly a century and a half we had only the briefest listing of his topics as given by one of his hearers to Smith's friend Dugald Stewart. Then, luckily, a manuscript of almost 400 pages turned up in the garret of a country house. It was copied from the classroom notes of an intelligent student, and was edited and published by Edwin Cannan in 1896. We are less concerned with the major portion dealing with public and private law, which Smith never found time to expand. Our gratitude is for more than a third of the report presenting Smith's treatment of "Police," the term he used to embrace "the opulence of a state," including taxation, manufactures, and commerce. Here, in summary, is the *Wealth of Nations*, stated at least a dozen years before that treatise was completed. Some passages are word for word the same. Memorable features of the finished work—the pin factory, wise rules of taxation—are already used. Absent from this earlier version are insights which Smith was to get later in France, as also the stress on colonies prompted by approach of the American Revolution. The report of the lectures shows that the argument of the *Wealth of Nations* had taken shape in Smith's mind from British example, years before Smith had knowledge of French advocacy.

Now came a new chapter in Adam Smith's life, which helped

to point his learning, further improved his social graces, and assured him of financial independence for arduous years of writing. The Glasgow professor was besought by Charles Townshend—soon to be chancellor of the exchequer and author of unhappy duties on imports of the American colonies—to tutor Townshend's stepson, the young Duke of Buccleugh in continental travels. Smith was to receive annually £300 and expenses and the same stipend as long as he lived—twice his income from the College. It was common then for distinguished scholars to accept such appointments, but Smith took the unusual step of resigning his chair instead of going on leave.

Professor and pupil posted first to Paris (February, 1764) for a short reunion with David Hume, then secretary of the British Embassy. Hume dispatched them with *open sesame* letters of introduction to principal personages in the provinces. Eighteen months in Toulouse were followed by briefer stays in Languedoc, Bordeaux, and especially Geneva, where Smith repeatedly visited his admired Voltaire. In the summer of 1764, before he became engrossed in a round of entertainments, the traveler had "begun to write a book in order to pass away the time." This was the *Wealth of Nations*, into which he put much that he saw and heard of good and bad public administration, commercial practices, and conditions of the people. It was a quarter-century yet till the French Revolution; Smith was generally optimistic about the country, and not alone in failing to detect signs of the cataclysm that oppressions would produce.

The climax of the tour was in the return to Paris for ten months (December 1765-November 1766). Here as Hume's friend, and for his own merits (since the *Theory of Moral Sentiments* had preceded him), Smith was immediately welcomed to the effervescent company of the physiocratic philosophers and the hostesses of intellect and position whose salons they frequented. These apostles of liberty revolved about the king's physician, François Quesnay. Among those known familiarly to Smith in Paris were Dupont, Morellet, Mercier de la Rivière, Mirabeau, and Turgot. Those of the coterie or sect were writers and propagandists in revolt against the restraints of centralized government. Their preachments of individualism and freedom helped prepare for the French Revolution. They would banish most social and economic controls in favor of natural law. Their maxim was *laissez faire*—let spontaneous forces operate. Land was the only productive factor. Manufactures and commerce were sterile. Therefore public revenue should be drawn entirely from land rents. They were champions of the peasants, being robbed by nobles and monopolists. Quesnay's *Tableau Economique*, published in 1758, was an ingenious, if mystifying, graphic representation of the generation and circulation of wealth.

In Quesnay's rooms at Versailles and in similar gatherings of the French economists, Adam Smith heard much that confirmed his previously formed preference for let-alone policy. These spirited exchanges in Paris left him with the conviction that agriculture was the prime—though not the sole—productive activity. Unlike his new friends, he assigned usefulness to industry and commerce as well, though he did exclude personal and professional services, as of flunkeys and hair-dressers, even teachers and lawyers. As we shall see, he afterward, in the *Wealth of Nations*, gave high but qualified praise to the physiocrats and would have dedicated his great work to Quesnay had not that innovating philosopher and reformer died before the treatise was ready for the press. Particularly, Smith adopted into his own system what he had not possessed before, a concern for the just distribution or sharing of income among economic classes.

The Scottish professor's life with the physiocrats was not all intellectual excitement and pleasurable parties. He was embarrassed when one of the French ladies fell enthusiastically in love with him and was vexed to know how to discourage her overtures. He was anxious when his young charge, the Duke of Buccleugh, contracted a severe fever; Smith watched constantly at his bedside until Dr. Quesnay was fetched. Then came sudden tragedy when the Duke's younger brother, who had joined them, was murdered in the street. This abruptly ended the visit.

While Smith tarried in London (winter and spring, 1766–67) the American colonies had won a round in the waxing fight with the mother country. Refusal of merchants of Boston, New York, Philadelphia, and Charleston to order—or pay for—English goods brought the exporters of London, Bristol, and Glasgow about the ears of the Rockingham ministry. The Stamp Act of Smith's friend Townshend, which so incensed the Americans, was repealed. This wise retraction was undone, however, by the Declaratory Act, claiming the right of Parliament to bind the colonies in all cases whatsoever. In the midst of these rumblings the king dismissed Rockingham, and Shelburne, a Secretary of State in Chatham's ill-assorted ministry, begged Smith's advice on colonial policy. We note only that Smith's counsel leaned to the side of liberal treatment of the Americans.

Returning to Kirkcaldy, Smith settled down in his mother's house to six solid years of labor on the book he had commenced in France. The stately residence in the High Street where the bulk of the *Wealth of Nations* was composed was pulled down more than a century ago, but a tablet on the existing building signalizes the spot, and the narrow passage that runs beside the garden is called Adam Smith's Close. Resisting his friend Hume's importunities, the recluse seldom visited Edinburgh. Except for solitary walks on the sea sands, he stuck in his study. He stood before the fireplace, dictating to an amanuensis. When puzzled for the right word, he would rub his head against the wall. The pomatum in his wig left an unsightly smudge. Maybe more authors should deface more plaster.

Adam Smith deceived himself in supposing that he could complete his book by the early winter of 1772 at the latest. Bad health, "arising from want of amusement and from thinking too much upon one thing," combined with other occasions of delay. But the real prolongation of his labors was because, having arrived in London with the manuscript, (May 1773), he found much to add to his treatise. The contest with the American colonies was entering its final phase. Within a few months East India Company's tea was dumped into Boston harbor. The king and his cohort in Parliament punished Boston by what all the colonies called "Intolerable Acts." The first Continental Congress (September 1774) severed trade with the Mother Country, which retaliated by forbidding the colonies' commerce with any other nation. Burke, in his celebrated plea for conciliation, tried vainly to reverse this trend; Adam Smith agreed that the political loyalty of the Americans would follow from cultivating, not menacing, economic cooperation with Britain. Two years after Smith reached London the fighting war had commenced with the battles of Lexington, Concord, and Bunker Hill. Hardly was Smith's *Wealth of Nations* off the press (March 1776) than the colonies formally declared their independence.

During these momentous controversies Adam Smith was all ears. He consulted intimately with Benjamin Franklin, the prime source of American information, and Dr. Richard Price, not less the advocate of colonial rights, as amendment of the manuscript progressed. Sir Joshua Reynolds, Samuel Johnson, Burke, and Gibbon were others with whom he conversed familiarly. Smith's biographer, John Rae, rightly declares that the innumerable illustrations from the condition and growth of the American colonies "constitute the experimental evidence of the . . . truth of the book, without which many of its leading positions had been little more than theory."

It is significant that the *Wealth of Nations* and the Declaration of Independence issued at almost the same moment. The first proclaimed economic liberty, the second announced political freedom. The two together marked the beginning of the end of mercantilism and feudalism. True, Britain did not adopt free trade fully for seventy years, and the rights of man, startlingly militant in the French Revolution, suffered ironic reverses before the creed was widely accepted. But the old order of restraints on the market and on democracy had been memorably challenged.

The *Wealth of Nations* appeared in two handsome quarto volumes at the price of £1:16s. In spite of initial neglect by reviewers, the work sold so briskly than ten English editions were required by 1800, and translations into French, Italian, Spanish, and Danish multiplied. From the first, ministers borrowed from the book in policies of taxation and commerce, and soon it was familiarly quoted in Parliament. However, Smith's liberal system did not escape censure, for it was confounded in frightened minds with demands—economic, political, and ethical—issuing from the French Revolution. The Lord Chancellor felt obliged to explain that Smith's teaching contained nothing "inimical to the principles of civil government, the morals or religion of mankind," such as were associated with abhorrent French doctrine.

Two years after the appearance of the *Wealth of Nations* Adam Smith was named one of five Commissioners of the Customs of Scotland. This seems to have been a recognition by Lord North, prime minister and chancellor of the exchequer, of the contribution of Smith's book, which North had put to practical use in the public finances. The compliment was the greater since North was a Tory, while Smith remained a firm Whig. The salary was £600 a year, and the Duke of Buccleugh insisted that his old tutor retain his pension. In a roomy house in Panmure Close in the Canongate quarter of Edinburgh, Smith lived comfortably with his mother and cousin. He entertained his intimates at famous Sunday night suppers and was host to distinguished visitors to the town. He spent his leisure in his large and varied library, and took pleasure in generous private charities.

He performed the duties of his office conscientiously, though they prevented him from undertaking further scholarly work, such as completion for publication of his Glasgow lectures on government. With close friends he founded the Royal Society of Edinburgh. His wisdom was sought in favor of free trade for Ireland. It may be as well for his reputation that he lived out his last years in useful public duties and pleasant social intercourse without producing more volumes. In any event in his last illness Smith insisted that friends, summoned for the purpose, destroy in his presence sixteen folders of manuscript. He seems to have been partial to his *Theory of Moral Sentiments* above the *Wealth of Nations*, but he was unlikely to add to the fame of the latter.

He was buried in the Canongate churchyard under a simple stone that needs no lengthy inscription. The best known likenesses of Adam Smith are small ceramic medallions by James Tassie. They show a bold profile—high forehead, eyeballs noticeably protruding, somewhat aquiline nose, firm mouth and chin. Smith was of middle height, full but not stout in figure, notably erect in carriage. His large gray or light blue eyes are said by one who knew him to have beamed with "inexpressible benignity."

Adam Smith's life among traders, shippers, manufacturers, public men, and philosophers prepared him to announce a new economic era. The revolution he heralded was swift and sweeping because, fitting his personality, his preachment was calm and rational. His task was easier because he championed forces of freedom and individual initiative which were already gaining momentum. Nor was he obliged, like Marx, to plead for powerless masses. He spoke to no mass at all, but to each man's self-interest. While the implications of his doctrine were profound for the development of democracy, his was not a political appeal. He proposed no cultural upheaval. True, his changes could not be accomplished without hurting some in the established order of society, the privileged monopolists. But these were few, and their advantage depended on the will of Parliament. What he urged was a shift of governmental policy for the benefit of the whole community. His argument was on the plane not of rights, but of expediency. He supported his argument with economic reasoning, not with ethical principle.

His campaign for commercial liberty was ready to be won at the time when he commenced it. Mercantilism, or governmental direction of economic activity, had outworn its usefulness. Time had been when public oversight, promotion, and protection were serviceable, even necessary. Private capital, experience, and ability to bear risk were too little to prosper without collective guarantees. Statesmen like Colbert supplied both stimulus and resources. But when numbers of individuals, eager and able, were volunteering and asking no more than opportunity, controls became superfluous, indeed positively restrictive. In this situation the wits of statesmen were outmatched by the zestful contrivance of citizens.

Now for a view of the chief features of Adam Smith's masterpiece, *An Enquiry into the Nature and Causes of the Wealth of Nations.*

He began with sentences which give a key to the whole work: "The annual labour of every nation is the fund which originally supplies it with all the necessaries and conveniences of life which it annually consumes. . . . According therefore, as this produce, or what is purchased with it, bears a greater or smaller proportion to the number of those who are to consume it, the nation will be better or worse supplied with all the necessaries and conveniences for which it has occasion." He was soon speaking of the produce of the land and labor of every country. He was saying that wealth is not in the precious metals, which the mercantilists so much cherished, but in goods, whether used as capital (to produce more goods) or consumed directly. He was shifting attention from sterile "treasure" to the work of the people applied to natural resources.

This emphasis on "necessaries and conveniences of life" was the new era in economic teaching which Adam Smith inaugurated. Almost two centuries earlier another Smith—Captain John Smith of the Virginia colony—had illustrated the same truth when he weaned the men of Jamestown from their passion for treasure. "There was no talke, no hope, nor worke, but dig gold, wash gold, refine gold, load gold." John Smith compelled them to cut down trees and saw them into clapboards to be returned to England to procure supplies. Not the gold mine, but another hole in the earth, the sawpit, was the source of gain.

This homely preachment, that wealth is work, formed Adam Smith's text throughout. He elaborated this theme in all its bearings. His entire treatise is derived from this fundamental proposition announced at the very outset.

He moved promptly to his task with another famous observation: "The greatest improvement in the productive powers of labour, and the greater part of the skill, dexterity, and judgment with which it is any where directed, or applied, seem to have been the effects of the division of labour." He may have taken the phrase, "division of labour," from Mandeville's *Fable of the Bees* (1714), where the merit of specialization is praised in two forms, separation of employments (different workmen making arrows, garments, or watches), and breaking up each trade or calling into particular processes. Smith, also, embraced both degrees of division of labor, and argued the benefits further than any predecessor had done.

Smith dramatized the principle as demonstrated in "a very trifling manufacture; . . . the trade of the pin-maker."* He explained that "a workman not educated to this business . . . could scarce . . . with his utmost industry, make one pin in a day, and certainly could not make twenty. But in the way in which this business is now carried on, not only the whole work is a peculiar trade, but it is divided into a number of branches. . . . One man draws out the wire, another straights it, a third cuts it, a fourth points it, a fifth grinds it at the top for receiving the head; to make the head requires two or three distinct operations; to put it on, is a peculiar business . . . ," so that the whole was divided into some eighteen operations. Even a factory with ten workers turned out 48,000 pins in a day, or 4,800 for each worker, which was perhaps

---

* The example of a pin factory had been cited years earlier in Chambers' *Cyclopaedia* and by Delaire, a physiocrat (see Edwin Cannan's edition of *Wealth of Nations*, Modern Library, 1937, 5 n.), but Smith may have transposed what he himself had seen in a small nail factory at Kirkcaldy.

5,000 times as many as a man trying to make a whole pin could produce. "In every other art and manufacture, the effects of the division of labour are similar. . . ."

He illumined the means of this startling economy of effort through division of labor. First, the skill of a workman is increased when he performs the same simple operation countless times; "practice makes perfect." Second, specialization saves the time that is lost in adjusting to a different set of tools and another process. Smith, the keen observer, remarked that "A man commonly saunters a little in turning his hand from one sort of employment to another." This slow pace is seen in country workers who are obliged to pass, twenty times a day, from this job to that. Third, machines, which so greatly augment production, are apt to be invented or improved by those whose whole desire is to "find out easier and readier methods of performing their own particular work." Smith related that a boy attending one of the first steam engines discovered that he could save his constant hand labor by use of a string that automatically opened and closed the valve admitting steam to the cylinder.

Smith might have added another economy from the division of labor, namely, uninterrupted application of capital. No tools lie idle, as some must where the worker puts down one to take up another.

The counterpart of division of labor is cooperation between specialized producers. These exchange their surpluses with each other. This "is not originally the effect of any human wisdom, which foresees and intends that general opulence" which division of labor brings about. Rather "It is the . . . consequence of a certain propensity in human nature . . . to truck, barter, and exchange one thing for another." Each, wishing to serve himself, acknowledges the like motive in others. "It is not from the benevolence of the butcher, the brewer, or the baker, that we expect our dinner, but from their regard to their own interest. We address ourselves, not to their humanity but to their self-love, and never talk to them of our own necessities but of their advantages."

Here, simply stated, is the selfish motive, operating in every individual in the society, which brings exchangers together and permits each specialized producer to secure what he requires of others. The vast and intricate cooperation is accomplished by no over-all plan, but piecemeal and unconsciously. The system works without deliberate organization, without, for instance, intevention of government. This is the secret of the let-alone policy which Adam Smith urged.

Of course the complacent view that self-interest achieves the public benefit has many exceptions, some of which Smith recognized. Developments since his time have destroyed the validity of the maxim "every man for himself, and the devil take the hindmost." The self-seeking incentive which received Smith's blessing has resulted in concentrations of power which press too many individuals into the ranks of the hindmost who fall to the mercies of the devil. The rough equality of opportunity which the Scots philosopher envisioned turned out to be fatuous. Competition—each person giving the least and getting the most he could contrive—was the self-acting mechanism supposed to preserve a fair level of fortunes. But hit-or-miss competition, at best involving waste and painful casualties, has a wicked way of generating combinations. These concentrations refute Smith's optimistic prescription. We may not justify self-interest to the point where it practices exploitation. When masses of the population are made to suffer, society itself—that collective conscience which slumbered in Smith's pages—rises to protest.

Each item in Smith's treatment has become a staple of economic exposition. Thus he pointed out that division of labor is limited by the ability to make exchanges, or by the extent of the market. Among "the lone houses and very small villages . . . scattered about in . . . the Highlands of Scotland, every farmer must be butcher, baker and brewer for his own family." Perfection of the arts and industry, therefore, belongs to populous ports enjoying access to the whole world as market for products of every sort of labor. This was a forecast of the reach of her commerce when Britain soon became, in accordance with Smith's teachings, "the workshop of the world."

He explained the awkwardness of giving one product directly for another (barter), and showed how exchanges are facilitated by use of "some one commodity or other, such as . . . few people would be likely to refuse." He reviewed the numerous sorts of generally acceptable goods which historically have been employed—cattle, hides, salt, sugar, tobacco—and came finally to the precious metals, stamped to certify weight and fineness, as the preferred form of money. He was alive to the advantages of substituting "paper in the room of gold and silver money," for it "replaces a very expensive instrument of commerce with one much less costly, and sometimes equally convenient." This took him to a lucid account of "the circulating notes of banks" which he considered "best adapted for this purpose," and thence to the functioning of banks of issue. Later in the book, supporting his main thesis, he declared that "Money, . . . the great wheel of circulation, the great instrument of commerce . . . though it makes a . . . very valuable part of the capital, makes no part of the revenue of the society." Only "the annual produce of land and labour" constitutes "the real revenue of every society."

Aside from the benefits of the intervention of money in buying and selling, what "rules determine . . . the relative or exchangeable value of goods?" Smith warned that "after the fullest explication I am capable of giving it," the subject of value and price may "appear still in some degree obscure," since it is "in its own nature extremely abstracted." Smith's caution to the reader betrayed, in fact, uncertainty in his own mind on this central feature of economic theory. His doubt was wholly natural in a pioneer groping for an answer to a critical query. His solution set a pattern which was followed, with variations, for a hundred years. His exposition of value influenced every ramification of doctrine. It ran in the blood stream, as it were, of the systems of his successors. Otherwise a buttress of orthodoxy, it was put to uses by Marx which Smith could not possibly guess. Smith's belief could not have persisted so long—and it now enjoys a new lease of life through spread of Communism—without containing elements of truth. If we may make the distinction, its truth is moral rather than economic in the technical or mechanical sense. A century after the *Wealth of Nations* another school made a departure in the marginal utility concept of value.

"The word value," Smith observed, "has two different meanings, and sometimes expresses the utility of some particular object, and sometimes the power of purchasing other goods. . . . The one may be called 'value of use;' the other, 'value in exchange.' The things which have the greatest value in use have frequently little or no value in exchange; and on the contrary, those which have the greatest value in exchange have frequently little or no value in use. Nothing is more useful than water: but it will purchase scarce any thing. . . . A diamond, on the contrary, has scarce any value in use; but a very great quantity of other goods may frequently be had in exchange for it."

It is value in exchange, or price, which Smith went on to discuss, but we must pause at this point to note his confusion concerning value in use. If we comprehend all water, the totality of water, it unquestionably has higher use value than the totality of diamonds. But this is a comparison of abstractions which have no practical meaning. What we value, actually, is portions of water, a gallon or a cupfull at a time. Similarly, we do not set a value on the complete existing stock of diamonds, but on this or that particular gem. Now any one gallon of water, while additional quantities are available, has in fact not great but little value in use. The use that is dependent for its satisfaction upon possession of a particular gallon is unimportant. By the same token, however, each diamond—diamonds being scarce—serves an urgent need. The "paradox of value" that bothered Adam Smith does not exist. Water has little value in exchange because—in units—it has little or no value in use. Diamonds have high value in exchange because—again in units—diamonds have great value in use. We estimate usefulness in connection with abundance or scarcity. Usefulness as modified by quantity of a good available is well expressed in the word utility. This means degree of usefulness belonging to any one portion of a stock of goods. This gives us the utility notion of value referred to above. If we wish to refine the idea, we must speak of marginal utility, or the utility of the last or least unit which we desire and are able to possess. So much for correction, or resolving of a contradition which Smith thought he saw between value in use and value in exchange.

It is obvious that marginal utility seeks to define value from the demand side, or from the consumer's estimate of his satisfaction from acquiring a good. Adam Smith, and all others with him for a century, entertained a cost theory of value. For Smith the prime cost was labor. "Labour was the first price, the original purchase money that was paid for all things. It was not by gold or by silver, but by labour, that all the wealth of the world was orginally purchased; and its value, to those who possess it, and who want to exchange it for some new productions, is precisely equal to the quantity of labour which it can enable them to . . . command."

He gave the simplest of illustrations. "If among a nation of hunters . . . it usually costs twice the labour to kill a beaver which it does to kill a deer, one beaver should naturally exchange for or be worth two deer." But Smith was quick to enter a reservation which many who later drew deductions from the dogmatic labor theory of value were prone to neglect. True, he said, "In that early and rude state of society which precedes both the accumulation of stock [capital] and the appropriation of land, the proportion between the quantities of labour necessary for acquiring different objects seems to be the only circumstance which can afford any rule for exchanging them for one another. . . . In this state of things, the whole produce of labour belongs to the labourer. . . ." But as soon as particular persons accumulate capital, and use it to provide materials and subsistence to workmen, then, in purchasing the product, "something must be given for the profits of the undertaker . . . who hazards his stock in this adventure." The workers may no longer claim the whole product (or its value) by right of their labor. "The value which the workmen add to the materials . . . resolves itself in this case into two parts, of which the one pays their wages, the other the profits of their employer. . . ." Nor are "profits . . . only a different name for the wages of a particular sort of labour, the labour of inspection and direction." Profits bear no proportion to hardship or ingenuity of supervision. "They are regulated altogether by the value of the stock employed, and are greater or smaller in proportion to the extent of this stock." We need not repeat his illustration differentiating profits from what have come to be called "wages of superintendence."

Similarly, "As soon as the land of any country has all become private property, the landlords, like all other men, love to reap where they never sowed, and demand a rent even for its natural produce." The worker now, to have access to land, "must give up to the landlord a portion of what his labour either collects or produces. This portion, or, what comes to the same thing, the price of this portion, constitutes the rent of land, and in the price" of most commodities "makes a third component part." Here is another subtraction from the value of the product to which labor has contributed.

It is to be noticed that Smith included rent as an element in price. His friend David Hume, as soon as he read the *Wealth of Nations*, protested against this, but Smith persisted in his error. Rent, as Ricardo and others were to point out, is a payment for land superior in quality to that which barely repays the labor and capital used in cultivating it. The product of this marginal land returns nothing to the landlord, its price contains no rent component. Rent measures a differential advantage. As we shall see when we come to Ricardo, rents, say of agricultural lands, are high or low because the price of grain is high or low, not the other way around. Rent is a result of price, not a cause of it.

Having posited so much, Adam Smith proceeded to distinguish between "the natural and market price of commodities." The natural price is what will compensate the contributions of labor, capital, and land—that is, what will return wages, profits, and rent—at their ordinary rates prevailing in the society. The market price, depending on the relation between supply and effective demand at a particular time, "may either be above, or below, or exactly the same with . . . natural price." It is the natural or "central price, to which the [market] prices of all commodities are continually gravitating." Conformity of market price to natural price might be prevented, among other causes, by monopolies which Smith always antagonized.

The Scots writer was less concerned with the distribution or sharing of income among claimants than with other features of the economy. In this complicated area he was not so successful as elsewhere. He was apt to be suggestive rather than selective and decided. In spite of his long mulling over the manuscript and revisions of successive editions of the book, his rules were frequently inconsistent with each other. In treating the determination of wages, for example, he put forward most of the explanations among which, since his time, choice has been made and which have been separately defended. The subsistence theory, bargain theory, wage fund, and residual claimant doctrines may all be attributed to Smith. His most pervasive assumption was that "The wages paid to journeymen and servants of every kind must be such as will enable them, one with another, to continue the race of journeymen and servants, according as the increasing, diminishing, or stationary demand of the society may happen to require."

He everywhere showed his partiality to workers, just as he was critical of the exactions of landlords. Thus "The interest of [those who live by wages] is strictly and inseparably connected with the general interest of the society. Whatever either promotes or obstructs the one, necessarily promotes or obstructs the other." But of the landlords, "Every increase in the real wealth of the society, every increase in the quantity of useful labour employed within it, tends indirectly to raise the real rent of land . . . the proprietors of land . . . are the only one of the three orders [workers and capitalists the others] whose revenue costs them neither labour nor care, but comes to them, as it were, of its own accord, and independent of any plan or project of their own."

He esteemed the services of capitalist employers, whose stock "puts into motion the greater part of the useful labour of every society. The plans and projects of the employers of stock regulate and direct all the most important operations of labour, and profit is the end proposed by all those plans and projects. . . . Merchants and master manufacturers are . . . the two classes of people who commonly employ the largest capitals, and who by their wealth draw to themselves the greatest share of the public consideration." But, Smith warned, their actions and counsels were motivated by their aims of private profit. "The interest of the dealers . . . in any particular branch of trade or manufactures, is always in some respects different from, and even opposite to, that of the public. To widen the market and to narrow the competition, is always the interest of the dealers." Widening the market benefits the public, "but to narrow the competition . . . can serve only to enable the dealers, by raising their profits above what they naturally would be, to levy, for their own benefit, an absurd tax upon the rest of their fellow-citizens. The proposal of any new law or regulation of commerce which comes from this order . . . ought never to be adopted till after having been long and carefully examined, not only with the most scrupulous, but with the most suspicious attention." Selfish gain, though the mainspring of the economy, must not be allowed to wield legislative control.

As to distributive shares, Smith did not differentiate clearly between profits and interest, as indeed was not done until much later when enterprisers became more distinguishable from capitalists.

Adam Smith lavished effort to discredit the prevailing "commercial or mercantile system" of restraints on imports, colonial policy, and other interventions of government, such as bounties and drawbacks. His method was not horatory, but refuted by intensive examination of results. Quietly, candidly, with wide knowledge purposefully applied, and allowing exceptions where appropriate, he terminated, as far as one economist could do it, several centuries of misconception.

"That wealth consists in money," he began, "or in gold and silver, is a popular notion which naturally arises from the double function of money, as the instrument of commerce, and as the measure of value. . . . A rich country, in the same manner as a rich man, is supposed to be a country abounding in money; and to heap up gold and silver in any country is supposed to be the readiest way to enrich it." Locke endorsed this view, while others urged that a nation must accumulate gold and silver to have the wherewithal to carry on foreign wars. "In consequence of these . . . notions, all the . . . nations of Europe have studied, though to little purpose, every possible means" of amassing the precious metals within their borders. Thomas Mun (*England's Treasure by Forraign Trade*, 1664), in common with other merchants, combated prohibition on export of gold by showing that expenditures abroad could conduce to a favorable balance of trade. When foreigners must return more gold than they received, this was a way for a country which had no mines to acquire treasure. Mun's argument, said Smith, was solid in asserting that export of gold and silver in trade might be advantageous to a nation. But it was erroneous in supposing that government must exert itself to attract the precious metals more than "any other useful commodities, which the freedom of trade, without any such attention, never fails to supply in the proper quantity."

The plea for a favorable balance of trade was addressed to parliaments and councils of princes, "who were conscious . . . that they knew nothing about the matter," by merchants "who were supposed to understand trade." So governments were convinced, and Mun's recommendation "became a fundamental maxim in the political economy, not of England only, but of all other commercial countries." This obsession with foreign trade, Smith declared, was misplaced. Every country would have done better to promote the "inland or home trade, the most important of all, the trade in which an equal capital affords the greatest revenue, and creates the greatest employment to the people . . ."*

---

* We shall see later that Henry C. Carey particularly praised Smith for espousing domestic commerce.

The commodities within a country, largely the product of its own industry, will always enable it to secure in exchange the goods, as also the money, that it needs from abroad, so far as it has means to pay for the imports. Governments should have no concern to regulate the distribution of commodities, gold included, between countries, for trade is the automatic regulator. If there is a surplus beyond effectual demand at home, it will find its way to foreigners in spite of every legal penalty. If there is a dearth of gold, credit or paper money will come into action and commodities will be produced to be sent abroad to supply the deficiency. The precious metals, of high value in small bulk, are most "easily transported from one place to another, from the places where they are cheap, to those where they are dear, from the places where they exceed, to those where they fall short of . . . effectual demand."

In reply to the argument that gold must be hoarded lest it be wanted to support foreign wars, Smith showed that "Fleets and armies are maintained, not with gold and silver, but with consumable goods. The nation which, from the annual produce of its domestic industry, from the annual revenue arising out of its lands, labour, and consumable stock, has wherewithal to purchase those consumable goods in distant countries, can maintain foreign wars there." He appealed to fact. In the last French war, ending only thirteen years earlier, Britain laid out some £60 million in distant countries. But as the circulating gold and silver in Britain could not have exceeded half this amount, all of the metallic money, if it was money that supported operations abroad, "must . . . have been sent out and returned again at least twice" in the short period of six or seven years "without any body's knowing anything of the matter." How ridiculous, then, for government to attempt to prevent the export of the precious metals! Britain doubtless spent some gold at the seats of war, but this gold she had "annually purchased, either with British commodities, or with something else that had been purchased with them; which still brings us back to commodities, to the annual produce of the land and labour of the country, as the ultimate resources which enabled us to carry on the war." This was his constant story; wealth is commodities, wealth is work, "the real revenue . . . of the society."

Thus, "It is not by the importation of gold and silver, that the discovery of America has enriched Europe. . . . By opening a new and inexhaustible market to all the commodities of Europe, it gave occasion to new divisions of labour and improvements of art. . . . The productive powers of labour were improved, and its produce increased in all the countries of Europe, and together with it the real . . . wealth of the inhabitants."

What were the devices of mercantilism to procure and keep gold? Smith named them. Restrain imports of foreign goods, especially from countries with which the balance of trade was supposed to be disadvantageous. The methods were duties or outright prohibitions. On the other hand, encourage exportation by drawbacks (canceling taxes on home-produced commodities and reimbursing import duties if the goods were later exported), or by bounties (bonuses to nourish up home manufactures), by favoring treaties, and by establishing colonies that offered near-monopoly markets.

Adam Smith patiently demonstrated the falsity of each of these forced expedients. We may not follow his penetrating reasoning except as illustrated in a few famous passages of the *Wealth of Nations*. Tempting individuals to certain forms of production by protections or privileges was at best useless and was apt to be wasteful. "No regulation of commerce can increase the quantity of industry in any society beyond what its capital can maintain. It can only divert a part of it into a direction into which it might not otherwise have gone; and it is by no means certain that this artificial direction is likely to be more advantageous to the society than that into which it would have gone of its own accord." Every individual, by employing his capital to his own greatest benefit, "generally, indeed, neither intends to promote the public interest, nor knows how much he is promoting it. By preferring the support of domestic to that of foreign industry, he intends only his own security; and by directing that industry in such a manner as its produce may be of the greatest value, he intends only his own gain, and he is in this . . . led by an invisible hand to promote an end which was no part of his intention."

"What is the species of domestic industry . . . of which the produce is likely to be of the greatest value, every individual . . . can, in his local situation, judge much better than any statesman or lawgiver can do for him. The statesman, who should attempt to direct private people in what manner they ought to employ their capitals, would not only load himself with a most unnecessary attention, but assume an authority which could safely be trusted, not only to no single person, but to no council or senate whatever, and which would nowhere be so dangerous as in the hands of a man who had folly and presumption enough to fancy himself fit to exercise it."

However, Adam Smith was no dogmatist. He admitted circumstances under which freedom of trade should or might be restrained. The Act of Navigation of 1660 which undertook to give to British (including colonial) shipping and sailors a practical monopoly of the commerce of their own country he pronounced "perhaps . . . the wisest of all the commercial regulations of England." It aimed to diminish the menacing maritime power of Holland and to augment the naval strength of Britain. In so doing it limited British trade, but Smith earnestly supported it because "defence . . . is of much more importance than opulence." Similarly, if a home product was taxed, it was proper to tax the import of that commodity. He did not rule out restrictions in two other cases. One was retaliation when a foreign nation imposed high duties or prohibitions on import of British manufactures, though the effort should be to secure the repeal of the foreigner's restriction. Secondly, Smith advised that, if protection was to be withdrawn from a home industry, it be done only gradually lest "a great number of people should . . . be thrown all at once out of their ordinary employment."

Having dispatched the mercantile system, Adam Smith praised its opposite, the "agricultural system" of his French friends, the physiocrats, as "the nearest approximation to the truth that has yet been published upon the subject of political oeconomy." He could treat it more briefly, however, because it was an ingenious speculation only, nowhere practiced. He approved the physiocrats' scheme because it represented the wealth of nations as consisting, "not in the unconsumable riches of money, but in the consumable goods annually reproduced by the labour of the society." Further, these philosophers considered "perfect liberty as the only effectual expedient for rendering this annual reproduction the greatest possible." But he had a serious reservation. In holding "the labour which is employed upon land as the only productive labour," the physio-

crats were "too narrow and confined." Smith himself believed
that "the labour of farmers and country labourers is certainly
more productive than that of merchants, artificers and manufacturers." However, "The superior produce of the one class . . .
does not render the other barren and unproductive." He took
pains to show how the work of merchants and manufacturers
did "fix and realize itself in some . . . vendible commodity."
This distinguished them from menial servants who were truly
"barren or unproductive." (Of course we today accord productivity, sometimes of the highest order, to governors, churchmen, lawyers, physicians, men of letters, opera singers, and
others whom Smith excluded because "the work of all of them
perishes in the very instant of its production." Their contributions are not as evanescent as Smith supposed, but mainly we
call these productive because they satisfy wants).

Of Smith's discussion of public revenue we may notice only
his celebrated "four . . . maxims with regard to taxes in general." They are usually called his canons of taxation, which
enjoin equality, certainty, convenience, and economy. In his
words, "I. The subjects of every state ought to contribute
towards the support of the government, as nearly as possible,
in proportion to their respective abilities; that is, in proportion
to the revenue which they respectively enjoy under the protection of the state. . . . II. The tax which each individual is
bound to pay ought to be certain, and not arbitrary. The time
of payment, the manner of payment, the quantity to be paid,
ought all to be clear and plain to the contributor, and to every
other person. . . . III. Every tax ought to be levied at the time,
or in the manner, in which it is most likely to be convenient for
the contributor to pay it. . . . IV. Every tax ought to be so
contrived as both to take out and to keep out of the pockets
of the people as little as possible, over and above what it brings
into the public treasury. . . ."

We may take leave of our economic Father Adam by quoting
his recommendation of "the obvious and simple system of
natural liberty. . . . Every man, as long as he does not violate
the laws of justice, is left perfectly free to pursue his own
interest his own way, and to bring both his industry and capital
into competition with those of any other man, or order of
men. The sovereign is completely discharged from a duty, in
the attempting to perform which he must always be exposed

to innumerable delusions, and for the proper performance of which no human wisdom or knowledge could ever be sufficient; the duty of superintending the industry of private people, and of directing it towards the employments most suitable to the interests of the society."

For Further Reading

Smith, Adam, *An Enquiry into the Nature and Causes of the Wealth of Nations.* Edited by Edwin Cannan, with introduction by Max Lerner (New York: Modern Library, Inc., 1937).

————, *Lectures on Justice, Police, Revenue and Arms,* delivered in the University of Glasgow by Adam Smith, reported by a student in 1763. Edited by Edwin Cannan (New Edition, New York: Kelley & Millman, 1956).

Rae, John, *Life of Adam Smith* (London: The Macmillan Co., 1895).

Hirst, F. W., *Adam Smith* (English Men of Letters series, London: The Macmillan Co., 1904).

Scott, W. R., *Adam Smith as Student and Professor* (Glasgow: Jackson, Son & Co., 1937).

Fay, C. R., *Adam Smith and the Scotland of his Day* (Cambridge, Eng.: Cambridge University Press, 1956).

Bonar, James, *A Catalogue of the Library of Adam Smith* (2d ed., London: Macmillan & Co., 1936).

Clark, J. M. and others, *Adam Smith,* 1776–1926 (Chicago: University of Chicago Press, 1928).

3

HEX ON SEX

Thomas R. Malthus

Malthus was the most controversial figure among economists. In so saying we confine the term to a particular doctrine (his "Principle of Population") and exclude the revolutionary ground-swell produced by the challenge of Marx. Of course there have been other arresting announcements, as of the anarchists and of Henry George in his "Single Tax," but the reverberation of these was due to organized movements in their behalf. The same has been true in lesser degree of the impetus supplied by Robert Owen, Fourier, and St. Simon. In our own day the recommendations of Keynes, less startling, swiftly passed into public policy. But for a bold pronouncement, standing alone, that of Malthus provoked the most resounding battle.

The irony of Malthus is partly personal, partly in economic development. He was the mildest man that ever declared a cruel verdict and laid a harsh sentence on humankind. His was a bolt from the blue, for nothing in his nature prepared for the storm he raised. A contrast as sharp is in the hopeless forecast of permanent poverty at just the moment when the energies of production were being released as never before, in the Industrial Revolution. A further singular feature is that the Malthusian furor has happened in two periods, the first in Malthus's lifetime and the second a century later in the contemporary world.

A caution is in order. If we center attention on Malthus's foreboding about population—what another called the "fearful pre-eminence" of "more men than corn"—we must not suppose that he was the author of one book. He was a classical

40

economist of a high order of capacity and performance, belonging in the triumvirate with Adam Smith and David Ricardo. His *Principles of Political Economy* (1820) is the rounded expression of his views and critical faculties, not to speak of his occasional tracts on a variety of subjects. Ricardo credited Malthus with originating the explanation of rent which oftener goes under Ricardo's name. Ricardo busied himself with extensive *Notes on Malthus* (long lost, but edited by Jacob H. Hollander in 1928), testifying to his respect for his friend's contributions. Malthus's treatment of the scope and method of political economy, as a blend of exact principles and wise policy, is fully applicable today.

Thomas Robert Malthus was born February 14, 1766, in Surrey, England. He was the second son of Daniel Malthus, a country gentleman of moderate means but enough to allow him full leisure to cultivate his tastes for literature (French and German included) and philosophy. Daniel's intellectual sympathies were as wide as all mankind, though he preferred for himself the secluded life of his pleasant old house, "The Rookery," where he puttered around his grounds with a keen appreciation of botany. At Queen's College, Oxford, he had followed his own devices, glad to remain at his books even during vacations, but left without a degree. Of Daniel's wife we know literally nothing except that she was the mother of a famous son and seems to have died before her husband.

In his agreeable surroundings—local to himself, for he sought no society in the county—it was easy for Daniel Malthus to hope and expect that others would enjoy similar happiness. A student of nature, he was also an admirer of human nature. With this penchant, he was so intimate with Jean Jacques Rousseau, who sought refuge in England about the time Thomas Malthus was born, that he became a dozen years later Rousseau's literary executor.

Following Rousseau's *laissez faire* prescription for education, Daniel let his sons ramble at will in their early years. Indeed Thomas continued to ramble when sent to his first tutor (Richard Graves, rector of Claverton near Bath), who paid little attention to Thomas and Thomas less to him. The same spirit of the maximum of self-discovery and minimum of discipline greeted young Malthus at an academy at Warrington conducted for the sons of dissenters. However, five years of this permissiveness served to fit Thomas for Jesus College, Cambridge, of which his master, Gilbert Wakefield, was a fellow.

Here he was fond of liberal, abstract studies, being especially good in mathematics. After taking his bachelor's degree (1788), he obtained his father's leave for additional years of reading, on his own plan, promising that after thorough grounding he would make useful application of his knowledge. His first essay, "The Crisis" (1797), at his father's urging he did not publish. Strangely at variance with his later opinion, he took no offense at Pitt's proposal to liberalize the poor law to encourage large families—this to furnish more recruits in the war then in its furious beginnings.

In this year Malthus took his master's degree, became a fellow of Jesus College, and obtained a curacy near Albury, the vicinity to which his parents had moved. Recently Thomas's reading and thoughts had turned from natural philosophy to political economy. It was inevitable that, on a visit to his father, the two fell to discussing William Godwin's *Enquirer,* which had just appeared. This was a follow-up of Godwin's more systematic *Political Justice* (1793) and illustrated the author's irrepressible belief in the prefectibility of man in society. This optimism was exactly to Daniel Malthus's liking, and he supported Godwin's enthusiasm with relish.

It is often observed that a dour, over-firm father will have a rebel for a son. The opposite happened in this instance. The father, romantic and visionary, found himself in his flights brought to earth by severely practical objections of his son. Discussion of Godwin's treatment of avarice and profusion "started the general question of the future improvement of society." Soon after, to clinch his arguments in rebuttal, Thomas sat down to write them out. "But as the subject opened upon him," he explained, "some ideas occurred, which he did not recollect to have met with before; and as he conceived, that every, the least light, on a topic so generally interesting, might be received with candour, he determined to put his thoughts in a form for publication."

This exploration and statement, with his father's encouragement, appeared anonymously the next year, 1798. *An Essay on the Principle of Population, as it Affects the Future Improvement of Society, with remarks on the Speculations of Mr. Godwin, M. Condorcet, and other Writers* was a loosely printed volume of fewer than 400 pages, some 60,000 words.

When Malthus committed his first thoughts to paper, the exuberant idealism of the French Revolution of 1789 had died in the Terror of five years later. From lifting up the hearts of the common people, frantic factional leaders (notably Robespierre of the Jacobins) had gone to thrusting heads of their political enemies under the guillotine, some 2,500 of them. The English people were unfitted, temperamentally and politically, to be attracted to the Revolution from the beginning. Theirs was a stratified society, content to discover betterment in piecemeal, constitutional fashion. They did not readily ignite in a flaming demand for equality; liberty for them was in law; fraternity did not go beyond respect from the "lower orders" and philanthropy approved by the wealthy. Now England was grappling with Napoleon, who had overrun Italy, dictated terms to Austria, and was threatening the British Empire by his invasion of Egypt.

The chief targets of Malthus's attack, Godwin and Condorcet, were among the few to persist in their utopianism, Godwin through many years, Condorcet in hiding from the Jacobins until he was captured and disappeared in 1794. Tom Paine's *Rights of Man* were in the way of becoming, not altogether through his own fault, the rights of Tom Paine.

If the French Revolution had soured, the Industrial Revolution at the time of Malthus' *Essay* had not unfolded its promise of increased production. Malthus was born about the time of the inventions of Hargreaves, Arkwright, and Watt. Soon Brindley and Telford were cutting canals and building roads. Manufactures would make Britain the workshop of the world, with London, Bristol, and Glasgow the ports from which she commanded the trade of the continents. But in the seventeen-nineties the transition from agriculture and home crafts was dismaying and cruel. Factories displaced some workers while they engulfed others. Population and poverty increased hand in hand. It would be a half century before the industrialists, demanding cheaper bread that they might pay lower wages, succeeded in removing tariffs on grain. The prevailing view in Malthus's time was that the poor were to be supported in their poverty, not be enabled to rise out of it. Before Malthus passed from the scene, the new potentialities of production and trade were evident. But by then, for better or worse, he was committed to a gloomy outlook and restriction of population. The accident of his argument with his father that led to the original *Essay* threatened to confine him for life to exploring a particular problem. He was like an actor who is so notable in one role that he cannot get away from this success to play other parts.

Malthus was by no means the first to "see . . . unconquerable difficulties in the way to . . . the perfectibility of man and of society." It was a commonplace that increase of meat would be met by increase of mouths, so where was the gain, except in numbers? Malthus himself said of the first edition, "The only authors from whose writings I had deduced the principle which formed the main argument of the *Essay,* were Hume, Wallace, Adam Smith, and Dr. Price." These works were among "the few materials which were then within my reach in a country situation." Others had faced the same quandary— Dr. John Bruckner in 1767, James Steuart in the same year, and Joseph Townsend twenty years later.

If, as Malthus declared, many writers had taken notice of the "obvious truth . . . that population must always be kept down to the level of the means of subsistence," what did he add? No writer, so far as he knew, had "inquired particularly into the means by which this level is effected: and it is a view of these means, which forms . . . the strongest obstacle in the way of any very great future improvement of society." Malthus did more than define and illustrate the restraints on population. As James Bonar has observed, Malthus treated all phases of the problem "in their connection, perspective, and wide bearings." He was able to establish a principle and apply it to cases otherwise puzzling. No thinker is wholly original. If we give him a primary place, it is because he investigated a subject with more thoroughness than others and in doing so cast new lights upon it. This distinction does not exempt him from the limitations of his time. Malthus came at the end of one era (of dearth of production), and at the beginning of another, of comparative plenty. It was the former experience of social deficit which depressed him. Through science, invention, and improved means of transportation, hunger, as a familiar human misery, was on the way to being removed unless in exceptional cases. But Malthus belonged to yesterday. He assumed that what had been would continue into the future.

While Malthus was too pessimistic, Godwin and Condorcet

erred the other way in being too optimistic. Malthus himself said later, "It is probable that, having found the bow bent too much one way, I was induced to bend it too much the other, in order to make it straight." In this contrast the merit could be claimed by Malthus. He founded his reasoning on fact, he investigated history. The Utopians whom he combated were fancy free. They could give wing to their exalted hopes because they were in the realm of imagination. Their conclusions were reached by deduction from principles that pleased them. Malthus, given a few postulates, proceeded inductively from experience. The truth, as time revealed, lay somewhere between them.

Said Godwin, "There is no characteristic of man which seems at present . . . so eminently to distinguish him . . . as his perfectibility." And in a later edition of the *Political Justice,* "the voluntary actions of men are in all instances conformable to the deductions of their understanding." He explained in revision of his first bald statement, "By perfectible, it is not meant that [man] is capable of being brought to perfection. But the word seems sufficiently adapted to express the faculty of being continually made better and receiving perpetual improvement." So much for modification of perfectibility. But Godwin's vision of the far future was sufficiently alluring. Human life would be extended indefinitely, so there would be no need for marriage to produce offspring, and the sex instinct would be done away by intellectual development. "The whole will be a people of men, and not of children. Generation will not succeed generation, nor truth have . . . to recommence her career every thirty years. Other improvements may be expected to keep pace with those of health and longevity. There will be no war, no crimes, no administration of justice, as it is called, and no government. Besides this, there will be neither disease, anguish, melancholy, nor resentment. Every man will seek with ineffable ardor the good of all."

In opposing such speculations Malthus explained, what is not to be doubted, that he did not desire to find them visionary. "I ardently wish," he declared, "for such happy improvements." Evidence was against their realization, but he hoped that critics of his essay could prove him mistaken. In such case he would "gladly retract his present opinions, and rejoice in a conviction of his error."

Now to the *Essay* itself. Malthus immediately resolved that he would not proceed on mere conjectures; probable cause for a belief must be shown. "A writer may tell me that he thinks man will ultimately become an ostrich. I cannot properly contradict him. But before he can expect to bring any reasonable person over to his opinion, he ought to shew, that the necks of mankind have been gradually elongating; that the lips have grown harder, and more prominent; that the legs and feet are daily altering their shape; and that the hair is beginning to change into stubs of feathers. And till the probability of so wonderful a conversion can be shewn, it is surely lost time and lost eloquence to expatiate on the happiness of man in such a state; to describe his powers, both of running and flying; to paint him in a condition where . . . each man's share of labour would be light, and his portion of leisure ample."

Malthus objected that near-perfection or a carefree state could never be reached because population would always press against the food supply. He offered two postulates: "First, That food is necessary to the existence of man. Secondly, That the passion between the sexes is necessary, and will remain in its present state." Godwin had no grounds for his supposition "that the passion between the sexes may in time be extinguished." (Godwin had said, as noted above, that "voluntary actions of men are . . . conformable to . . . their understanding." Godwin enthroned reason above the sex instinct). Malthus, on the contrary, found "no progress whatever" in this department.

Then he came to his third basic proposition, which is known to every student, namely, "that the power of population is indefinitely greater than the power in the earth to produce subsistence for man." This is because "Population, when unchecked, increases in a geometrical ratio. Subsistence increases only in an arithmetical ratio. A slight acquaintance with numbers will show the immensity of the first power in comparison of the second." The effects of these two unequal powers must be kept equal by "a strong and constantly operating check on population from the difficulty of subsistence," and this check "must . . . be severely felt by a large portion of mankind."

Nature distributes life with a profuse hand, but life is limited to the supply of nourishment. And the check that keeps the two in balance? "Among plants and animals its effects are waste of seed, sickness, and premature death. Among mankind, misery and vice. . . . Consequently, if the premises are just, the argument is conclusive against the perfectibility of the mass of mankind." The body of the book is Malthus's appeal to experience which "invariably confirms" his sobering forecast.

He would test his proposition about people tending to increase geometrically and food only arithmetically. He would settle for the rate of growth of population in the United States of America, where conditions were most favorable. There population had been found to double every 25 years. If the produce of England and Scotland, by breaking up more land, could be doubled in the first 25 years, that would be an accomplishment. This produce could not be quadrupled in the the present amount. This increase is evidently arithmetical. next 25 years; the utmost possible would be to increase it by Malthus did the simple figuring to show that after a century the people would number 112 millions, while the food supply would support only 35 millions, "which would leave a population of seventy-seven millions totally unprovided for."

An escape in emigration was ruled out when he applied his formula to the whole world. Suppose the then population of the world to be one billion, the human species would increase in the ratio of 1, 2, 4, 8, 16, 32, 64, 128, etc., and subsistence as 1, 2, 3, 4, 5, 6, 7, 8, etc. In two centuries and a quarter the population, if unchecked, would be to the means of subsistence as 512 to 10, in three centuries as 4096 to 13, and in two thousand years the disparity would be almost incalculable.

Suppose the fear of lowering one's station in life, or of outright want and seeing his children in rags, restrains from "early attachment to one woman." Monogamy Malthus considered, under sanction of marriage or not, "the dictate of nature and virtue." This abstention "almost necessarily, though not absolutely so, produces vice." This is the price of one check on population. Yet in even the most vicious societies, "the tendency to a virtuous attachment is so strong, that there is constant effort towards an increase of population. This . . . constantly tends to subject the lower classes . . . to distress, and to prevent any great permanent amelioration of their condition." No "permanent amelioration" because, if conditions of life are tolerable, workers will increase their numbers. But food not being immediately increased proportionately, the lot of the workers is worsened. With labor cheap, production of food will rise to restore the old balance. Laborers being again fairly comfortable, the restraints to population are loosened, and the story is repeated. This oscillation or vibration of population is obscured by causes which Malthus named. The principal one was the silence of history concerning "the manners and customs of that part of mankind [the working people], where these retrograde and progressive movements chiefly take place." But the existence of this seesaw of population was undoubted.

This observation of Malthus was the foundation of Ricardo's subsistence theory, or what the sarcastic Lassalle called the "iron law" of wages. It was that workers would tend to get enough to maintain them and keep up the race of workers, with no long-time betterment. As soon as their lot improved they would take out their good fortune in having more children, more children would survive, there would be more applicants for work, and wages would fall.

Malthus put it in the most general terms by saying that "population does invariably increase, where there are the means of subsistence, the history of every people . . . will abundantly prove." And he referred, as so many times, to the necessary checks of misery or vice as "these too bitter ingredients in the cup of human life."

Not until well into the *Essay*, in considering the pressure of population on food supply in civilized nations, England typically, did Malthus develop the force of the "preventive check." The "positive check" included hunger, famine, sickness, pestilence, vice, evil living conditions in great cities, and war. The preventive check, refusal to marry early or to marry at all, applied principally in the middle class and upper groups of the lower classes. In these, prudence often restrained from the fatality of a large family that would bring parents and offspring to want. Gentlemen with small income, farmers, artizans, tradesmen, down to footmen and housemaids were in this category. Among the laboring poor this self-denying foresight operated feebly from numerous causes. Ignorance, lack of earning capacity, and habits of hand-to-mouth existence figured. But Malthus stigmatized, as a powerful contributor to reckless marriages and population growth, public poor relief which removed the salutary dread of destitution.

The poor laws of England, costing some £3,000,000 annually, "though they may have alleviated a little the intensity of individual misfortune, . . . have spread the general evil over a much larger surface. . . . It may at first appear strange, but I believe it is true, that I cannot by means of money raise a poor man, and enable him to live much better than he did before, without proportionably depressing others in the same class." If the food produced in the country remained the same —and Malthus thought the poor law did nothing to increase it—a larger share to some meant smaller shares to the remaining.

This was comfortable doctrine for the wealthier classes. In good conscience they could begrudge their forced contributions for the indigent because these increased the distress. The poor laws tended "to create the poor which they maintain." First, they increased population without increasing food. Second, provisions consumed in workhouses by the least valuable and least industrious part of the population deprived worthier persons.

Dependence should be made disgraceful. A man who would go to the alehouse, not deterred because he might leave his family on the parish, might hesitate to waste his earnings if he knew that, in the event of his sickness or death, "his family must starve, or be left to the support of casual bounty." Malthus proposed a few reforms in the poor law. Stop all parish relief in supplement of wages. For cases of extreme distress, establish county workhouses supported by taxes on the whole kingdom, where the fare would be meager, and all must work who could do so. A corollary would be, abolish the laws of settlement, which confined relief to those belonging to the particular parish. This would stimulate independence and permit workers to go where there was employment. Further, hold out "all possible encouragements . . . to agriculture above manufactures." This would increase healthy work and the food supply and raise wages on the land. Being better off, and with no prospect of going to the parish for assistance, the farm worker would be more inclined "to enter into associations for providing against the sickness of himself or family."

As to these last recommendations, note that Malthus still thought of England as primarily an agricultural country, or at least a country self-contained. Though England was on the eve of sending manufactures to all the world and importing much of her food in return, Malthus did not sense this means of providing for her population. It is not so surprising that he should have argued for sick-benefit clubs more than a century before England adopted social insurance.

Malthus then commenced to show in more detail why the visions of a perfect society must be dashed by scarcity of food in the face of rising population. Dr. Robert Wallace (*Various Prospects of Mankind, Nature, and Providence,* 1761) recognized this danger; but like some others, he said it could not be imminent until a period so far distant as not to be worth troubling about. The whole earth must be intensively tilled before we need fear for subsistence. But Malthus objected that "At every period during the progress of cultivation, from the present moment, to the time when the whole earth was become like a garden, the distress for want of food would be constantly pressing on all mankind. . . . Though the produce of the earth might be increasing every year, population would be increasing much faster; and the redundancy must necessarily be repressed by the periodical or constant action of misery or vice."

He took more space in pricking the bubble of Condorcet (*Esquisse d'un Tableau Historique des Progrès de L'esprit Humain*—Sketch for an Historical Picture of the Human Mind, 1795). First he feelingly praised Condorcet's devotion to his ideals in the face of bestialities of the Reign of Terror in France. Cordorcet steadfastly hoped for the perfect society while he was himself virtually under sentence of death from the degraded Jacobins. Malthus swiftly sketched the degenerated behavior that mocked the philosopher's dreams. Condorcet must be noble to withstand the spectacle of "one of the most enlightened nations of the world, after a lapse of some thousand years, debased by such a fermentation of disgusting passions, of fear, cruelty, malice, revenge, ambition, madness, and folly, as would have disgraced the most savage nation in the most barbarous age. . . ."

Condorcet, like Wallace, was sensible of the problem of overpopulation but deferred it to a remote era. By that time the renovation of society might be expected to cancel the danger. Want, misery, sickness would be banished and the life of a human being would be lengthened without assignable limit. But, said Malthus, the notion of earthly immortality flew in the face of all experience. Condorcet would "make facts bend to systems, instead of establishing systems upon facts." In all known millenia the maximum of man's life had not increased. Suppose by eugenics the span might be stretched; though "I may not be able . . . to mark the limit, at which further improvement will stop, I can very easily mention a point at which it will not arrive." Bakewell had bred Leicestershire sheep for small heads and legs in order to increase the meaty parts of the animal, but if he kept at it forever, "the head and legs of these sheep would never be so small as the head and legs of a rat." Malthus made no apology for patiently exposing the Frenchman's absurdities. "When paradoxes of this kind [human immortality on earth in a perfect society] are advanced by ingenious and able men, neglect has no tendency to convince them of their mistakes."

And how would Condorcet combat the menace of too many vigorous Methusalahs, male and female, in that distant paradise? Why, either by "a promiscuous concubinage, which would prevent breeding [!], or . . . something else as unnatural." But to remove the difficulty in this way must be to destroy the very virtue in society which was Condorcet's object.

Malthus bore down harder on Godwin, who conjectured that, in a society ruled by reason and benevolence, laws of property would cease to oppress. Malthus objected that it is not human institutions, but "deeper seated causes . . . that . . . render turbid the whole stream of human life." Suppose, with Godwin, all the ills of English society done away, and a simple sufficiency of produce divided according to everyone's wants. There would be no marriage, but sexual attachments would be formed at will. "It would be of little consequence, according to Mr. Godwin, how many children a woman had, or to whom they belonged. Provisions and assistance would spontaneously flow from the quarter in which they abounded, to the quarter that was deficient."

What would happen? An immediate upsurge of population. Since every cause of depopulation would have been removed, "the numbers would inevitably increase faster than in any society that has ever yet been known. Malthus repeated his earlier comparison of population growing by multiplication and food supply by addition only. Further, by no amount of forcing, with more cultivators and more fertilizer, could the land be made to yield the same increase year after year. He did not name the law of decreasing returns in agriculture, but that is what he was expounding, as elsewhere in his *Essay*. With the added produce of the earth shrinking and population doubling and redoubling, disaster must follow. "Alas! what becomes of the picture where men lived in the midst of plenty. . . . This beautiful fabric of imagination vanishes at the severe touch of truth. The spirit of benevolence . . . is repressed by the chilling breath of want. The hateful passions that had vanished, reappear." No social institutions, which Godwin blamed, would have failed. In fifty years at the utmost nature would have checked further population by precipitating the old violence, injustice, misery, and starvation. Malthus spelled out the sorrowful correctives that must return Godwin's children of light to the familiar darkness.

This disillusioning recital compelled notable reformers who wrote after Malthus was dead—for example, Marx and Henry George—to combat his dire prediction. How would it profit if they destroyed bad institutions, only to encounter Malthus's retrogression due to a surplus of population? By their time, as we shall see, they could exploit a fallacy in Malthus's forecast which he himself later partially admitted. But more of that when we come to the revised second edition of the *Essay*.

In several passages toward the end of his essay Malthus expressed his general pessimism about the future of humankind. Because of the principle of population he did not look for "any very marked and striking change for the better, in the form and structure of general society; by which I mean, any great and decided amelioration of the condition of the lower classes of mankind, the most numerous, and . . . the most important part of the human race."

Can we find any consolation in this gloomy outlook? Yes, Malthus the clergyman was equal to it. The last chapters are a sermon on the familiar theme that the Almighty has decreed sufferings for our good. Without the stimulus of want we should not be excited to effort, physical, mental, and moral. Malthus says in several places that men in society should make all the ameliorations possible in the human state. But actually he does not believe much can be done toward producing, not an earthly paradise, but a more tolerable lot for the masses. He is not a reformer of social institutions. He accepts "the established administration of property, and the apparently narrow principle of self-love" as the springs of civilization, indeed of "all the finer and more delicate emotions of the soul." He deplores great inequality of fortunes between the classes of proprietors and laborers, but doubts "whether a government could with advantage to society actively interfere to repress" this injustice. He does not quite go the length of saying, "Earth is a desert drear, Heaven is my home," but almost that.

For Malthus the prospect of reorganizing society did not exist. He was Newtonian in proclaiming the supremacy of natural law. In this he went beyond Adam Smith and even his friend Ricardo, for he dealt specifically not with wealth but with human welfare. He submitted humbly to the curse laid on the first man and first woman when they were expelled from the Garden of Eden.

Fortunately, in his period when *laissez faire* was triumphant, his religiosity did not save him from a chorus of protest against his desperate doctrine.

In the second edition of the *Essay*, 1803, of which he acknowledged himself the author, Malthus presented a less drab prospect for mankind. The first edition had been a spur of the moment performance, argumentative rather than expository, and with little supporting data. To justify himself, in answer to critics, he resolved to give the whole question further examination. Collecting materials on the operation of the principle of population currently, he visited the continent twice. He went in 1799 to Germany, the Scandinavian countries, and to part of Russia, the only regions which the war then permitted an Englishman to visit. Three years later, the Peace of Amiens allowed him to travel in Switzerland and France. He supplemented his observations and conversations in his journeys with diligent reading in the accounts of explorers in far quarters of the world.

Aside from abundant illustrations of his central contention, the revised work developed a third defense against pressure of population on the food supply. He explained in his preface that "I have so far differed in principle from the former [statement] as to suppose the action of another check to population which does not come under the head either of vice or misery." This was "moral restraint" in the form of refusal to marry until a man could expect to support the children he would bring into the world. He had included this "preventive check" earlier, as we have noticed, but now he gave it a new emphasis which to the minds of most readers brightened the outlook for social improvement. In further concession, he "endeavoured to soften some of the harshest conclusions of the first Essay."

Moral restraint was in every view the best check on excess population. "The period of delayed gratification would be passed in saving the earnings which were above the wants of a single man, and in acquiring habits of sobriety, industry, and economy, which would enable him in a few years to enter into the matrimonial contract without fear of its consequences. The operation of the preventive check in this way, by constantly keeping the population within the limits of the food though constantly following its increase, would give a real value to the rise of wages and the sums saved by labourers before marriage, very different from those forced advances in the price of labour or arbitrary parochial donations which, in proportion to their magnitude and extensiveness, must of necessity be followed by a proportional advance in the price of provisions. As the wages of labour would thus be sufficient to maintain with decency a large family, and as every married couple would set out with a sum for contingencies, all abject poverty would be removed from society, or would at least be confined to a very few who had fallen into misfortunes against which no prudence or foresight could provide."

Of course, if this preventive check of moral restraint was to combat the old enemies, the positive checks of vice and misery, men must practice chastity in the period of waiting for prudent marriage. Promiscuity would doubly increase the dependent population: numbers would mount, and laborers would lack competence to amplify production. Thus wages would fall and at the same time cost of provisions would rise.

Nor did Malthus for a moment allow escape from these evil consequences of promiscuous sex indulgence by use of artificial methods of birth control. Condorcet had approved these devices. Malthus did not describe but on every occasion abhorred them. They were unnatural, vicious, morally and socially degrading. Malthus was a moralist as well as a utilitarian.

He by no means surrendered his original thesis that "the passion between the sexes," unless checked by some means, would call to nature's table more mouths than food. Some of his erstwhile critics were jubilant that Malthus had now contradicted himself. By admitting the power of prudential restraint he had opened the way to constant social betterment. This was true. Malthus admitted—or gladly agreed, for he was the ardent friend of improvement—that as he had overstressed passion, he had too much restricted the prospect of increasing production of food. But he insisted that the peril to which he pointed inveterately lurked. The process of eradicating poverty, vice, crime, misery, pestilence, famine, and war would be arduous, slow, and in constant danger of counteraction.

Meantime, as a stimulant to prudence, he proposed that, after due notice, parish relief should be abolished. The poor could not, as of right, claim public maintenance. The disregardful would suffer when it was withheld, but this would be the inescapable price of benefit to the whole society. The increasing proportion of the community dependent, after the peace of 1815, on parish assistance, and notable rise in taxes for this purpose, combined with Malthus's warnings to produce vigorous discussion of eligible remedies. The result was, in the year of Malthus's death, the New Poor Law of 1834 which ended home relief and placed administration under national auspices.

The *Essay* went through six editions in Malthus's lifetime, the last in 1826, and was translated into German and French. He constantly made additions and revisions, but only the second edition, with four times as much matter as the first, made significant change over his original formulation.

Recurrently since, most recently during the Great Depression of the nineteen-thirties, neo-Malthusians have repeated his alarms that the world, unless by means of positive and preventive checks on population, is staring starvation in the face. In developing countries aids to public health have precipitated a "population explosion" previous to any corresponding increase in food production or alteration of habits in favor of prudence. We are put on notice that the three-fourths of the world's people who are impoverished menace the more fortunate and self-disciplined minority.

In certain overpopulated countries, especially India and China, Malthus's doctrine, in its crudest form, has long been applicable and is so today. In advanced nations of western Europe and North America, where population growth is slowing or numbers are stationary, and where production of food and other necessities and comforts of life increase, his principle persists, though banished to the background.

Legal and religious objections to the use of contraceptives are being removed. It may be that Malthus was mistaken in supposing that mental activity and a variety of aesthetic and social enjoyments did not diminish the sex urge. As intellectual and a variety of emotional expressions are developed, perhaps mere physical gratifications are to a degree sublimated. The moral restraint of Malthus has been called into the service of preserving or improving the standard of living. The procreative instinct—certainly when combined with effective contraceptive means—appears to yield to the superior desire for security, education, an attractive home, entertainment, travel, and so forth.

In some instances, in the market economy at any rate, the burdensome surplus is one of bread and meat, not of men. Soil chemistry, seed selection, control of plant diseases, superior transportation, improved methods of preserving and storing even perishable foods, and knowledge of nutrition have made provisions available in quantities that have actually prompted destruction. However, the spectacle of too much food and fiber, of wheat and cotton ploughed under and young sows turned into soap is only local. Even in the places where resort is had to these expedients in the interest of price and profit, many struggle in poverty and hunger. And viewing the world as a whole, the message of Malthus still rings in human ears.

Aside from Malthus's direct contribution to the subject of population, he had a greater indirect influence through Darwin's theory of evolution. Darwin recorded that it was in reading Malthus's allusions to the prodigality of nature in scattering seed, and the struggle among animals and plants for food and room, that the idea of the *Origin of Species* (1859) popped into his mind.

That Malthus was a clergyman gave critics an obvious opportunity to contrast his holy office with his tolerance of the worst evils. "Parson Malthus," jibed Cobbett, "wants an act of parliament to prevent poor people from marrying young, and from having such lots of children." While profoundly religious, Malthus did not make the church his career. He never held more than a curacy, and that early in life. Later the Whigs (Lord Brougham) offered him a parish, but he declined it in favor of his son. At that time a large proportion of teachers and scholars were clerics; with Malthus academic pursuits clearly took precedence.

In 1805, possibly as the result of a meeting with Pitt at Cambridge, he was appointed Professor of History and Political Economy in the newly established Haileybury College in Hertfordshire. This institution gave a couple of years of general education to youths going out as servants of the East India Company. A colleague was Professor of General Polity and the Laws of England, while others offered Oriental languages, classics, mathematics, and natural philosophy. With the prospect of his chair at Haileybury, Malthus married Harriet Eckersall of St. Catherine's near Bath. The rural setting of the College, he wrote, was "very sweet, and vernal, and soothing, and fit enough to efface all recollections of hot, swarming . . . London from all good minds."

At Haileybury Malthus enjoyed thirty years of security and quiet for his studies and writing. Comparative quiet, that is, for the boys he taught were young, some only fifteen, and boisterous. Numbers were sons of directors of the India Company, and had little other fitness to become civil servants. They not only hazed each other, but in traditional insurrections directed missiles at their mentors. Sydney Smith, ever waggish, wrote that "The season for lapidating the professors is now at hand . . ." The "situation [of a friend joining the faculty] will suit him very well, peltings and contusions always excepted. He should stipulate for 'pebble money,' as it is technically termed, or an annual pension in case he is disabled by the pelting of the students. By-the-bye, might it not be advisable for the professors to learn the use of the sling (*balearis habena*)? It would give them a great advantage over the students." One would think Malthus could put up with these capers better than with the mental immaturity of his pupils. But he resolutely hoped that his efforts to give political economy to the older boys were not wasted, for, he reported, "they could not only understand it, but they did not even think it dull."

He became the official defender of the College against attacks upon it in Parliament. Lord Grenville feared that training future

Indian servants to themselves did not equip them with "English manners, English attachments, English principles, and, I am not ashamed to say, English prejudices." Malthus, chosen by his colleagues as a proven arguer, went to London to hear this speech. He replied in pamphlets that the students' behavior, in the classroom and out of it, would be better if the professors were given authority to expel recalcitrants and to deny graduation to an unfit fifth of the entrants. It seems a pity that the foremost economist of Britain in academic life was not given the facilities of one of the universities. Malthus escaped from his steady diet of juvenile association by regular attendance at meetings of the Political Economy Club and by systematic correspondence and visits back and forth with Ricardo and others who were adult indeed.

These friendships involved no embarrassment, as his teaching and occasional sermonizing in the college chapel may have done, from an impediment in his speech due to a hare lip. However, "I would almost consent to speak as inarticulately," said Sydney Smith, "if I could think and act as wisely." And Harriet Martineau, with whom Malthus had cordial exchanges at Haileybury and at her dinner table in London, was similarly excusing. In return for Malthus's praise of her accurate presentation of his ideas, she said she could understand him without her habitual ear-trumpet; "his vowels at least were sonorous, whatever might become of the consonants." Anyhow, tall and modestly self-possessed, his appearance and manner did much to offset his defect of pronunciation.

Malthus died of a heart attack while on a Christmas visit to his wife's family, and was buried in Bath Abbey. His epitaph, elaborate in the style of that day, was doubtless by his old college-mate, Bishop William Otter.

For Further Reading

Malthus, Thomas R., *An Essay on the Principle of Population,* 1798. Facsimile of first edition issued by Royal Economic Society, with notes by James Bonar (London: Macmillan & Co., 1926).

Ashley, W. J., ed., *Parallel Chapters from the First and Second Editions* of *Malthus's Population,* 1798:1803 (New York: The Macmillan Co., 1895). Besides a comparison, this book affords a judicious abridgment of the two principal editions.

Malthus, Thomas R., *Principles of Political Economy, Considered with a View to their Practical Application,* 1820. Reissue of second edition, with memoir by William Otter (New York: Augustus M. Kelley, 1951).

Bonar, James, *Malthus and his Work* (New York: Harper, 1885). Scholarly criticism, summary, brief biography.

Godwin, William, *An Enquiry Concerning Political Justice and its Influence on General Virtue and Happiness,* 1793. Edited and abridged by R. A. Preston, with foreword by Lindsay Rogers (New York: Alfred A. Knopf, Inc., 2 vols., 1926).

Condorcet, Antoine Nicolas, *Sketch for an Historical Picture of the Progress of the Human Mind,* 1795. Translated by June Barraclough, introduction by Stuart Hampshire (New York: The Noonday Press, 1955).

Vogt, William, *Road to Survival* (New York: Wm. Sloane Associates, 1948). Lively recent example of Malthusianism.

4

DIMINISHING RETURNS

David Ricardo

Plaques on the walls of the cathedral at Bath, England, testify that numbers who sought the waters of that place were disappointed in their hopes of health. Fortunately the sojourn of Mrs. David Ricardo was beneficial, for she lived to an old age with spirited pretensions. More important for the world of ideas, she was accompanied to Bath by her husband, a London broker, who found time a little heavy on his hands in that resort of the ailing and the leisured. Wandering into a circulating library he came upon Adam Smith's *Wealth of Nations*, "and turning over a page or two ordered it sent to his house. He liked it so much as to acquire a taste for the study."

We do not know the precise date (about 1799?) of this meeting of minds of the Scottish philosopher and the City banker. The circumstance marks the beginning of the second phase of development of the "classical" study of political economy. Ricardo, practically concerned in financial operations, was peculiarly fitted, in experience and talents, to be the pupil and then the improver of the older master. The economic image, seen through Adam Smith's lens, was broad but in many parts vague. Ricardo, the man of affairs, adjusted the focus for sharper definition. Ricardo, too, shifted the scrutiny. Smith, as was natural at the outset, was preoccupied with the production of wealth. Ricardo, more than a generation after Smith, when problems of production were on the way to solution, explored distribution, or the sharing of income among the various classes of producers. Smith and Ricardo are the foremost names in the first scientific formulation of economic principles.

David Ricardo was born in London, April 19, 1772, the third of many children of Abraham Ricardo and his wife Abigeal del Valle. The Ricardo family during a hundred and fifty years had been expelled from Spain, found temporary refuge in Italy, were attracted thence to the credit capital of Europe in Amsterdam, and with the commercial ascendancy of England, the economist's father settled across the channel. The elder Ricardo prospered as broker and merchant, obtained from the Crown the rights of permanent residence, and secured full license in the Royal Exchange. His integrity as a trader took the form, in his religious life, of firm, even intolerant attachment to his synagogue and the traditions of the Sephardic congregation. This was natural in a refugee from oppression and prejudice who had nonetheless made a place for himself and guarded every means of his safety.

David received the practical schooling calculated to fit him for a business career. This included two years in Amsterdam, when he lived in the home of an uncle, studied doubtless in the famous Talmud Tora attached to the Portuguese synagogue, learned the Dutch language, and was introduced to the commercial concerns of his relatives. At fourteen he became the precocious helper in his father's counting house. Here he eagerly discharged responsibilities beyond his years. In this respect, as in several others, he reminds us of his contemporary Alexander Hamilton, who was a junior merchant when most boys were entrusted with no more than their own pocket money.

By the age of twenty-one David Ricardo was no longer an apprentice in finance. Nor was he submissive to his father in choice of a wife. She was a Quakeress, Priscilla Ann Wilkinson, daughter of a neighboring surgeon. Marriage outside the Jewish faith expelled David at a stroke from paternal roof and business partnership. The elder Ricardos and the young couple were reconciled a few years later, as well they might be, for the home established by David and Priscilla was notably happy, blessed by eight children. The off-shoot from the ancient stock was flourishing, too. Principal members of the stock exchange, already convinced of David Ricardo's integrity and talents, rallied around their youthful friend, so suddenly thrust on his own, to put support and opportunity in his way. Their confidence was rewarded by his swift progress to reputation and riches.

While still in his twenties he accumulated handsome resources and might then, if he chose, have retired from active business to devote himself to the studies which were to make him celebrated in the development of economic thought. As it was, he combined intellectual inquiry with ever greater pursuit of the pound sterling. Such leisure as he could snatch he occupied with branches of mathematics, chemistry, and mineralogy. He fitted up a private laboratory and was an early member of the Geological Society. His first concern with physical science and cultivation of habits of exact reasoning helped prepare for his later investigations in a more complicated field. He was not the first nor the last to begin with natural laws and go on to areas of human relationships and institutions. While he was fond of quantitative statement, Ricardo did not become a mathematical economist. Rather by his skill in deductive method, arguing from accepted general principles to fruitful particular conclusions, he opened the way for pioneers in the application of mathematical analysis such as Jevons. Ricardo perfected economic logic, but did not appeal to logarithms.

We would be mistaken, however, to suppose that Ricardo was not impelled to abstract reasoning by daily observation of and personal participation in extraordinary events and stresses of his period. The Industrial Revolution and the Napoleonic wars raised a whirlwind that churned every phase of public and private life. As in the demonstration in physics in which several forces meet at a point, Ricardo, as a dealer in credit, was at the center of tensions. New demands were put on British agriculture to feed armies across the channel and sustain the swelling home population. Workers were being drawn with accelerating speed from farms into factories, from cart and plow to anvil and loom, from country cottage to city slum. Mechanical inventions typified by Arkwright and Watt furnished industrial profits, which were promptly placed under command by the exchequer to support the furious long war. In spite of intensified taxation the public debt between 1793 and 1816 multiplied more than four times. Here was a call for new financial devices to match those in production of wealth. Ricardo was the man to help summon resources of unexampled magnitude, with a sophistication that served both national need and his private advantage.

Ricardo rose to affluence and financial sway amidst events which invited speculation, but by the same token demanded information and a nice calculation of chances. News of military fortunes on the continent inspired rapid alternation of hopes and fears. The bank restriction of 1797 caused a premium on gold, together with fluctuations in the foreign exchanges and in prices of foodstuffs already jumpy enough from blockade and uncertain harvests. Ricardo, following the success of his independent operations, was able to aid the Chancellor of the Exchequer as one of a limited number of loan contractors. These specialists in finance furnished the treasury certainty by bidding to underwrite the new debt issues. As the war progressed, these public borrowings came in swifter succession and greater magnitude. As a contractor, Ricardo committed subscribers in advance and proposed to take a loan at a price. The contractors aided the Exchequer with their counsel as well as with their credit.

An illustration of Ricardo's patriotic reliability was afterward related in the House of Commons. When other contractors recommended a loan of £24,000,000, Ricardo, "greatly to his credit, observed to the chancellor of the exchequer, that if he considered his own interest merely, he must agree with his brother contractors; but if he were to consult the advantage of the country, he should advise the application of the sinking fund, and a loan of £12,000,000 only." Ricardo's public response to this tribute was characteristically honest and modest: "He had . . . given the opinion which he had long entertained. He should have sunk into the earth before those who had long known his sentiments if he had given any other; but he knew that those gentlemen who had given a contrary opinion had given it just as conscientiously; for great and sincere differences of judgment on this subject existed in the city."*

Already attracted to economic study, Ricardo was now encouraged to formulate and express his views. The first influence in this direction was his friendship with James Mill, commencing in 1807 and continuing in unbroken intimacy for the

---

* See Jacob H. Hollander, *David Ricardo, a Centenary Estimate* (Baltimore: The Johns Hopkins Press, 1910, pp. 38–40). The present brief sketch of Ricardo and his contribution owes most to Professor Hollander's perceptive essay.

remainder of his life. Mill, philosopher, critic, soon the historian of British India, was Ricardo's mentor who became his disciple and expositor. Systematic and industrious, James Mill lacked the limberness and creative faculty of his more famous son, John Stuart, who was to mark the transition from *laissez faire* to social reform. But the elder Mill, in addition to exact scholarship, enjoyed the wide acquaintance among publicists, writers, and editors which he used to usher the busy broker into intellectual and literary circles. Not that Ricardo had been unmindful of the flow of economic discussion in books, controversial pamphlets, and particularly in the *Edinburgh Review,* but James Mill drew him into personal participation.

A more specific stimulus was in monetary events which fixed Ricardo's attention both as financier and as economic critic. Bank paper, not convertible into gold, increased in volume by some 15 per cent in less than two years following November, 1808. In the year 1809 the exchange with Hamburg fell 3 shillings, from 30s. 8d. to 27s. 8d., and the price of gold bullion ruled 15 per cent or more above the mint price. The premium upon gold in terms of inconvertible paper became the conspicuous feature of the "bullion controversy" which first brought Ricardo, as an analyst, to public prominence. Thereafter, in a brief decade, his power of penetration and the naked candor of his mode of statement made him the acknowledged master in pronouncements on confronting problems and in comprehensive treatment of principles of political economy.

Ricardo commenced with the habitual diffidence in communicating his views which contrasted with bold confidence in his results. Moved to dissent from James Mill's review of Thomas Smith's *Money and Exchange,* Ricardo sent an unsigned contribution, on "The Price of Gold" to the Morning Chronicle at the end of August, 1809. Ricardo's light was not to be hid under a bushel. In the next couple of months he published in the same columns replies to attacks by "A Friend to Bank Notes but no Bank Director," (actually his friend and fellow broker Hutches Trower). In his rejoinders Ricardo got so far as to sign his initial, "R." He got further in keeping the record straight, for he discredited plausible partisan excuses and arguments that proceeded from mental confusion.

Ricardo insisted forthrightly that the Bank of England had

issued too much paper money and was causing inflation. We may give his reasoning in the conclusions of the Bullion Committee of parliament whose inquiry he inspired: (1) "That the variations of the exchange with foreign countries can never, for any considerable time, exceed the expense of transporting and insuring the precious metals from one country to the other." (2) "That the price of Gold Bullion can never exceed the mint price, unless the currency in which it is paid, is depreciated below the value of gold." (3) "That the paper currency is now excessive, and depreciated in comparison with gold, and that the high price of Bullion and low rates of exchange are the consequences as well as the sign of such depreciation."

Others assigned different reasons for the lowered estimate, at home and abroad, placed on the value of English paper money. Thus Sir John Sinclair "takes much pains to inform us, that the increase of our commerce and of our public revenue require an additional amount of circulating medium." To which Ricardo answered, "Who has denied it? . . . But . . . if no increase of Bank Notes beyond such necessity had taken place, no depreciation could have occurred . . . it is the excess above this amount, only, whilst the Bank possesses the confidence of the public, which causes depreciation." Those who presumed to measure the quantity of note issues against the volume of commerce declared "that the amount of bank-notes has not increased in a greater proportion than the augmentation of our trade required, and therefore cannot be excessive." Ricardo gave penetrating reasons for his reply that this assertion "would be difficult to prove, and if true, no argument but what is delusive could be founded upon it." He dealt similarly with complaint of his critics that "He attributes a favourable or an unfavourable exchange *exclusively* to a redundant or deficient currency, and overlooks the varying desires and wants of different societies, as an original cause of a temporary excess of imports above exports, or exports above imports."

Those who would not admit that "this depreciation in the actual value of bank-notes has been caused by the too abundant quantity which the Bank has sent into circulation" had another dodge. The bank-notes, it was offered, "are the representatives of our debased silver coin, and not of our standard silver." But, Ricardo rejoined, "This is not true, because the law . . . declares silver to be a legal tender for sums only not exceeding 25 *1.* [pounds] except by weight," and he stated the consequence. "If the Bank insisted on paying the holder of a bank-note of 1000 *1.* in silver coin, they would be bound either to give him standard silver of full weight, or debased silver of equal value, with the exception of 25 *1.* which they might pay him in debased coin. But the 1000 *1.* so consisting of 975 *1.* pure money, and 25 *1.* debased, is worth more than 1112 *1.* at the present market value of silver bullion." Ricardo contended throughout that "for near a century gold has been the standard metal. But if a change have taken place, and silver be now the standard of value, and consequently bank-notes the representatives of the silver coins, this" as he demonstrated, "will not remove the difficulty."

Ricardo was more than the practical man perfectly versed in the practices of finance and commerce. Unlike many of his fellows "on 'Change," who made light of theory, he founded his observations on "the admitted principles of political economy" as expounded by the best writers. "Merchants," Ricardo remarked in the course of the bullion controversy, "may understand the details of business—they may give much useful information; but it does not therefore follow that they are qualified to give sound opinions on points of theory and science. Glass-makers and dyers are not necessarily chemists, because the principles of chemistry are intimately connected with their trades." Because he appealed to pervasive economic forces, Ricardo was not misled by current "facts" which seemed to be at variance with them. While his pursuers entangled themselves in thickets of apparently contradictory evidence, Ricardo pressed through to his object. Not that he ignored refutation citing particular experience; he often paused to show, with patience, exactly why supposed disproofs were specious.

As he proceeded in his newspaper letters and short pamphlets, posing his own proposition, answering attackers, and supporting the report of the Bullion Committee with which he substantially agreed, he became animated in thrust and parry. If he had difficulty in composition, it is not betrayed in these spirited exchanges. In all, however, he was modest and considerate of those who differed from him. Though his dissents were emphatic, his mode was never harsh or belittling toward his opponents.

As his concern was for the public good, so he aimed to be helpful to the proprietors of the Bank of England whose overissue of notes, if continued, invited peril to the nation's economy. "We have advanced so far in this ruinous path," he declared, "that we are beset with dangers on every side;—to proceed will inevitably plunge us into increasing and accumulated difficulties, from which we shall be unable hereafter to extricate ourselves; and to return, though by far the safest course, will be attended with trials which will require a great degree of ability, integrity, and firmness to surmount."

Ricardo believed the reform recommended by the Bullion Committee, that the Bank after two years should be required to redeem their notes in specie, was too summary. Probably the Bank at such short notice could not provide itself with sufficient bullion to meet this mandate. Instead, the premium on gold of some 17 per cent, "proving a depreciation of the currency of nearly 15 per cent," could be corrected "by more gentle means" in which he hoped all parties would agree. He proposed to make the resumption selective: "Let the Bank . . . be required by Parliament to pay (if demanded) all notes above 20 *l.*—and no other, at their option, either in specie, in gold standard bars, or in foreign coin (allowance being made for the difference in purity) at the English mint value of gold bullion, viz. 3*l.* 17*s.* 10½ *d.* per oz., such payments to commence at the period recommended by the Committee." This limitation might be extended for three or four years, "and if found advantageous, might be continued as a permanent measure." For reasons which he detailed, circulation of the smaller notes notwithstanding, "Under such a system the currency could never be depreciated below its standard price, as an ounce of gold and 3*l.* 17*s.* 10½*d.* [in paper] would be uniformly of the same value."

The disturbances of war produced clashes of interest among groups and classes. The currency controversy posed the advantage of creditors (through resumption of specie payments and higher value of money) against that of debtors if the greater plenty of money were continued. Ricardo's involvement was in the first instance technical, had to do with the causes of economic manifestations and only incidentally with social policy. But the next question that centered in Parliament was frankly a contest between historic economic sectors in the community. The theoretical explanation, while original and of permanent influence, was at the time of small concern to the public.

The struggle over the corn laws (import duties on grain, chiefly wheat) was bound to be acute as soon as the final defeat of Napoleon loomed. The combatants were on the one hand landlords, composing the ancient class economically, politically, and socially dominant in England. On the other hand were the rising industrial enterprisers. The issue was, shall Parliament protect the traditional aristocracy or favor the capitalist innovators? The familiar, cherished past, or the clamorous future? The patterns of rural life, or the demands of burgeoning manufacturing cities and towns? The owners of country estates for centuries had been social arbiters. Opposing them were members of the middle class, no longer simply merchants and petty tradesmen, but pioneers in production with power machines, employers of hundreds or thousands of operatives.

Actually, distress of the landed gentlemen developed before the peace. Efforts to raise more food by extending cultivation to poorer soils and use of better methods resulted in abundant harvests. Prices were further depressed by imports from Ireland and impending return to gold payments. But the prospect of the future, when grain would flow in from the continent and from America unhampered by blockade, embargo, and hazards of capture at sea, was more alarming. What then would happen to rents already imperilled? Fears of landlords contrasted with hopes of captains of industry. If the price of bread fell these employers could and would pay less in wages to their factory workers. Their costs of production thus reduced, their profits would rise correspondingly. The collision of classes was head-on. Landlords wanted higher import duties to preserve the home market. Manufacturers argued for free trade. Not only did industrialists require unimpeded imports of grain to keep wages down, but they could better sell their textiles and hardware abroad if other countries could sell foodstuffs to England and earn pounds with which to pay for English goods.

If threatened drastic decline in land rents formed the problem, the question in the minds of discerning thinkers was, what makes rents go up or down? By economic rent they meant— what we mean today—payment for the use of land or other natural resources, exclusive of any improvements or capital investment. Rent, as the term is employed in everyday speech, usually embraces buildings, fencing, drainage, terracing, fertilizing, and so forth, and in this sense includes interest on capital and profits of enterprise. The economist's rent is compensation for mere land, "the original and indestructible qualities of the soil," or, in the case of urban land, not its fertility but the convenience of its location.

With the law of rent needing to be defined, several writers offered the same answer at about the same time—Malthus, Edward West, and Robert Torrens, as well as Ricardo. Though he was not the first, Ricardo gave the principle the most precise definition and cleared away misconstructions that marred the exposition particularly of Malthus. Ricardo's reasoning was offered early in 1815 in his "Essay on the Influence of a Low Price of Corn on the Profits of Stock." His argument was that as population and the demand for food increase, resort must be had to inferior soils less convenient to market, or to additional application of capital and labor to lands already in use. In either case the return, or "the profits of stock," will decrease. But the owners of lands will demand from tenants, in rent, the whole produce above what the tenants contribute in capital and labor. Competition among tenants (farmers in the case of agricultural lands) will reduce them all to the returns of the tenant on the land which barely repays cultivation. By the same token, all that is yielded on the superior lands, above the minimum return from the marginal or "no rent" land, will be demanded by landlords, since they are the owners. Economic rent, then, is a surplus, depending in amount upon the differences in quality or location of lands.

The operation of rent, therefore, with increasing needs of society for foodstuffs and raw materials, skims off the excess above what will content the most necessitous cultivator. The result is that while profits and wages tend toward a minimum, rents automatically rise. Ricardo showed that rents must be high if and because the price of corn is high, not the other way around. He observed, "It is now universally admitted, that rent is the effect of the rise in the price of corn, and not the cause; . . . the only permanent cause of the rise in the value of corn, is an increased charge on its production, caused by the necessity of cultivating poorer lands; on which, by the expenditure of the same quantity of labour, the same quantity of produce cannot be obtained."

Two possible sources of confusion in the reader's mind must be removed. The returns to the cultivator or other tenant of which we speak are income *per unit* of capital and labor. The user of better land will realize a higher total return, but that is because he employs more units of investment. The product of his last unit of investment, which will be no more than common profits and wages, is of course his; he contributed the capital and labor, with no assistance from the landowner. But the portions of his total product resulting from earlier and more profitable investment must be surrendered to the landlord. In other words, the occupier of better land, except that he has the opportunity of employing on it his larger capital and greater amounts of labor, is reduced, in percentage return, to the condition of the cultivator of the least productive soil.

A further question may be disposed of. What is the effect on profits of improvements in methods of production, say the introduction of machinery and cheaper means of transportation? These economies are contributed by capital and labor. The completely passive landlord had no part in bringing them into existence. The increased product which these betterments make possible therefore belongs to the investor. The result of improvements in cultivation, while population remains the same, will be to raise the margin of the use of land. The poorer soils, previously needed, will now be abandoned. Profits will rise, rents will fall.

We have noted that the contentions between classes of claimants on government favor—primarily agriculturalists and industrialists, or land and capital—fastened Ricardo's attention on the relative importance, for England's progress, of shares in the national income. Profits and interest, rather than rent or wages, commanded his steady preference. Higher profits furnished the source of capital accumulation, on which depended economic advance. Ricardo's impulse was partly from the teachings of Adam Smith, partly from the spectacular achievements in industry which enabled England to triumph in the war, partly from his own involvement in finance. Capital and its gains became increasingly the national pole-star.

Indeed Ricardo's emphasis on diminishing returns in agriculture, with consequent increase of rents, was not for its own sake, or to fend off higher import duties on grain, but to show the damage to industrial profits. He argued that restriction on the importation of corn raised its price, higher cost of food compelled increase of wages, higher wages reduced profits and interest. This was manifest in agriculture. That was bad enough, but the ill result was communicated, for "it is the profits of the farmer which regulate the profits of all other trades." Competition would not permit returns in manufactures or commerce to rule higher than in the least profitable employment. Again, "the general profits of stock depend wholly on the profit of the last portion of capital employed on the lands."

Ricardo could not convince Parliament to his view. Of what weight was a pamphlet of the ablest reasoner against the frantic demand of landlord and farmer for higher import duty to protect against the calamitous drop in grain prices, with worse in prospect? The law of 1804 imposed a fixed duty while wheat sold under 63 shillings a quarter (eight bushels, one-fourth of a ton). Amendment in 1815 prohibited imports so long as the price at home was under 80 shillings. This resulted in fluctuating prices, which did not satisfy its sponsors. New clamors for remedy returned Ricardo to the attack, both in pamphlet and in Parliament. He urged gradual progress toward "a substantially free trade in corn." But it was almost a quarter-century after his death that the corn laws were repealed (1846).

About the time of the corn law controversy, but not because of that agricultural discussion, Ricardo, like many another business man who had achieved success, bought a country estate— Gatcomb Park in Gloucestershire. For some years he shuttled back and forth to London, but more and more he treasured the quiet of rural life in which he pursued his economic studies without interruption. We have from Maria Edgeworth a glowing picture of the domestic scene, including a vignette of a charade: "Mr. Smith, Mr. Ricardo, Fanny, Harriet, and Maria *crowing*. Ditto, ditto, *combing* hair. Mr. Ricardo, solus strutting, a *coxcomb*, very droll." Ricardo's unaccustomed coachmanship on the steep roads of the country neighborhood drew from Sydney Smith the report that "a new surgeon has set up in Minchin Hampton"—the nearby town—"since Mr. Ricardo has taken to driving."

Ricardo's only treatise was the *Principles of Political Economy* published in 1817. It is notable for giving the subject scientific coherence as against the looser philosophical character of Smith's *Wealth of Nations*. As we have seen, Ricardo developed the "laws" of distribution (governing rent, profits, wages) rather than dwelling on means of efficient production as Smith had done. He contributed a fresh analysis of international trade. He traced the shifting and incidence of taxes, showing who are the final payers, in whole or in part, of different duties. Throughout, his method was deductive, deriving particular consequences from assumed firm premises. His early attachment to geology and chemistry carried over to give his description of social behavior a formality, a precision, even a rigidity which he had applied to the physical sciences.

His treatment of value, while it bulks large, was not written for its own sake but for the purpose of establishing his previously taken position on the relation of wages and profits. A rise in wages causes a fall in profits, because higher wages do not compel a rise of prices by which the employer may compensate for his increased costs, and may in fact result in lower prices. In successive editions of the work Ricardo modified his dictum that value proceeds from and is measured by the labor embodied in a commodity or service. His alterations and concessions resulted from the criticisms of Malthus and others, but more from his own disturbing doubts about the accuracy of his first bald statement of the doctrine. Capital employed in production was itself stored-up labor. Thus if much fixed capital is applied (machines and plant) and little circulating capital (used to acquire materials and pay wages), the amount of labor embodied in the product will be different from the labor transferred if ready capital in the "mix" is great in proportion to the relatively permanent capital. This difference does not trouble the theory, but it makes "embodied labor" an uncertain measure of value. And what about a product whose value is increased not by expending on it more labor, but simply by a period of waiting before the commodity is consumed, as with aged wines? And scarcity presented a variant of this problem, as in the instance of old masterpieces of painting or unique jewels.

Perplexed, Ricardo worked around to practical abandonment of embodied labor as the measure of value. He ended by concluding that gold is the measure of value. This is as much as to say that the value of a good is what a purchaser will give for it. This shifts the criterion of value from cost to use, from supply to demand, from objective to subjective measure. It comes close to admitting what Jevons and the Austrian economists declared years later, that value depends on marginal utility, or the satisfaction derived from the last unit of a commodity or service which consumers will demand. Ricardo did not take this step into consumers' estimate of value, afterward defined by others in terms of psychology and differences in needs, tastes, and purchasing power.

For better or worse Marx lingered in Ricardo's contentment with a labor theory of value, and made it, with its corollaries, the dependence of Communist preachment. As Ricardo left the subject of distribution in the *Principles*, rent was the surplus from better lands above the product of labor and capital bestowed on the poorest land; wages would not rise permanently above subsistence level; profits and wages were antithetical, but both were depressed by the progress of rent; the rate of interest was not altered by a general rise in prices.

Ricardo, and Robert Torrens about the same time—we need not enter into the vexed question of precedence—advanced beyond the mere territorial division of labor in describing conditions of international trade. A country would do well to export a product in which it enjoyed an advantage over other countries, Ricardo pointed out, and in return supply itself with specialties of its neighbors. It might have an absolute advantage in two products, and yet choose to take one of them from abroad. The reason lies not in the verdict of the mystified Adam Smith, "a certain propensity in human nature . . . to truck, barter and exchange one thing for another"; the explanation is that the country with an advantage in two products has a superior comparative advantage in the one it exports. Therefore it will economically devote its production to the commodity in which it has the greatest advantage and obtain the other by trade.

Though Ricardo was a man of much modesty, he came increasingly before the public. Once engaged in a pamphlet discussion, he pursued it. His formal *Principles* established him as a chief expositor of economic doctrine, often relating to pressing questions of policy. His increased participation in the forum of opinion, and doubtless the urgings of his friends, persuaded him to seek election to Parliament. With no inclination toward a political campaign, the convenient and at that day familiar method was to purchase the seat of a "pocket borough."

Ricardo is supposed to have made a loan of £25,000 (some believed more) without interest to the proprietor who determined the votes of the few electors of Portarlington in Queens County in Ireland. Ricardo never so much as visited his constituents, who in 1819 returned him to the House of Commons in fulfilment of the bargain. This corrupt practice, in the case of Ricardo anyhow, gave the public the benefit of superior legislative talents. Though at first rising to speak, Ricardo was alarmed at the sound of his own voice, he was always heard with attention, for he expressed himself on questions in which his authority was admitted—currency, the Bank, taxation, agricultural distress, and trade. His warm sympathies made him the friend of parliamentary reform, civil rights, and the motives, though not the prescriptions, of Robert Owen. Of no party, his views were frequently called for from both sides of the House.

Ricardo was in his usual health, happily planning visits from old friends to Gatcomb Park, when he was suddenly attacked by an infection of the ear which in a few days reached the brain. He died September 12, 1823, and was buried on the estate of a daughter near Chippenham, Wiltshire.

The need of an investigator for association and discussion with persons of similar curiosity was supplied in Ricardo's case by serious regular correspondence (with Malthus, McCulloch, Trower, etc.), by visits back and forth, and especially in meetings of the Political Economy Club. It was founded in 1820, perhaps as a consequence of more informal gatherings under Ricardo's roof. He never missed a meeting when he could be present to pursue common inquiries with those just mentioned and Torrens, Tooke, James and John Stuart Mill, Senior, Grote, Sydney Smith, and more. The Political Economy Club, with its informed, critical exchanges, became Ricardo's university seminar.

We have portraits and a bust of Ricardo, and several who knew him well gave descriptions of his personal appearance and disposition. He was somewhat below middle height, had an open, friendly expression of face, with shining dark eyes. He hated anything like presumption and was considerate of others, in individual relationships and in his generous charities.

It is ironical that Ricardo more than others should have furnished the kernels of two reform philosophies that went vastly beyond any application he would have made of his doctrines. The labor theory of value, unhappily coupled with the subsistence theory of wages, was the inspiration of Karl Marx's socialist forecast. It could not have been different; the ubiquitous assumption of the London broker that "the labour of the country . . . constitutes its only real source of wealth" was bound to set vibrating every sense of a poor refugee champion of the rights of exploited workers. The teaching of the prime exponent of capitalism was readily transmuted into the revolutionary cry, "Workers of the world, unite! You have nothing to lose but your chains!"

Similarly from Ricardo's demonstration that land value is a social product, and that the landlord's exaction of economic rent depresses both labor and capital, came the demand of Henry George that society must reclaim in tax what society has created. Henry George, it is true, wished not to destroy but to preserve capitalism, with its premises of private ownership of man-made means of production, competition, and the price system. He believed that recapture of rent by the community would free individualist forces for beneficial operation.

It is not here implied that Ricardo was the first to tell the tale, or that Marx and George were the first to adorn it with a moral. The development of economic thought is not so exactly identified with particular persons. Rather, these are mentioned for their conspicuous influence.

For Further Reading

Ricardo, David, *The Principles of Political Economy and Taxation,* 1817. Introduction by William Fellner (Homewood, Ill.: Richard D. Irwin, Inc., 1963). In Irwin Paperback Classics.
———, *Notes on Malthus' "Principles of Political Economy,"* edited with introduction and notes by J. H. Hollander and T. E. Gregory (Baltimore: The Johns Hopkins Press, 1928).
Hollander, Jacob H., *David Ricardo, A Centenary Estimate* (Baltimore: The Johns Hopkins Press, 1910). A most valuable brief account.
Ricardo, David, *Works and Correspondence,* edited by Piero Sraffa and M. H. Dobb (Cambridge, Eng.: Cambridge University Press, 1951, 10 vols.). Vol. X has biographical material.
Turner, John R., *The Ricardian Rent Theory in Early American Economics* (New York: New York University Press, 1921). Helps in understanding such dissenters as H. C. Carey.

5

NURTURE, NOT NATURE

Robert Owen

Generous, but opinionated; inventive but dogmatic; planful in an age that celebrated chance; immersed in the miseries of mankind, but ever sublimely hopeful; of lowly origin, he stood before kings—such was Robert Owen. Probably no thinker or advocate was more influential for social reform in his own day or, through movements which he inspired, reaching to ours. Though his career was strewn with disappointments, we may truly speak of the success of his failures.

Owen (1771–1858) was born in Newtown, Montgomery-shire, Wales, next to the youngest child in the large family of a saddler. As his constant preachment was to be that man's character is made for him through circumstances, and not by him through his own design, we are not surprised to find that to his earliest experiences he ascribed effects on his later life and opinions. From the age of four or five he was the eager pupil of the village schoolmaster. One day, hurrying to the class, he swallowed his piping "Flummery" (porridge) so fast that his stomach was scalded and he fell in a faint. "In that state I remained so long, that my parents thought life was extinct. However, after a considerable period I revived; but from that day my stomach became incapable of digesting food, except the most simple. . . . This made me attend to the effects of different qualities of food on my changed constitution, and gave me the habit of close observation and of continual reflection; and I have always thought that this accident had a great influence in forming my character." In spite of this damage to his stomach, Robert Owen managed to get along, through strenuous years, to the age of eighty-seven.

Besides flummery he devoured all the books he could lay

hands on—biography, history, novels, even Harvey's *Meditations among the Tombs* and Young's *Night Thoughts*. When only seven he became his teacher's usher, assisting in instructing his younger fellows. He deplored having his talents set above the accomplishment of other scholars. "Such competitions," he later recorded, "are unjust, because, as no two organizations are the same, there can be no just comparison between the . . . efforts of any two individuals,—while the successful one is thus taught vanity, and the unsuccessful, jealousy and hatred." Fond of dancing class, he had compassion for "the girls . . . if they could not obtain the partners they liked. . . ." Their distress was afflicting. "I have long thought that the mind and feelings of young children are seldom duly . . . attended to. . . . I am now conscious there was much real suffering in that dancing-room, which, had there been more knowledge of human nature in the dancing-master and in the parents of the children, might have been avoided."

At nine the boy quit school for work in a neighbor's drapery (dry goods) shop. But soon, determined to see the wider world, he got his parents' consent to let him seek employment in London when he should be ten. With forty shillings in his pocket he posted off atop the night coach. After a few weeks with an older brother in Holborn, friends secured him a place as apprentice to James McGuffog, a prosperous draper in Stamford, Lincolnshire. McGuffog's signature now sells for a tidy price because he was the kind master of Robert Owen. The apprentice rapidly became a little man of business, a judge of fine fabrics and a favorite in waiting on the gentry who were McGuffog's customers.

The boy's religious devotion at this period was to be expected. His doubts aroused by contentions between sects were not so usual. More surprising was his considered conclusion that "Christian, Jew, Mohamedan, Hindoo, Chinese and Pagan" were all in error. One's character was forced upon him by his environment, was not created by his own soul's striving. He abandoned "all belief in every religion which had been taught to man" in favor of "the spirit of universal charity,—not for a sect or a party, or for a country or a colour,—but for the human race, and with a real and ardent desire to do them good." This sounds premature in a child, but it was a conviction that was elaborately illustrated throughout his life.

His apprenticeship completed, Owen shifted to a larger shop on London Bridge. Here, through interminable hours, he served not the carriage trade but cash customers for cheap goods. His next move, luckily, was to Manchester, already in the late seventeen-eighties the focus of the developing Industrial Revolution, notably in "spinning cotton by new and curious machinery." While still clerking in a retail store Owen got to know a mechanic who had found out the means of making "mules" (the latest advance in production of yarn). With borrowed capital and materials obtained on credit these two employed forty men building excellent equipment for sale to rapidly rising and expanding mills in the vicinity. Owen fortunately sold out before mismanagement by his partner threatened the enterprise. With his share of completed machinery Owen began, on a small scale, to spin cotton.

Owen heard that Drinkwater's new mill, only partially in operation, unexpectedly required a manager. In a sort of "double-take"—at first paying no attention but then resolved to apply—he hastened to the owner. When his youth was overcome (he was not yet twenty) the salary he demanded astonished Drinkwater. It was more than all other eligibles together had requested. Owen replied that he was making that sum (£300) in his own business, invited Drinkwater to see the proof in his books, and Owen was engaged.

His impulsiveness presented him with a challenge, for of much of the machinery and many processes from cotton to yarn he knew nothing. Furthermore, how was he to organize the work of 500 men, women, and children? With studious application, Owen was soon in command of the situation. He improved conditions for the workers and spun the finest yarns in England, fit for weaving into muslins, and sold the product at a premium price. In 1791 he tested the first American sea island cotton ever sent to Britain. While achieving reputation as an expert manufacturer, unlike others in the trade who were "generally plodding men of business, with little knowledge and limited ideas," Owen welcomed intellectual contacts. In an informal group that held its meetings in Manchester College he was intimate with John Dalton, the chemist then defining his atomic theory, with Samuel Taylor Coleridge, and others who came to distinction. Invited into the inner circle of the Literary and Philosophical Society of Manchester, he at first gave papers on the cotton industry, but then was emboldened to avow his theological dissent and to insist that good or bad characters were the result of social environment. He had learned what he could of the chemical discoveries of Lavoisier and Chaptal, and one evening announced that "the universe appeared . . . to be one great chemical laboratory; that all things were chemical compounds, and that man was only a complicated chemical compound." His notion far antedated biochemistry as we have come to know it!

Not the least of Owen's coterie of "enquiring friends" and a fellow lodger in Brazen Nose Street, Manchester, was Robert Fulton, deep in inventions for canal construction and navigation. Fulton was as fertile in projects as he was lean in pocket, and Owen advanced him small sums—minute when compared to the ultimate momentous success of the steamboat which these loans served to forward. Briefly these two young enterprisers were in formal partnership; but when Fulton found other resources, Owen preferred to withdraw, and Fulton remained his debtor for £100, never repaid. The generous Owen looked on "the little aid . . . which I gave to enable him to bestow so great advantage on his country and world, as money most fortunately expended."

Another celebrated figure entered Owen's story. Samuel Oldknow of Mellor, who occupied a special place in the genesis of textile manufacture, was about to marry Drinkwater's daughter. He wanted to bring the two firms under one ownership. Drinkwater's earlier engagement to take Owen into partnership with him was an embarrassment. How satisfy a wealthy son-in-law and not lose a valued manager? Drinkwater, who knew nothing of the practical conduct of the business, proposed that Owen forfeit the prospect of partnership and name his own salary as superintendent of the mills. Owen indignantly produced his contract and threw it into the fire, declaring "I never will connect myself with any parties who are not desirous to be united with me; but under these circumstances I cannot remain your manager with any salary you can give." He later reflected, with some contradiction, that his "was an act of feeling, and not of judgment. . . . the previous circumstances in which I had been placed created these feelings, and I could not have acted otherwise at that time."

Robert Owen had not long to regret his exit from Drinkwater's employ, for his talents were in ready demand in a new enterprise, the business of which took him on errands to Glasgow. Here he chanced to be introduced to Caroline, eldest of five daughters of David Dale, "an extensive manufacturer, . . . merchant, banker, and [independent] preacher." Miss Dale suggested that Owen might like to visit the falls of the Clyde and her father's mills at New Lanark thirty miles above Glasgow. On seeing this "primitive manufacturing Scotch village," doubtless because of the improvement it invited, Owen remarked to a companion, "of all places . . . I should prefer this to try an experiment I have long contemplated."

Repeated walks with Caroline on the Glasgow Green ripened the friendship, but a year passed before the bashful Robert, pointedly prompted by a mutual confidante, declared his love for her. She replied that he must obtain her father's consent to the courtship. This seemed to her hopeless; she would not marry without it, and added the cold comfort that she must live and die unwed. Owen had not met the formidable father, whose wealth and excessive religiosity promised to put a young and free-thinking stranger at a disadvantage in pretending to his daughter's affections.

But, not for the first time, commerce aided cupid. Miss Dale had told Owen that her father, wishing to retire and with no son to take over his affairs, was willing to sell New Lanark. He could not trouble to renovate the four old mills which were feeling the competition of newer factories rapidly multiplying. An application to Dale to know whether the report was true offered an excuse for pressing love's suit. The old gentleman, possibly suspicious of Owen's motive, doubted the sincerity and ability of his caller as a prospective purchaser of a large property. This pricked the young Englishman's pride. He explained that he was a practiced cotton spinner in partnership with elders of sufficient capital. After thorough investigation of the mills by Owen and his friends, and of Owen himself by David Dale, New Lanark was sold, lock, stock, and barrel, to the Manchester firm for £60,000, Owen's own price. This was in the summer of 1797, when Robert Owen was twenty-eight. In process of taking over New Lanark he lived at Old Lanark a mile away. The quintet of Dale girls were to vacate the family's summer home at the mill village, but the new owners begged that they complete their usual stay. This gave abundant opportunity for outings of Robert and Caroline "among the beautiful scenery on the banks of the Clyde, and," said he, "our time was thus spent very much to our satisfaction."

The father, getting wind of the walks and talks, brought his daughter back to Glasgow, but Owen followed on many errands of business. The frosty parent gradually thawed during two years. His co-director of the Royal Bank of Scotland, Scott Moncrief (and his lady) vouched for Owen's worthiness. Thus assured, and won by Owen's candor, Dale welcomed the marriage in his own house. The patient preliminaries came to a summary close. "The Reverend Mr. Balfour . . . requested Miss Dale and me to stand up, and asked each of us if we were willing to take the other for husband or wife, and each simply nodding assent, he said, without one word more—'Then you are married, and you may sit down,'—and the ceremony was all over."

The young couple repaired to Manchester, but soon moved to New Lanark where the mills demanded Owen's constant management. The date was January 1, 1800; a new century in social thought and action had commenced.

When, as G. D. H. Cole put it, Owen "entered on his new kingdom,"* the Industrial Revolution was in its first surge. Economic and social life were thrown into confusion by the application of water and steam power to newly invented machines. Beginning with cotton manufacture, the transformation spread to iron and steel, to transport, and made new drafts upon coal production. Rural villages burgeoned into factory towns and cities. Country people abandoned their obsolete spinning wheels and hand looms and were pressed into urban slums. Capitalist enterprise took on a new dimension, Britain commanded the trade of the world, and needed it to support the war against Napoleon. Enthralled by the prodigiously mounting output, Parliament abdicated any responsibility for control of working conditions. The "cotton lords" and their counterparts in other industries, intoxicated with miraculous profits, answered only to their rapacity. The common people, largely illiterate and dislodged by the occupational upheaval, were ruthlessly exploited. The aristocracy numbly acquiesced in the greed of business innovators. Children of tender years—

---

* *Robert Owen*, p. 67.

at first little paupers handed over by parish authorities, but soon youngsters in families of factory operatives—were engulfed in the mills and mines. We must remember that in the absence of public education it was universally expected that children must work, but the suddenly intensified demand for labor subjected them to worse usages. They were now confined in hot lint-filled spinning rooms for twelve, thirteen, even longer hours, from the ages of five or less.

In this organized chaos decades passed before human degradation was resented and reluctantly corrected. The mushroom industrial cities were virtually without representation in Parliament; and long after they got it the propertyless workers remained without voice and had few champions. Robert Owen was among the foremost in the first half of the nineteenth century to confront and seek to solve public social problems.

He began by brightening the corner where he was—his own factory village of New Lanark. To renovate the lives of the people there by providing a good environment was important in itself for their benefit and, incidentally, for the profit of the business enterprise, but from the beginning this was intended to be only a local demonstration of what could be universally achieved. "I had now," he said, "to commence in earnest the great experiment which was to prove . . . by practice, the . . . principles of truth . . . to commence the most important experiment for the happiness of the human race that had yet been instituted at any time in any part of the world." While Owen has been thought of as the founder or inspirer of small, self-contained utopian communities—"vest pocket editions of the New Jerusalem" Marx called them—these were in fact to be only examples, for nobody was more all-embracing in his plans than Robert Owen.

Though David Dale, by comparison with other mill owners of the time, was benevolent, Owen found the population of New Lanark dirty, drunken, immoral, ignorant, and thievish. There were 1300 in families and 400 or 500 "pauper children, procured from parishes." If he had tried the usual method of reducing evils by punishments he must have many jailed, transported, even hanged for their habitual crimes. This would "keep them in a state of constant ill-will and irritation." It would not correct causes of their misery and misconduct—"the long day's work which they had to undergo," the bad housing, and the exorbitant prices they paid, on credit, for the inferior goods they consumed. Instead he used earnings of the mills, so far as his profit-minded partners would allow, for improving physical facilities. He erected clean, convenient homes, dried up the grog shops, sold food and clothing at a 25 per cent saving to the purchasers, quit employing parish children, and set about educating those that remained. Colleagues predicted failure, indeed ruin, from his unheard-of program. The most stubborn obstacle was the hostility of the workpeople themselves, who long suspected that the new manager (an Englishman who was to them a foreigner) meant to extract more gain from their increased exertions.

What decisively won the workers' confidence was Owen's action in paying them their wages during four months of the American embargo on exports of cotton, when the mills had to be shut down. Seven thousand pounds thus distributed, "without a penny deducted from the full wages of anyone," was convincing proof of good intentions.

Owen shortened work hours to ten and three-quarters in the day, and employed no children under the age of ten. This bold stroke, such a departure from the prevailing practice of squeezing out the last energies of the workers, increased their physical fitness and alertness, added to their contentment, and, though this was a subordinate purpose, boosted production and profits. One gentle persuasion was to hang near every worker's machine a block of wood, painted on the four sides black for poor, blue for better, yellow for good, and white for excellent. The side of the "silent monitor," as Owen called it, turned uppermost reported the performance of the previous day. Gradually, as Owen walked through the mills, he found the dark colors giving way to lighter.

The main attraction that brought thousands of visitors to New Lanark from all parts of Britain and from the Continent and America was Owen's school. Inherited from Dale's regime he found one faithful, old-fashioned schoolmaster trying to cope with upwards of four hundred youngsters, endeavoring to teach the older ones to read if they could remain awake after a dozen hours at the machines. Owen promptly set about changing this make-believe into a progressive scheme of education embracing infants of eighteen months up to adults of twenty years. He adopted what he favored from the systems practiced by Lancaster, Bell, Pestalozzi, and other pioneers, but added superior methods of his own. It was not until 1816 and after two changes of partners that he was able to erect a large new building for his "Institution for the Formation of Character." It was principally a school, but contained reading and recreation rooms for grown-ups. Training of the younger children, especially, abandoned completely the customary catechism and learning by rote. Owen substituted, in the most modern fashion, supervised play, particuarly dancing, singing, and marching. "They give health, unaffected grace to the body, teach obedience and order in the most imperceptible and pleasant manner, and create peace and happiness to the mind, preparing it in the best manner to make progress in all mental acquisitions."

Against objections of the parents, he withheld books until his tots were six, and believed himself that ten was not too old to begin with the printed page. "The children were not to be annoyed with books; but were to be taught the uses and nature . . . of the common things around them, by familiar conversation when the children's curiosity was excited so as to induce them to ask questions. . . . The schoolroom for the infant instruction . . . was furnished with paintings, chiefly of animals, with maps, and often supplied with natural objects from the gardens, fields, and woods." The subtle lesson was that all living creatures, from starfish to elephants, are products of their varying environment. By such means rational development was encouraged; "with these infants everything was made to be amusement." To witness these wonders came bishops, members of Parliament, nobility of foreign lands. Owen recorded, "I have seen as many at once as seventy strangers attending the early morning exercises of the children. . . ." The Grand Duke Nicholas, afterward Czar of Russia, with his suite, made a delightful sojourn. Remarking on the alarms of Malthus, the Grand Duke, on leaving, addressed Owen: " 'As your country is over-peopled, I will take you and two millions of population with you, and will provide for you all in similar manufacturing communities'."

Children above ten were generally obliged by their parents to work in the mills, so their schooling, more conventional than that of beginners, must be in the evening under the severe handicap of fatigue. Nowhere in the school at New Lanark were there punishments or rewards, since, as character was made for and not by the individual, Owen saw no place for personal blame or praise.

William Cobbett, not without his own intensities, was just the fellow to scoff at Owen's schemes. Being at New Lanark, he recorded, "I was rather curious to know whether there was any reality in what we had heard about the effects of the Owen 'feelosofy.' The building which Owen had erected was used as a schoolroom; and here I saw boys . . . and girls . . . carrying on what was called education. There was one boy pointing with a stick to something stuck up upon the wall, and then all the rest of the boys bawling out what that was. In one large room they were all singing out something at the word of command. In another . . . there were eighteen boys and eighteen girls, the boys . . . in Highland dresses, without shoes on, naked from three inches above the knee, down to the foot, . . . each having a girl by the arm, . . . the girls without . . . shoes and stockings; and there were these eighteen couples marching . . . to the sound of a fiddle . . . with great regularity and elegance." Though these were children swathed in tartans, Cobbett, in a pang of prudery, was alarmed lest such "half-naked lads and girls" were being educated for "pre-mature marriage" that would never "check population."

Owen pointed out that his reforms at New Lanark, which so astonished visitors, were confined to a manufacturing community and were subject to many compromises, particularly the need to make profits from the business enterprise. But his limited demonstration gave him a hankering to prove, with a freer hand, that favorable circumstances would produce happiness and virtue in all mankind. His opportunity came when, following the Napoleonic wars, the problem of poverty became more insistent than ever. Mechanical and scientific means of increasing output, enormously stimulated by the long conflict, became a mockery in the economic letdown that resulted from the peace. When markets contracted, efforts to reduce costs forced the further substitution of machines for human labor. Mass unemployment and spreading destitution in the midst of potential plenty alarmed the propertied, ruling class. Poor rates were more burdensome, but mounting distribution of public relief was self-defeating because it encouraged larger families. How long would paupers, thus systematically multiplied, remain merely receptive and not resort to forms of violence that would threaten the familiar social order?

A meeting at the City of London Tavern in 1816, presided

over by the Duke of York and attended by principal churchmen, politicians, business men, and economists, considered remedies for the prevailing distress. A continuing committee, with the Archbishop of Canterbury as chairman, heard Owen's testimony, which pointed to what we have since called technological unemployment. He afterward embodied his views in a formal report, which was also submitted to a select committee of the Commons inquiring into the poor laws.

In this report Owen emerged from the precincts of New Lanark and proceeded, by swift stages, the proclaimer of a "New Moral World" by means of cooperation. Earlier, he declared, machine processes in industry and chemical advances in agriculture had reduced costs and prices, and war demand absorbed the swelling output. But peace was disastrous to human workers expelled by the recent inventions. With reduction of wages, the home market was viciously contracted. (Here was a hint of the failure of mass purchasing power, later signalized as a prime cause of depression). What to do? Abandon the use of machinery? Besides being stultifying, one country could not do it and survive in competition with other countries. Allow wholesale starvation? Even the most confirmed Malthusians would flinch from that.

Owen's expedient was "Villages of Cooperation," in each of which 500 to 1500 people would produce, on the land and in workshops, mostly for their own use. Surpluses would be sold to meet interest on the investment, which could be made by benevolent individuals or by public authorities. Goods might also be exchanged between villages. Near the center of the tract would be a large building in the form of a hollow rectangle (a "Parallelogram") housing living apartments, a common dining room and kitchen, nursery, schoolrooms, library, and shops. Thus the poor, instead of being a public expense and degraded, would sustain themselves in a wholesome and elevating environment; only the smallest part of their output would enter an already overstocked market. He did not now urge complete equality of the villagers, for his proposal was at first a constructive substitute for prevailing minimal relief of the unemployed in demoralizing idleness.

Though Owen was manifestly fitted to give evidence, the parliamentary committee, after two days of debate, refused to hear his testimony. The members were obsessed by the fear

that the good life in the cooperative communities would release all the springs of population growth. But Owen's written
report was printed entire in leading London newspapers. He
blanketed the country with 30,000 copies of these and repub-
lished them in a pamphlet, of which 40,000 were quickly
distributed. This "front attack" cost Owen £4000, but his
blast against pauperization, and his remedy in Villages of
Cooperation became the excited topic of conversation throughout the kingdom. He had supporters aplenty; persons of
wealth were attracted by the promise of lowering the poor
rates. But the Malthusians, economists and other, were loud
in dissent. Relieved of personal responsibility, Owen's protegés
in the communities would beget children without limit. Malthus
himself, in the sixth edition of his *Essay on Population* (1817)
delivered himself against Owen: "if the higher classes of society
were bound to proceed in the system according to its . . . intention . . . the whole nation would shortly become a nation of
paupers with a community of goods." Malthus foresaw by
Owen's scheme "a state of universal poverty and distress."

A feature of Owen's plan, strange for a foremost industrialist
who favored superior means of production, was his preference,
in his villages, for cultivation by the spade, not by the horse-
drawn plough. True, it would emply more hands, but reversion
to a primitive method would "in a very short time plunge [the
spade-wielders] into *aggravated* misery." But with Owen, spade
husbandry was not a caprice. Mistakenly relying on a limited
experiment, he actually believed that turning the earth into "a
highly cultivated garden" would prove most efficient. This
advice was a target of his economist opponents.

Owen reached a climax in overflow meetings in the City of
London Tavern in August 1817, attended by the mighty of the
land. New Lanark and the villages of cooperation were now
pushed into the background, and he resolved on clearing the
way for the regeneration of mankind. "Knowing . . . that unless
a deathblow could be given to all the false religions of the
world, there could be no hope for man's liberation from the
bondage of ignorance, disunion, and misery;—and feeling that
in my then situation I was the only individual living who had
the slightest chance to accomplish such a task—I resolved to
dare the deed. . . ." With considerable drama he declared to
his audience: "hitherto you have been prevented from even

knowing what happiness really is, solely in consequence of the . . . gross errors . . . that have been combined with the fundamental notions of every religion that has . . . been taught to men. . . . By the errors of these systems [man] has been made a weak, imbecile animal; a furious . . . fanatic; or a miserable hypocrite. . . ."

Owen's denunciation of religions shocked his hearers, and recoiled upon him with increasing force for the remaining years of his apostleship. We say apostleship because Owen held to "a consistent practical religion, based on different ideas of the Great Creating Power of the Universe." He was in fact a deist, though henceforth he was apt to be called atheist and infidel. He now forfeited his character of altruistic business man which had recommended him, put on the mantle of prophet, and with the progress of time fancied himself messianic. Was this a touch of madness or simply ardent candor in a devoted spirit? Whatever one wishes to call him, he had given an easy handle to opponents of all his schemes. But also he had made himself, as Cole observes, "the father of Socialism and of many movements."*

Meanwhile Robert Owen had taken the lead in urging factory legislation which in other hands became a principal welfare development in Great Britain and in all industrialized countries of the world. His representations to fellow manufacturers and to members of Parliament carried the proof of his own reforms in his New Lanark mills. Until Owen gave his impressive impetus, the only curbs on employers driving children of five years and upwards for outlandish hours (sometimes reaching nineteen a day) had been by the local magistrates of Manchester (1797) and in Peel's Act of 1802. The latter applied only to "apprenticed" (pauper) children in cotton factories and was a mere approach to correction of abominable conditions.

In 1815 Owen called manufacturers of Scotland to a meeting to petition Parliament for two purposes: to remit the import duty (four pence per pound) on cotton, and give relief to children and others in all textile mills—cotton, wool, flax, and silk. The factory owners were instantly unanimous for removing the tax on cotton, but not one would second the motion for protecting the workers. Owen therefore took his own measures. He published his resolves and posted to London. Lord Liver-

---

* *Robert Owen*, p. 149.

pool's government agreed to take off most of the tax on raw cotton and favored restrictions on ages and hours of children if Owen could get a bill for that purpose introduced in Parliament. Owen applied to influential members and got Sir Robert Peel, in the Commons, to sponsor a law to limit hours in all mills to ten a day, no children to work before the age of twelve years and then only after they had been taught to read and write. Owen wanted no select committee of Parliament to investigate and debate whether protracted hours at the machines were injurious to infants, but Peel consented to it and began his concessions to the hostile manufacturers by eliminating all but cotton mills from the proposal.

During two sessions of Parliament Owen attended the committee daily. He confronted two arguments of the powerful industrial interest. First, "masters ought not to be interfered with by the legislature in any way in the management of their business." This was the favorite cry of *laissez faire*, approved by infatuated economists and reverberated by "cotton lords" as an axiom of British prosperity. When this demand was finally overruled, objectors sought to prove that keeping young children to their tasks for fourteen hours or more in close, humid mills did them no harm. Here Owen's testimony to the contrary was irresistible unless he could in some way be discredited. Alarmed manufacturers dispatched two of their number to Lanark "on a mission of scandal-hunting." They found an eager ally in a neighboring parish clergyman who imparted that Owen in his proceedings was treasonable to Church and State. The inquisitors paid the rector to go with them to London to prefer his charges to Lord Sidmouth, Secretary of State. Lord Sidmouth rebuked them in short order, praising Owen's example.

But the select committee found new dodges for delay and dilution of the bill. Owen tried to overcome disingenuous opposition not only by his testimony but with pamphlets showing that the mill owners themselves, as well as the country and the factory children, would profit by the reforms he begged for. After two years he quit in disgust, and others, including the remarkable Richard Oastler, took over for two years more of tortured committee discussion. When passed in 1819 the bill was mutilated; children might work at nine years for twelve hours exclusive of mealtimes; there was no provision for enforcement. Decades passed before what Owen projected was accepted.

The Industrial Revolution munitioned Britain and her allies in the Napoleonic wars, but, correspondingly, extraordinary war demand for goods and workers was necessary to utilize the newly discovered means of increasing production. Owen was the most original of those called on to cope with "the revulsion from war to peace" which "created universal distress among the producers in the British Islands." In the last year of the struggle Britain spent £80,000,000 above peacetime to supply the war. As Owen said, "On the day on which peace was signed, this great customer of the producers died, and prices fell as the demand diminished. . . ." In the midst of this acute distress Owen formulated, in new scope, his plan for the future of society.

Arkwright and Watt had burst the bonds of commercial exchange. How could potential blessings be enjoyed without the penalties of depression, unemployment, and poverty? In a *Report to the County of Lanark* in 1820 Owen declared that gold and silver were no longer adequate to the needs of the market, let alone a more just distribution of goods and services. As "labour . . . is the source of all wealth," so the "natural standard of value is . . . human labour, or the combined mental and manual powers of men called into action." The unit of value should be the wealth that an average laborer could produce in a day. It was only from labor, liberally remunerated, that high profits could be paid for agricultural and manufactured products. The labor theory of value was familiar, but the rights of the worker in his product were at this time by no means recognized.

To exchange labor for labor, Owen contended, would result in happiness, steady abundance, and progress. Money—"an artificial standard of value"—though serviceable at an earlier stage of the economy, had "blindly urged [man] forward to create, but deprived him of the wisdom to enjoy." Owen then outlined, more fully than earlier, the character and benefits of cooperative communities sharing "intrinsic" or labor values, avoiding the destructive selfishness of profit-seeking market operators.

Efforts to finance pilot villages in England had fallen through. Owen had met obfuscation and encrusted prejudice in the tradition-ridden society of Britain. Some of his partners in the New Lanark mills, after consenting to his program of reform, had second thoughts and pestered until he dropped cherished features of the schools. His memorials pleading for international action in favor of workers were presented to the Congress of Sovereigns at Aix-la-Chapelle (1815), but he found himself opposing "the habits created by . . . irrational surroundings . . . in all countries" of Europe. Feeling thus frustrated in "every attempt . . . to practically benefit poor suffering ill-used humanity," he resolved to take his message and offer his example in America. Here was a newer, freer society that promised to be more responsive to his endeavors.

He set sail in 1824, resigning all but a financial connection with New Lanark. He bought the lands of the Rappites, a German peasant community on the banks of the Wabash River in Indiana, which was dissolving. For 30,000 acres he paid a pound an acre, including a substantial village with homes, church, and workshops. In addresses in the hall of the House of Representatives in Washington, attended by President Monroe, President-elect J. Q. Adams, and other notables, he proclaimed his reasons for coming to America to establish his "New System of Society." In accepting or rejecting his vision, he declared, "the rulers of these states . . . will have to decide upon the destinies of the human race, both in this and in future generations." Already known by reputation, he lectured in other cities in furtherance of his invitation to "the industrious and well-disposed of all nations" to join him in his model community of New Harmony.

The New Harmony community lasted something over three years, 1825–28. Owen summarized the causes of failure: "the attempt was premature to unite a number of strangers not previously educated for the purpose, who should carry on extensive operations for their common interest, and live together as a common family." Nor was his modified trial of "what could be done by those who associated through their own choice and in small numbers" more successful. Owen lost four-fifths of his fortune in New Harmony, about £40,000.

Those who responded to his invitation to the banks of the Wabash were too diverse in background, motive, and degrees of unfitness. Robert Dale Owen, the founder's son, did not mince words in saying the colony attracted "waifs and strays from surrounding society; men and women of crude, ill-considered, extravagant notions; nay, worse, vagrants who regard the latest heresy but as a stalking-horse for pecuniary gain, or a convenient cloak for immoral demeanor." The backwoods families who flocked in first had nothing in common with the intellectuals, many of them Europeans, whom Owen imported in the "Boat Load of Knowledge" on his return to the community early in 1826. These two groups were divided especially by the evangelical, fundamentalist religious practices and dogmas of the frontier folk and the free-thinking of the foreigners. "Original sin," the habitual presupposition of the countrymen, clashed with Owen's constant contention that character was conferred not by the curse of Eden but by circumstances of one's journey on earth. The activities in which most could unite were recreational, concerts and singing, but the local people were scandalized at dancing, and on Sunday, and in the church!

Owen began New Harmony with a prudence which he soon discarded. He explained to his followers at the outset, "It is . . . no light thing for men and women of all ages, to change the habits to which they have been accustomed from infancy; and many difficulties must be at first encountered, and many struggles with our old feelings while the work of regeneration shall be going forward. . . ." But within a few months he abandoned his resolve to keep all in his own control while every villager received in proportion to his production. He resigned management to an elected committee and proclaimed community of property.

Few were qualified, even where inclined, for systematic work in the fields and shops, though these kinds of labor must be the basis of any social refinements in the colony. The ravenous hogs left by the Rappites rooted up the little garden patches while the Harmonyites debated constitutions of community government.

Owen, by now a missionary to the whole world, was too restless to fasten himself to the exacting task in this lonely settlement in the wilds. His long absences invited discord. When he would return his benign presence was a temporary balm, but he seemed to have lost his faculty for efficient management and he smiled on what to other eyes was approaching destruction. He was by turns too paternalistic and neglectful.

For a time the schools, enrolling two hundred pupils under

talented teachers, prospered. But the different instructors were wedded to their individual ideas, and at one point each seceded with his own students.

Owen had a protracted contest with William Maclure, educator and geologist, who had put a substantial capital into the venture. Their differences did not illustrate harmony among principals. Maclure for a time drew off into his own colony, and other leaders with their devotees separated themselves permanently. This would have been well enough at a later stage if the central community had flourished, but so near the beginning division was a sign and cause of weakness.

Owen came out of it with much land, which he gave to his four sons, who for a while continued at New Harmony and became American citizens to the benefit of American society in several ways. Robert Dale Owen with his colleague Fanny Wright entered on a long career in public education, labor organization, and defense of civil liberties. Thus New Harmony left a larger legacy through the very dispersal of its gifted members.

Robert Owen himself was anything but dashed by the brief history of his enterprise. His enthusiasm for a "New System of Society" and a "New Moral World" soon took him scouting in the British West Indies and thence to Mexico for a fresh opportunity to found a model community. It was probably just as well for his own comfort and what remained of his fortune that he was not granted a strip of Texas (then Mexican territory) for a further and grander experiment in America.

On his return to England in 1829 Owen's efforts were more diffused than at New Lanark and New Harmony but were more influential. Hitherto he had looked to men of wealth and position as patrons of his enterprises, and he never ceased to count such among his friends. But now he became identified with the masses of workers in projects of labor exchanges and labor unions. Both of these movements led, without Owen's direct participation, to consumers' cooperatives, which multiplied beyond all anticipation. Workers in these years were astir to get a reform of Parliament that would give them votes and representation. When the result in 1832 was to shift power from the landed class to the capitalist-oriented middle class, workers in their disappointment were ready to turn from political expedients to economic self-help.

Owen gave impetus to cooperative societies already in

existence and he founded others. The aim of all, whether of producers or of consumers, was to accumulate funds to establish cooperative communities such as Owen had long urged. In practice, the means became the end, which was fortunate. Owen's National Equitable Labour Exchange commenced in Gray's Inn Road in 1832 but soon moved to Charlotte Street, Fitzroy Square, thereafter a center of Owenite activities. Workers depositing their products received labor notes with which they bought the goods of others. The notes reflected the value, the skill, and not simply the time, of the labor expended, but they were not sufficiently accurate and the exchange, and others patterned after it, were left with over-priced goods that could not be sold. The scheme embodied Owen's insistence that labor was the cause of value and that the medium of exchange should be not gold or silver or government paper money, but a unit of labor.

The labor exchanges disappeared in the preference of workers to organize in labor unions. Owen first enlarged a local effort at Birmingham into the Grand National Guild of Builders, men of all the crafts who would erect structures without relying on capitalist employers. After abortive attempts the project failed from the aggressive hostility of master builders who locked out their workers unless they promised to have nothing to do with the Guild. This was only an episode, for promptly (1833) Owen was the prime organizer of the Grand National Consolidated Trades Union. Existing unions, cooperative, and benefit societies, formed a nucleus to which new ones in every trade and industry, and agriculture, were rapidly added until the loose membership numbered maybe a million men and women. But dissolution was as swift. Support of strikes was too burdensome, lockouts were ruinous, trade depression was an over-all blow. The sentence of a half-dozen farm laborers of Tolpuddle in Dorchestershire, who had newly joined the Consolidated Union, to seven years' transportation was a spectacular backset. The project was grandiose. Time was to show that discipline, in unions according to crafts, must precede more comprehensive organization. But Owen had given the labor movement its first conspicuous lift which it never afterward completely lost.

Nothing could deflate Robert Owen's ebullience. He resumed his crusade for a New Moral World—through lectures, books, tracts, manifestoes, newspapers, congresses. His organ, the

Crisis (later with change of name) will surprise any reader with the variety and zeal of his activities. For three years he was governor (and benevolent dictator) of a new Village of Cooperation, Queenwood in Hampshire, but it fell victim to his extravagant financing. While Owen soared increasingly into heights of social ethics, those he had inspired with his philosophy began to devote themselves to the humbler undertaking of cooperatively owned food stores. The Rochdale Equitable Pioneers of 1844 were his disciples, and their practice of distributing profits according to members' purchases started the cooperative movement which has spread around the world.

In old age, comfortably maintained by prosperous sons, Owen never ceased his dreams nor neglected any opportunity to impress his conviction of their early realization. In his last years, ironically, this apostle of the rational became a believer in spiritualism, and through mediums conversed with Jefferson, Franklin, Shakespeare, Napoleon, the Duke of Wellington, his beloved Duke of Kent (father of Victoria), and the prophet Daniel as his familiars. Long before that he had lost his grip on reality. However, he is not to be judged by this lack of focus toward the end. Maybe he was always a little mad, but his sense of evils in the world was calculated to drive a generous mind and heart to extremes.

In his last illness, at eighty-seven, he asked to be taken to Newtown in Wales and to the very house in which he was born. He revived sufficiently to plan meetings to renovate education in the place, then quietly fell asleep, forever. He was buried beside his parents in the churchyard.

In his long and incessantly active lifetime he did more than others to promote social betterment. His particular reforms—of factory conditions, education, and the promotion of cooperatives and labor unions—were ultimately successful, as the present day attests. But of superior benefit was the changed emphasis in securing human happiness which he contributed. He endlessly repeated those words of the Lord's Prayer, "Thy kingdom come on earth." He did his mighty best to relieve the soul's anxiety by exhorting men to improve their lot here below. If this was materialism it was of a noble sort, worthy of raptures.

All who came later to correct social sorrows owed much to his good will toward the world. They might be revengeful where he was charitable, they might proclaim cleavages where

he strove for harmony, incline to bitterness where he was
hopeful. But all must labor in his vineyard of the here and
now. How keen was his perception! Later philosophers espoused
determinism. Among modern psychologists are those who call
themselves behaviorists. Robert Owen, much earlier, had
pointed to the force of circumstances: "man's character is made
for him, not by him."

For Further Reading

Owen, Robert, *A New View of Society and other Writings*. Introduc-
    tion by G. D. H. Cole (New York: E. P. Dutton & Co., Inc.,
    Everyman's Library, 1927). See especially "Report to the County of
    Lanark," 1820.
———, *The Life of Robert Owen*, 1857. (New York: Alfred A. Knopf,
    Inc., 1920). Autobiography, most valuable for period covered, to
    1822.
Owen, Robert Dale, *Twenty-seven Years of Autobiography. Threading
    my Way* (New York: G. W. Carleton & Co., 1874). Especially
    for New Lanark.
Podmore, Frank, *Robert Owen: A Biography* (London: Hutchinson &
    Co., 2 vols., 1906). Most detailed life.
Cole, G. D. H., *Robert Owen* (2nd. ed., London: Macmillan & Co.,
    1930). More summary than Podmore, superior on economic
    movements.
Harvey, Rowland Hill, *Robert Owen, Social Idealist* (Berkeley: Uni-
    versity of California Press, 1949). Lively portrait by an American
    scholar.
Morton, A. L., *The Life and Ideas of Robert Owen* (New York: Monthly
    Review Press, 1963). Selections from Owen's writings are topically
    arranged.

6

CIRCUMSTANCES ALTER CASES

Friedrich List

Friedrich List (1789–1846) was the first to dwell prominently on the relative character of economic truth. He argued
that economic principles are not hard and fast laws, universally
applicable without regard to time or place. Instead he favored
policies that are appropriate to particular conditions. His
system was not absolute and dogmatic, but flexible and selective. His thought was dynamic, emphasizing not only change
but purposive economic development. His images were not of
the static, still-life variety; the forces he comprehended are in
motion, constantly acting upon each other. He offered a lively
picture of constant change, and change which may be directed
to desired ends. An economy in List's mind need not obey
foreordained rules. On the contrary, it could be deliberately
molded to accomplish the wishes of the society.

List abandoned the *laissez faire* advice and the natural law
assumption of his predecessors. He defied ex cathedra pronouncements. Man was not made for the economy, but the
economy could be fashioned by and for man. He decried let-
alone individualism and seized on the powers of the organized
community. Thus his was properly political economy, utilizing
guidance, promotion, and correction by government.

Generally Adam Smith and others of the classical school
reckoned that what was good for the merchants in a Glasgow
street was good for persons in the whole world. They extended
a shop-keepers' economy to embrace all peoples everywhere.
Not so, said List. Between individuals locally and the universe
of individuals comes an all-important entity which the classicists

omitted, namely, the nation. The nation may have interests and purposes different from those of individuals. Smith supposed that the conflict of individual aims would produce the common benefit. List interposed a conscious, collective will, that of the state. The nation might have to discipline its own citizens, and, at periods, be hostile to other nations. List, unwilling to trust to chance, but enamoured of organization, focused on government as the determining force in economic society. List held that division of labor, which Smith celebrated, highly desirable as it is, demands the counterpart of coordination of specialists. Smith's prescription of free trade, a hands-off role for government, could not bring about the required integration of efforts.

In the first place, nations did not remain at peace with one another, and war would leave an agricultural people, say, unsupplied with manufactured goods. More than this, there must be closer geographic cooperation between farmers, artizans, manufacturers, merchants, and financiers than world free trade provided. A nation must foster a variety of occupations if the people in the several branches of production were to be of greatest mutual assistance. Only a community embracing within itself many callings could be inventive and progressive. List's thesis was that two is more than twice one. Intimate interchange and interdependence are the invigorating forces which he cherished.

Adam Smith's system was one of values represented by physical commodities. List showed that these goods themselves are of less importance than the capacity to produce them. Commodities yield a temporary and uncertain benefit. They wear out, may be destroyed, or become obsolete. The ability to replenish and improve upon them is what must be nourished. In the current phrase, "know how" is superior to mere consumables. Consequently List condemned Smith's exclusion of artists, physicians, governors, scholars and the like furnishers of services from the category of producers because they did not offer tangible commodities that could be bought and sold. Actually, philosophers and scientists were the pioneers of social advancement.

We must not think that the classicists whom List constantly criticized did not comprehend different stages, or degrees of progress in peoples. They were too much aware of their world and of history not to recognize retrogression in some societies, inertia or stagnation in others, or a course of betterment in a third sort. But they did not incorporate growth as the central feature of the life of communities as List did. The classicists had no receipe for getting from one condition to a better except to rely on the actions of individuals in serving their selfish interests. The very premise of the classicists' ideal ruled out anything like collective planning. Modern day economic planners, bent on insuring the welfare of advanced countries and developing backward ones, had a forerunner, a century earlier, in Friedrich List. He was eager to use what his opponents called artificial means of generating improvement.

We shall see that if and when all or most nations had been brought, by his several expedients, to something like equal maturity in their economies, List was as ready as the next to agree that a system of free exchanges between them was in order. Then and not until then was he on all fours with classical trade doctrine, willing to let down tariff barriers, forego bounties and other encouragements to domestic production, and invite the widest commerce to operate unhindered. In the preparatory periods, however—of varying duration for different countries—he reverted to many of the objects and methods of the mercantilists whom the classical economists had sought to supplant.

Pledged to social control, as against free-style individualist competition, List necessarily stressed wise enforcement of public laws. For him legislation in furtherance of national development was not enough. Statutes on the books came alive only as they were skilfully put into practice. He was one of the earliest proponents of what we now call the arts of public administration. Administration is the capable arm of executive authority, the omnipresent, practical connection between the citizen and his government. Thus knowledgeable public administration, as Alexander Hamilton insisted before List, can make all the difference between a negligent and a competent, forward-moving society. We shall better appreciate List's thought by a sketch of his career, the influences that bore upon him, and the influence which he in turn exerted.

List was born at Reutlingen in Württemberg, a small state in pre-Imperial Germany. He had a distaste for his father's tanyard where he was put to work as a boy. His aversion was not to the smells of the soaking-vats, but to the inefficiency of the primitive methods used in handling and treating the hides. From the first he was intent on economy of production, urging that machinery should supersede muscle. His father found the boy's protests unfilial, so Friedrich departed for a larger field of operation—government administration—in which he spent much of his life in one way and another. Perforce he began modestly as a clerk in municipal offices of neighboring towns, including Ulm and Tübingen. He looked higher, and passed examinations which gave him appointment in the civil service of Württemberg.

By the age of twenty-seven he was ministerial under-secretary. He attracted the special approval of Von Wangenheim, the minister, by a pamphlet critical of bureaucracy and out-lining plans for the University of Tübingen to train public officials. Von Wangenheim appointed List Professor of Staats-praxis (we should say Public Administration). List's teaching of reform was applauded by his sponsor, with the result that both minister and professor were removed by the king, sup-ported by obtuse nobles and intrenched office-holders. It was the story of the tannery over again, and not the last time that List was to suffer from the hostility of parochial stupidity and jealousy. List was always prone to put his ideas into action.

The offense which particularly provoked dismissal from his university chair was his extracurricular advocacy as president of an association of merchants and others. His proposal was to abolish internal trade barriers in the German states. This enlightened movement was inspired by the defeat of Napoleon, 1815, which ended the Continental blockade. German manu-facturers and sellers were no longer protected against foreign imports, but neither could they enlarge their home trade area because the frontiers of the component states were studded with custom houses. Germany, commercewise, was like an egg crate, with tariffs hampering the distribution of goods beyond the most local limits. Industry and commerce were boxed in by this outmoded provincial system.

Germany presented a doleful contrast to the United States of America. At war's end British vessels, ready-laden, slipped their cables and dumped on the wharves of Boston, New York, Philadelphia, and Charleston superior wares in such surplus that they were auctioned at give-away prices. American manufactures, fostered during the European conflict, were few, crude, and expensive by comparison, and were threatened with destruction. Fortunately, national protective duties were brought to the rescue and the American market was uniformly open to our producers. Soon List was to play a part in further development of American industry, and he never forgot the example set by this country for Europe in eliminating the internal tariffs which prior to the Constitution had thwarted our economic progress.

In continuing to urge commercial union for Germany, List was denied the influence he would have enjoyed from official position. He was elected by his loyal native place of Reutlingen to the Württemberg National Legislative Assembly, only to have the ministry forbid him taking his seat. He labored privately, in publications and visits to government and business leaders in different German capitals, to flatten trade walls. Again elected to the Württemberg Assembly (1822) a petition for a German common market, inspired by List, was rewarded by his expulsion from the legislature and a sentence of ten months' imprisonment.

The enmity of the king of Württemberg followed List in his flight to Strasbourg. Ejected there, he sought refuge at Baden with the same result. In Paris General Lafayette was cordial, as he had been many years before to the Irish refugee, Mathew Carey, and invited List to accompany him on his return visit to the United States, to which Lafayette was going as guest of a greatful nation. But, patriotic and dutiful, List posted back to Württemberg to seek the king's pardon. The royal answer was to have him arrested and thrown in the Asberg fortress. The "hard labor" prescribed for him was punishment as cruel, for a creative man, as the rockpile—meaningless mechanical clerical tasks. He was released after some months of this drudgery only on compulsion of forfeiting his citizenship and departing instantly from Württemberg. One would think the king's revenge was satisfied, but no, he again had his erstwhile subject chased from France. It seemed that nowhere in Europe could List escape persecution. He determined to accept Lafayette's invitation of two years before, and with his wife, three young daughters and stepson, followed the Marquis to America.

Lafayette's tour of the United States was a triumphal progress. Every city, town, and house where he was entertained preserves to this day recollections and mementoes of the old hero's visit. Thus List, as Lafayette's friend, met the principal men of America under the most favorable auspices. Among those he came to know were President Andrew Jackson, Madison, John Adams, Jefferson, Clay, Webster, John Marshall, Edward Livingston, Emerson, and Stephen Girard.

On his way to Havre to take ship for America he had written: "I hope that the United States will afford me a fine example in proof of my assertion [that Adam Smith's "free intercourse system holds back a nation's development"]. They followed Smith's theories till their whole industry lay in ruins, and then began to follow the system which the theorists abhor. We shall see how they fare under it." He did see, up and down the coast, inland to Pittsburg and on to Harmony founded by his fellow-Württemberger, George Rapp. At this time (1825) the champions of protection for America's infant industries were succeeding. The tariff of 1816 had been bettered by that of 1824, and preparations were in the making for pressing the advantage. Societies for encouraging manufactures and "internal improvements" (turnpikes, canals, soon railways) had the ear of Congress and much of the country. List understood this ferment, probably better than most of the American propagandists.

He applied for American citizenship, and, seeking German-speaking neighbors, he settled his family on a small farm near Harrisburg, Pennsylvania. On these few acres he exhausted his strength and his means to no avail. He was more successful as editor of a German-language newspaper, *Der Adler* (*The Eagle*), in Reading. His articles and editorials excited the admiration of protectionists centered at Philadelphia under the sponsorship of Mathew Carey, Ingersoll, Colwell, and other leaders of the Pennsylvania Society for the Encouragement of Manufactures and the Mechanic Arts. At their urging List published in his paper twelve letters to Charles J. Ingersoll, vice-president of the Society. He repudiated Adam Smith's free trade system as injurious to American development, and espoused instead protection of home industry. He supported his argument at every turn with illustrations from American experience and contemporary conditions. The Society reprinted his pieces in a pamphlet, *Outlines of American Political Economy* (Philadelphia, 1827).

List's polemic was superior as protectionist propaganda, but its enduring significance went far beyond the purpose of the moment. He declared in effect that economic "laws" are neither universal nor permanent in application. Rather, circumstances alter cases. A country must adopt policies appropriate to its stage of progress, pursue them so long as they serve, and be prepared to abandon or reverse these means when a further stage of development has been achieved. In opposition to the classical *laissez faire* dogma he introduced an "American Political Economy" suitable to this young nation's needs. Smith and his followers took for granted that what was useful for Britain was valid for the world.

Not so, said List. The Scots philosopher took in too much territory. Between the individual traders of a single locality and the cosmos of peoples came a neglected element, namely, different political societies in varying degrees of economic maturity. These countries or nations had special requirements which might well run counter to any general prescription.

In the summer of 1827 List attended the Harrisburg Protectionist Convention and addressed the two houses of the Pennsylvania legislature. List now in spectacular fashion practiced what he preached. The Schuylkill Canal (Port Carbon to Philadelphia) had recently been completed, and neighboring anthracite coal deposits were beginning to be exploited. With Reading friends List acquired several thousand acres of coal lands north of Pottsville and laid out the town of Tamaqua. But how get the coal to the canal with twenty-two miles of hills and rock-strewn river lying between? The answer must be a railroad, but longer than others constructed in the area. List's wealthy friend Girard supplied funds for the Little Schuylkill Navigation, Railroad and Coal Company. The line was finished in short order (September 1831). Mules hauled the coal wagons on wooden rails topped with strap-iron. Two years later, when the steam locomotive had been proved in England and been tried in America, List's railroad put two engines in service. Later the line was extended and for a century has been part of the main Reading Railroad system.

List's ambitions extended far beyond this local railway. "In the midst of the wilderness of the blue mountains of Pennsylvania," he wrote, "I dreamed of a German railroad system. It was clear to me that only through such a thing could the

. . . commercial unification [of Germany] come into full reality." He would go back to his homeland to erase internal trade barriers, surround the German nation with a tariff to protect its industries, and tie all parts of the country together with a network of railways. "Germany and the return to Germany always lie in the background of my plans," he confided.

He was grateful for his appointment as United States Consul at Leipzig, and he later occupied the same post at Stuttgart. His official duties were light, and he gave himself with untiring enthusiasm to the project of unifying Germany economically and politically. He wrote articles, edited journals, informed, argued, organized. The first response was in the construction of railroads, beginning in 1835. Generals and statesmen saw the benefits from this development and supported List's efforts. Soon the Zollverein (customs union) was making progress under his urging, and improved transport and freer trade stimulated each other.

List had long meant to set forth the reasoning and practical value of his reforms in a substantial treatise. The vigorous campaign in England for repeal of that country's corn laws (import duties on grain and other foodstuffs) promised to lower manufacturing costs there. German industries, less mature, were threatened with disastrous competition. This impending damage troubled List when he wrote the work by which he is chiefly remembered, *The National System of Political Economy* (1841). As the title shows, the nation—not the individual nor the universe of individuals, as with the *laissez faire* school— was his focus. Value, in the sense of consumption utility, must be less the purpose of a nation than capacity to produce values.

A country in an undeveloped state should put no obstacles in the way of imports, for it requires manufactured goods, capital, skills, experience, contacts with the world of learning and science. List cited Spain and Portugal as such nations; in our day many of the new republics of Africa and countries of southeast Asia and the Near East are in this category. When a society has commenced to vary its economy, has made a start in industry and supply of credit, these means must be deliberately nurtured by protective tariffs, bounties, and other encouragements until its facilities are brought to maturity. This policy will entail a temporary sacrifice for the sake of later precious acquisition. Faculties of education, ingenuity, inventiveness, organization, and political discipline will contribute as much as physical instruments of manufacture, agriculture, and trade. List instanced Germany and the United States in the category of nations which must shield their young enterprises against the fatal competition of producers in more advanced countries. Nowadays Mexico, Brazil, and India may fall in this intermediate group.

Then when a nation's economy is efficient and resourceful, artificial stimulants should be discontinued, for it is now able to meet the offerings of other countries on even terms at home and abroad. When List wrote, only England was in this competent stage, and France was entering it; at present most nations of the western world and Japan have arrived at this maturity. List would say they now need the freest commercial intercourse with others, else their own productive powers must become sluggish, and tariffs, by raising internal prices, will enable domestic producers to exploit their own populations.

The mercantilists were enamoured of cash. Adam Smith preached that money is only the medium of exchange, and that wealth consists of goods, of commodities. List in his turn replaced commodities with capacities. "*The power of producing wealth,*" List declared, "is . . . infinitely more important than *wealth itself*; it insures not only the possession and the increase of what has been gained, but also the replacement of what has been lost. This is still more the case with entire nations (who cannot live out of mere rentals) than with private individuals." He referred to his own country: "Germany has been devastated in every century by pestilence, by famine, or by civil or foreign wars; she has, nevertheless, always retained a great portion of her powers of production, and has thus quickly reattained some degree of prosperity; while rich and mighty but despot- and priest-ridden Spain, notwithstanding her comparative enjoyment of internal peace, has sunk deeper into poverty and misery." List had received lessons in America which constantly informed his writings. Thus he went on to say that "The War of Independence of the United States . . . cost that nation hundreds of millions, but her powers of production were immeasurably strengthened by gaining independence, and . . . in the course of a few years after the peace she obtained . . . greater riches than she had ever possessed before."

Had List lived a few decades longer he would have witnessed

the truth of his observation in the aftermath of the Civil War in America. Despite losses of men and goods, the northern states, with varied knowledge and skills, and buoyed by victory itself, entered immediately on a period of rapid, indeed too rapid, industrial advance, especially in extension of railroads. The beaten southern states, by contrast, could not restore their physical wealth because their labor system, such as it was, had been destroyed, and they had no science or inventiveness or political morale. True, agricultural production (cotton) soon revived, but many decades passed before this section began to catch up with the rest of the country in industrial and urban development, and it lags to this day.

To take a later example, List's own Germany, which he had done so much to raise to economic efficiency, was crushed by World War I; she was deprived of her colonies and her merchant fleet, and was loaded with indemnities. Yet in two decades she was again menacing the world with her military might.

King Solomon, long before Adam Smith, observed that labor is the cause of wealth and idleness the cause of poverty. Smith, having impressed the same maxim, should have gone on "to put the further question, what are the causes of labour, and what the causes of idleness?" List pointed to "the spirit which animates . . . individuals, the social order which renders their energy fruitful, and the powers of nature which they are in a position to make use of . . . most depends . . . on the conditions of the society in which the individual has been brought up, and turns upon this, whether science and arts flourish, and public institutions and laws tend to produce religious character, morality and intelligence, security for person and for property, freedom and justice; whether in the nation all the factors of material prosperity, agriculture, manufactures, and trade, have been equally and harmoniously cultivated; whether the power of the nation is strong enough to secure to its . . . citizens progress in wealth and education from generation to generation. . . ."

Smith did not confine labor, the source of production, to mere bodily exertion, for he included the skill and judgment with which labor is applied in creating goods. His disciples failed to take the hint that might have induced them to improve on their master and develop the concept of "mental capital." Instead, J. B. Say, the French popularizer of Smith, and J. R.

McCulloch, Smith's Scottish follower, contracted political economy to the science of exchangeable values, and others reduced it further to "the science of exchange." Smith and his school, List declared, might have opened new vistas had they gone on from a mere theory of values of commodities to develop a theory of productive power. Lamentably, the classical doctrine sank "deeper and deeper into materialism . . . and individualism."

List complained that Smith "does not even assign a productive character to the mental labours of those who maintain laws and order, and cultivate and promote instruction, religion, science, and art." List pointed to the absurd contradictions which follow from excluding the supreme contributions of mind. "The man who breeds pigs is, according to this school, a productive member of the community, but he who educates men is a mere non-productive. The maker of bagpipes or jews-harps for sale is a productive, while the great composers and virtuosos are non-productive simply because that which they play cannot be brought into the market. [Of course, in our later day it is brought into the market, and at a high price.] The physician who saves the lives of his patients does not belong to the productive class, but on the contrary the chemist's boy does so, although the values of exchange (viz, the pills) which he produces may exist only for a few minutes before they pass into a valueless condition. A Newton, a Watt, or a Kepler is not so productive as a donkey, a horse, or a draught-ox (a class of labourers who have been recently introduced by M'Culloch into the series of the productive members of human society)." The excluded ones, whether by furthering morality, law, and order, or "by ennobling and raising the powers of the human mind," are "fitting men the better to produce values in exchange;" they are *producers of the productive powers.*

These immaterial stimulants and regulators of production reside in, are themselves the products of, organized society. For List's purposes this meant the nation. However, "The popular school of economists," he objected, "would have us believe that politics and political power cannot be taken into consideration in political economy. So far as it makes only values and exchange the subjects of its investigations, this may be correct; we can define the ideas of value and capital, profit, wages, and rent; we can resolve them into their elements, and

speculate on what may influence their rising and falling . . .
without thereby taking into account the political circumstances
of the nation. Clearly, however, these matters appertain as much
to private economy as to the economy of whole nations. We
have merely to consider the history of Venice, of the Hanseatic
League, of Portugal, Holland, and England, in order to perceive
what reciprocal influence material wealth and political power
exercise on each other."

For illustration List proceeded to "compare Poland with
England: both nations at one time were in the same stage of
culture; and now what a difference. Manufactories . . . are the
mothers . . . of municipal liberty, of intelligence, of the arts
and sciences, of internal and external commerce, of navigation
and improvements in transport, of civilisation and political
power. They are the chief means of liberating agriculture from
its chains. . . ."

List was never tired of elevating manufacture as the chief
partner of agriculture and commerce. As for landowners and
farmers, he took the simplest case of "those industries which
lie nearest and are most necessary to agriculture, e.g. flour
mills. . . . Compare, on the one hand, the value of landed
property and rent in a district where a mill is not within reach
of an agriculturist, with their value in those districts where this
industry is carried on in their very midst, and we shall find
that . . . there, under similar conditions of natural fertility,
the total value of land has not only increased to double, but
to ten or twenty times more than the cost of erecting the mill;
and that the landed proprietors would have obtained considerable advantage . . . even if they had built it at their common
expense and presented it to the miller." In fact, this "takes
place every day in the backwoods of North America, where, in
cases when an individual has not adequate capital to erect such
works entirely at his own expense, the landowner gladly helps
him by contributing labour, by team work, free gifts of lumber,
&c."

The same is true of all manufacturing industries, for "rent
and the value of landed property rise in exactly the same proportion with the proximity of that property to the town, and with
the degree in which the town is populous and industrious. . . .
The increase of . . . agricultural capital depends for the most part
on the increase of manufacturing capital; and nations which

do not recognize this truth, however much they may be favoured by nature in agriculture, will not only not progress, but will retrograde in wealth, population, culture, and power."

Adam Smith was mistaken when "he would make it appear that agriculture is far more valuable and important to a nation than manufactures." In doing so he "merely sanctioned the erroneous view of the physiocratic school, although in a somewhat modified manner." Here again the German economist was drawing on his observation in America, where Alexander Hamilton, urging protection for young manufactures, had been obliged to combat a preference for agriculture. Smith's dictum in favor of the superior productiveness of land had been complacently quoted against the arguments of our first pleader for rounded economic development. Following Hamilton and List, as we shall find, Henry C. Carey illustrated the mutual benefits of industry and agriculture in closest association with each other.

As a declared opponent of *laissez faire* and advocate of the responsibility of government in helping to shape a nation's economy, Friedrich List was constantly dissecting the recommendations of Adam Smith. But List was not a peddler of pet specifics. A thorough scholar, earnestly seeking to put economic thought and action on a new track, he understood previous views and the reasons which prompted them. Thus he spoke generously of "the great merits of Adam Smith. He was the first who successfully applied the analytical method to political economy. By means of that method and an unusual degree of sagacity, he threw light on the most important branches of the science, which were previously almost wholly obscure. Before Adam Smith only a practice existed; his works rendered it possible to constitute a science of political economy, and he has contributed a greater amount of materials for that object than all his predecessors or successors."

In pointing out Smith's shortcoming, however, List gave in a nutshell his own amendment or correction. That very peculiarity of Smith's mind by which, "in analysing the various constituent parts of political economy, he rendered such important service, was the cause why he did not take a comprehensive view of the community in its entirety; that he was unable to combine individual interests in one harmoniuos whole; that he would not consider the nation in preference to mere individuals; that out of . . . anxiety for the freedom of action of the individual producers, he lost sight of the interests of the entire nation. He who so clearly perceived the benefits of the division of labour in a single manufactory, did not perceive that the same principle is applicable with equal force to entire provinces and nations." Smith's "extraordinary acuteness" did not save him from a certain "narrowness and obliquity of his views" which prevented him, as Dugald Stewart said in another connection, from giving "a true and perfect representation according to all . . . dimensions and circumstances."

List gave the physiocrats of France shorter shrift. They wrongly blamed the degeneration of their agriculture on the mercantilist machinations of Colbert. The land of France "was cultivated by a peasantry languishing under a state of serfdom and personal oppression, who were sunk in superstition, ignorance, indolence, and poverty. The owners of the land [mostly clergy and nobility] . . . were devoted to frivolous pursuits, and had neither mind for, nor interest in, agriculture." This would not have been the doleful picture had "the great enterprise of Colbert been permitted to succeed." Revocation of the Edict of Nantes, within three years after Colbert's death, banished "half a million of the most industrious, skilful, and thriving inhabitants" (Huguenots), who added to the riches of Germany, Holland, and England. The "love of splendour and false ambition of Louis XIV, and the debauchery and extravagance of his successors," with other evils, "nipped in the bud the seeds which Colbert had sown."

The physiocrats, though "thoughtful men," were court favorites and friends of aristocracy and clergy whom they must not affront. So they chose to appear not as reformers, but as profound philosophers, though in the end it was the landed class whom they would compel to pay the whole support of the state. This elaborate tact, or obfuscation, did not conceal from List either the merit or the error of the physiocrats' substantive proposals. The purpose to teach "how the entire human race may attain prosperity" was noble. However, the ideal that "The welfare of the individual is conditional on the welfare of the entire human race" took no account of "any nation, of any war, of any foreign commercial measures: history and experience must be either ignored or misrepresented." The physiocrats failed to see, as did Smith and Say after them, "how the productive powers of a whole *nation* can be awakened, increased, and protected, and how on the other hand they are weakened, laid to sleep, or utterly destroyed; and how by means of those national productive powers the national resources can be utilized in the wisest and best manner so as to produce national existence, national independence, national prosperity, national strength, national culture, and a national future."

Commercial union, List pointed out, had always been prepared by political union. Before universal economic freedom could be enjoyed, every nation must reach something like the development of those best organized. Under existing conditions of the world, "the result of general free trade would not be a universal republic, but, on the contrary, a universal subjection of the less advanced nations to the supremacy of the predominant manufacturing, commercial, and naval power," (in that day, Britain). Therefore the system of protection, "inasmuch as it forms the only means of placing those nations which are far behind in civilisation on equal terms with the one predominating nation," offered "the most efficient means of furthering the final union of nations, and hence also of promoting true freedom of trade."

Quesnay had replied, point by point, to the refutations of his premature "cosmopolitical" system. "One is astonished at the mass of sound sense which he puts into the mouth of his opponents, and at the mass of mystical absurdity which he opposes to those objections by way of argument."

List, who had written his *Outlines of American Political Economy* with opposite views, swiftly described and dismissed the individualist opinions of Thomas Cooper's *Lectures on Political Economy*. Cooper, an Englishman of many talents, transplanted to the presidency of South Carolina College, made himself the particular foe of protective tariffs. A state in the Union which believed itself injured by such measures had full right to "nullify them." Cooper "denies even the existence of nationality; he calls the nation 'a grammatical invention,' created only to save periphrases, a nonentity, which has no actual existence save in the heads of politicians." And further, " 'Political economy,' he alleges, 'is almost synonymous with the private economy of all individuals; *politics* are no essential ingredient of *political economy*; it is folly to suppose that the community is something quite different from the individuals of whom it is composed. . . . The wealth of the community is nothing else than the aggregate of the wealth of all its individual members. . . .' "

Amidst his incessant labors for German political and commercial union and industrial progress, and poorly paid for his services, List enjoyed gratifications. The king of Württemberg in an audience acknowledged the injustice formerly done to his enterprising subject. "My dear List, I bear you no ill-will," he assured. "What a pity it is that twenty-four years ago we had not learnt to know each other as well as we do now!" List received the compliment of an honorary doctorate from the University of Jena. In 1844 a beneficial treaty for which he had long worked was concluded between the Zollverein, now embracing two-thirds of the inhabitants of Germany, and Belgium. His *National System of Political Economy* was published in May 1841 and a new edition was called for within four months. Subscriptions to found the *Zollvereinsblatt* gave him editorial and financial control of an influential journal.

These happy signs were soon clouded. In spite of increasing ill health, marked by distressing headaches,* he resolved to visit London to forestall, if he could, the injury Germany would suffer from impending repeal of the British corn laws. List believed that with cheaper food and raw materials British manufactures would expand more than ever, and less matured German industries would be overwhelmed. The Prussian government, which he must count on to further German protection, was already applauding the consummation of British free trade. "Last night . . . in the Upper House" of the English Parliament, he wrote in a letter of June 26, 1846, "I saw the Corn Law expire amid their Lordships' cheers." In the visitors' gallery of the House of Commons, buzzing with excitement, List was told, " 'Mr. Cobden wishes to make your acquaintance,' and a man still young, his eyes bright with intellect, held out his hand." Richard Cobden, the mortal foe of all List stood for, rallied him with the query, "Have you come over to be converted?"

They joked pleasantly enough, but List remained in London to press his plea for a commercial treaty, his desperate attempt

---

* Poor List, his pains may have been worse because he had a disproportionately large head for his short, stout body.

to save Germany, which must continue protectionist, from crushing competition. List's memorial, heartfelt but offered with no public authority, received from the British prime minister the courteous rejoinder that Germany would do best to follow in the free trade path.

List's torturing pains and sleeplessness oppressed him. He told a friend, "I feel as if a mortal disease were in my frame and I must soon die. If I am to lie sick, die, and be buried, I wish to do it in my own country." His body was broken, his spirit almost so. He made a last effort in a trip to Munich to establish a Society of Trade and Industry for Bavaria. Then he went to the little town of Kufstein in the Tyrol in hopes the mild climate would help restore him. Though he had sufficient money, when the host of the inn offered him pleasant quarters he replied, "I am too poor, give me the worst room in the house." The weather was "frightful," he spent much of his time in bed, and ate little. The morning of the last day of November he ventured out.

When he did not return by dark the landlord found in his room a letter scrawled to an old friend. "I have made several attempts to write to my family," it said, "to my precious wife, to my splendid children, but brain, hand, and pen refuse their service. . . . The blood rushes to my head and all is confusion. . . . I am on the brink of despair. God have mercy on those belonging to me. . . . God will reward you and my other friends for all you do for my wife and children. Farewell. Fr. List."

A search party found his body, covered with new snow, near the town. He had shot himself. Friends did come at once to the rescue of his family, and years later a monument was erected to him at Kufstein with subscriptions from all parts of Germany and Austria. "A defender of his country who toiled without reward," said the legend. But his countrymen thankfully recognized that he had commenced the building of the German Empire. That, in after time, Germany's political maturity did not match the economic maturity was not the fault of List.

For Further Reading

List, Friedrich, *The National System of Political Economy,* 1841. Translated by Sampson S. Lloyd, with introduction by J. Shield Nicholson (London: Longmans, Green & Co., 1928).

Hirst, Margaret E., *Life of Friedrich List and Selections from his Writings*. Introduction by F. W. Hirst (London: Smith, Elder & Co., 1909). Includes List's *Outlines of American Political Economy*, Philadelphia, 1827.

Rabbeno, Ugo, *American Commercial Policy* (2nd. ed., New York: The Macmillan Co., 1895).

7

ETERNAL OPTIMIST

Henry Charles Carey

The history of economic thought furnishes no clearer illustration of the influence of environment than in the system of the American, Henry Charles Carey (1793–1879). A second generation immigrant, his lifetime embraced the buoyant development of the fresh resources of a young nation subduing a continent. Democratic, ambitious, and of many skills, the people (with the exception of the slave South) were confident of making a better life for themselves. During his long span of life, the Union was extended from the Atlantic to the Pacific.

Rapid accomplishment in virgin surroundings inspired optimism. Bursting physical productivity, and new institutions devised at the will of the people to serve them, contrasted with the conditions and outlook of older societies in Europe and Asia. "Blessed is that country which has no history." Incrusted custom, stratified social classes, accumulated problems of the old world were notably absent in the new. Largely self-contained, we enjoyed the benefits of isolation. Carey could have adopted the formula of Dr. Emile Coué, "Day by day, in every way, I am getting better and better."

Therefore Carey exactly reversed typical contentions of English economists of his day. Especially he fingered his nose at Malthus and Ricardo. Besides, he inherited the inborn Irish distrust, not to say hatred, of the English and English pretensions. If one wishes to know how economic principles, instead of being enduring and universal, are relative to time and place, he cannot do better than discover the preachments of Henry C. Carey.

His story begins, in more ways than one, with his father, Mathew Carey (1760–1839). Born in Dublin and twice jailed for journalistic slanders on the British Parliament, he fled to Paris. There, encouraged by Franklin and Lafayette, he sneaked his passage to Philadelphia. No adopted son ever became more fiercely American. As editor, publisher, and pamphleteer, Mathew Carey was an engine for this country's development, especially through the Bank of the United States, protection to American manufactures, and promotion of "internal improvements" (canals and railroads). A refugee from his native, sorrowing Ireland, his venom against the tyranny of the British was lyrical. He would revenge the wrongs of Erin by helping mightily to fashion a nation to rival Britain's mastery. He passed on his wealth, influence, devotion, and fluency to his son. Mathew's ardent advocacies contain the genes which flowered in Henry Carey's philosophy.

Henry Charles Carey was born in 1793 in Philadelphia, had his whole career in that city, and was a principal contributor to its intellectual life. A precocious lad, his first economic education was in walks and talks with his father. Before he was twelve he had accompanied his father on business trips and for a few weeks was left in charge of the branch bookstore in Baltimore. At twenty-four he was taken into partnership and later was head of the firm Carey, Lea, and Carey, American publishers of Thomas Carlyle, Sir Walter Scott, and Washington Irving. In choosing works for his imprint and to satisfy his catholic curiosity he read prodigiously in many fields, as was reflected later in his own writings.

In his first economic writings, beginning with one on *The Rate of Wages* (1835) and including his *Principles of Political Economy* (3 vols., 1837–40), contrary to his father's teachings, he was a free trader. However, he already defined wealth in terms of social well-being, favored the national government as an instrument of economic progress, and was consistently optimistic in outlook. At the age of 42 he withdrew from active business to devote himself to economic and sociological studies. It may be that the failure of paper manufactures in which he had invested heavily helped convert him to the policy of protection.

Undeterred by abolition of the corn laws by Britain in 1846 and lowering of the American tariff to a basic revenue the next year, Carey was henceforth a leading advocate of protection. In this behalf, for nearly a decade, he was a regular contributor of editorials and signed articles to Horace Greeley's *New York Tribune*. He gave a coherence to Philadelpihia protectionist sentiment through intimate personal association with talented fellow-townsmen. The "Carey Vespers" were discussion meetings in his home attended by Stephen Colwell, William Elder, E. Peshine Smith, Robert Ellis Thompson, and often by visitors to Philadelphia who acknowledged Carey as master in a distinct American school of economic thought. The works, formal and occasional, which poured from his pen, were translated into a half-dozen European languages and into Japanese.

So vehement in his writings, in private life he was notably kindly. Until fairly recently an older generation of Philadelphians remembered him for his emotional intensity, his generous hospitality, and his handsome appearance, heightened in later years by a shock of snowy hair.

The starting point for an understanding of Carey's ideas is his belief in the power of association. Combined effort, mutual assistance, easy exchanges between producers of different commodities and services were for him synonymous with society. The primary importance which he assigned to an active, substantially self-contained community doubtless sprang from the sparseness of population in the vast new American continent. Alexander Hamilton, who profoundly influenced both of the Careys, father and son, had followed the same policy of keeping the people "close settled" on the eastern seaboard in the early stage of national economic development. Pioneering in wild lands to the westward must reduce workers to limited individual resources, depriving them of the benefits of cooperation. This scattering of population would hamper the intercourse necessary for economic progress and political unity. Concentration was desirable, dispersion was in every view retarding.

The other side of the coin of association was diversity of skills and occupations. It was the familiar principle that division of labor requires integration of specialists. The pioneer in the wilderness must supply himself with all that he needed in food, clothing, shelter, and tools to turn his isolated environment to his needs. At best his efforts would be meager in necessities and lacking in conveniences of life. He must be all workers rolled into one—farmer, mechanic, and merchant. Dependent entirely upon himself, his contrivances must be awkward and inefficient.

If, on the other hand, he remained in a community, he could be competent in his own calling because he had the advantage of proximity to other producers—carpenters, blacksmiths, masons, shoemakers, weavers. Variety in occupations in a neighborhood, with ready and active exchanges, stimulated ingenuity and enabled accumulation of wealth. The mere presence of more hands permitted, while it compelled, construction of roads, bridges, schools, churches, and means of defense and orderly government.

The limitations of the individual pioneer who went into the forest with axe, rifle, spade, and a sack of corn were illustrated in primitive societies, whether in earlier or in later times. Nature, though abundant, was resistant, was the master, and men could avail themselves of her riches only slowly and in the degree that they combined their labors. Carey constantly appealed to history, including anthropology. It was from the record of experience that he drew his theories, formulated his principles. Certainly the hopefulness and self-confidence of a young nation planted on a continent of huge potential resources gave a spring and optimism to all his thought. Undoubtedly his promising environment furnished his first prompting and inspired his reasoning. Had he lived in an old country, such as England or France, his enquiries would probably have led him to the pessimistic conclusions which he sought to correct in his contemporaries in those societies. Carey is a notable example of the influences, physical and social, which play upon the mind of an economist. Patently, his system was a report on what he saw about him. He manifested the relative character of economic principles. Truth in human relations is variable, applicable under certain conditions, invalid under other circumstances.

Carey's strength was in the sustenance he derived from his own place and time. He struck a new note of opportunity, he opened fresh vistas of accomplishment of men in subduing nature to their service. His was one answer to the narrow, almost despairing outlook of the members of the classical school typified in Malthus and Ricardo. At the same period at which Carey wrote in America the socialists in England, France, and Germany, whether Utopian like Owen and Fourier, or "scientific" like Marx, were giving a different retort to pessimism. The socialists, of whatever sort, revolted against institutions which had proved oppressive. They would substitute cooperation for exploitation. Carey shared their belief in a brighter future for mankind. Like them, he condemned many existing practices. But he was not a revolutionary, setting up a new form of society. He preached that poverty, misery, and injustice had never been necessary in the order of nature. In his America at any rate he wanted not so much correction of old abuses as conformity to wiser counsels. In contrast to the socialists he did not protest against the institution of private property or the motive of individual profit. On the contrary, these means to progress he cherished and wished to free them to operate for the benefit of all. He held, as ardently as the socialists did, to the gains from associated effort. But with Carey the mechanics of cooperation were to be different, resting on private incentive rather than on communal purpose as such. The distinction between Carey and the socialists will be clearer as we proceed with his thought.

We have said that Carey's merit was in his local—that is to say, American national—inspiration. As a consequence his weakness, as a formulator of doctrine, was in his claim that his system was universal. He presents a paradox. He, who did more than others to elevate appropriate economic policy, insisted that what he defined was general and enduring principle. It sounds condescending to observe that this is a common fault in self-taught philosophers. All thinkers and investigators, in the degree that they are original, we may say are self-instructed. How much poorer the world would be had not many gainsaid the accepted ideas of their time! At earlier periods there were no schools in the formal sense; organized bodies of scholars were few and far between. Further, imbuement in orthodoxy may be cramping or sterilizing in its effects. Perhaps a bold thinker is fortunate not to have been given mistaken directions by those exercising intellectual authority.

Yet there is a benefit and protection in mental discipline, which places a certain restraint on one's proposals. The social panacea is apt to be developed and urged by one whose idea, original and valuable, runs ahead of his information so that he does not take sufficient account of contradictions or of the resistance of obstacles. His wish becomes father to his thought.

Henry George, another who was molded by peculiar American conditions, falls in the same category of those who leap too easily from the particular to the general.

Not that Carey was lacking in learning. Far from it. He grew up in the atmosphere, indeed in the very trade, of books. He was an assiduous and resourceful reader. As we have seen, in the prime of life he retired from a successful business career to devote himself deliberately to economic investigation and advocacy. An honest man, he laid before his readers on every page evidence and authority for his conclusions, inviting them to judge for themselves. But, led by his own bright star, he was apt to see what suited his thesis and to neglect what opposed it. The same was true of many others of lesser gifts, but Carey would have profited by more neutral enquiry before he became committed to his special views.

Primitive, weak societies, like the individual pioneer, Carey declared, were obliged to commence their agriculture where the resistance of nature is least. They must settle on land clear of trees, like the ancient moors of England and Scotland, or with light growths of timber, such as pine, which could be removed with inferior tools and without excessive labor. This meant beginning on hillsides (or actually on hilltops, for defense) where the soil was thin and yielded small return to the poor cultivation which was all the ill-equipped little community could bestow. Aerial photographs taken in recent years for purposes of military reconnaissance, especially in England, reveal, on the almost barren sloping downs, traces of the plough reaching back hundreds of years, certainly to the middle ages. Hilltop settlements, crudely fortified, of which Old Sarum on Salisbury Plain is a famous example, dating from prehistoric peoples, are found in many parts of Britain and in other countries. These all testify, said Carey, to the fact that tillage and even grazing necessarily began on infertile, relatively open uplands whence most of the topsoil had been washed into the richer valleys. It was only with the growth of numbers and development of better tools than the stone axe (bronze, then iron, then steel) that early cultivators were able to advance into the lowlands. For here great forests of oak and other hardwoods must be cut, and the wet, flat lands must be drained before the rewarding deep humus could be utilized. Some of the very richest soils, such as in the Dismal Swamp of Virginia and North Carolina, and the Everglades of Florida, have not to this day been subdued to farming because available capital and effort are not equal to their conquest. If the draining of swamplands is attempted prematurely, as with the Jersey meadows across the Hudson from New York City in colonial times, the expenditure is wasted because the work is beyond the capacity of the society.

Carey made a wide historical and geographic survey to prove his contention that earliest settlements all over the world were on semisterile uplands which alone were eligible for weak and ignorant communities. With improved facilities, human and mechanical, gradually and after long ages, the superior resources of the earth were tapped.

Now this was a refutation of the fundamental assumption of the classical economists that growth of population compels resort to poorer and poorer soils. Carey believed that he exploded the doctrine of diminishing returns in agriculture and in the other extractive industries. Instead, the progress, he held, was from minimal to ever increasing returns, as society advanced in strength of numbers, science, and the powers of associated effort. The supposition of Malthus and Ricardo that the order of occupation is from the best sites to those which will barely repay cultivation, Carey contended, must be abandoned. These writers had calculated without the necessary appeal to historical facts. When they declared that the first farmer in a wild region will pre-empt the richest land, leaving that of second, third, fourth quality and so on to his successors, they supposed a capacity in the original settler which existed in their day but which the historical first occupier did not possess.

Thus Carey denied the theory of rent, which was that the higher return claimed by the owner of superior soils and sites was due to the difference in productivity of these as compared with locations which merely repaid the cost of use, and nothing more. The differences between the "original and indestructible qualities of the soil," which Ricardo made the basis of his doctrine, in fact ran the other way, said Carey. These highest faculties of the earth were availed of later, usually much later, not in the beginning. "The picture presented by Mr. Ricardo," said Carey, "differs totally from that which has . . . been presented. . . . The former, placing the settler on the lands of highest fertility, requires that his children and his children's children should, each in regular succession to the others, find themselves driven, by sad necessity, to the occupation of those capable of yielding smaller returns to labor—and that they should thus become, from generation to generation, more and more the slaves of nature. The latter [i.e., Carey's contention] placing the early settler on the poorer soils, exhibits his successors exercising constantly increasing power to pass to the cultivation of the richer soils—and becoming, from generation to generation, more and more the masters of nature, compelling her to do their work, and pressing steadily onward from triumph to triumph, with constant increase in the power of association, in the development of individuality, in the feeling of responsibility, and in the power of further progress."

It was an inevitable consequence of Ricardo's theory of rent that with the necessity of resort to less productive lands and locations the share of the product going to labor and capital decreased as rent claimed by the landowner increased. Carey taught the contrary: "In the early period of society, when land is abundant and people are few in number, labor is unproductive, and of the small product, the land-owner . . . takes a large *proportion,* leaving to the laborer a small one. The larger proportion yields, however, but a small amount, and both laborer and capitalist are poor—the former so poor that he is everywhere seen to have been a slave to the latter. Population and wealth, however, increasing, and labor becoming more productive, the land-owner's share diminishes in its *proportion,* but increases in its *amount.* The laborer's share increases not only in its amount, but also in its proportion, and the more rapid the increase in the productiveness of his labor, the greater is the *proportion* of the augmented quantity retained by him. . . ."

Before we can go further with Carey's discussion of the order of occupation of lands, or his treatment of rent, we must know his theory of value. It is the labor cost theory, but with his own twist. "Value is the measure of the resistance to be overcome in obtaining those commodities or things required for our purposes—of the power of nature over man." But as labor increases in efficiency—due to associated effort, inventions, and improvements of many sorts—the cost of production declines. With each advance, "the accumulations of the past become less valuable," and "decline in their power to command the services of the laborers of the present." The power of combination, using science and all the new facilities brought into action, is progressive. Though constantly less costly, labor's command over nature constantly grows.

Thus Carey's theory of value is the cost of *re*production. This is always falling. The older, cruder tools—say an axe of the bronze age—though it cost in labor vastly more than a modern steel axe, cannot exchange for more than the latter, and will surely fetch less becaues it is far less efficient. This cost of reproduction measure of value was an anticipation, by some seventy-five years, of a central idea of those calling themselves "Technocrats." During the Great Depression of the nineteen-thirties, taking their inspiration from Veblen, they elaborated on the prodigious advances in technology. A principal result of lowering costs was to lower values, or prices. They went on to warn that old debts, incurred for costly but inferior industrial equipment, would be difficult or impossible to discharge because better means of production, at the later date, could be had for less due to remarkable achievements in technology. The Technocrats cited arresting examples. An auto body, previously built up of parts bolted or welded, could now be stamped out by a single blow of a die on a sheet of metal. Bricks that had been formed practically by hand could be turned out by the latest machines at the rate of a hundred of the new for one of the old. Carey used similar illustrations in his own time, the high-speed rotary printing press superseding the manually operated flat-bed one, and so forth.

But how did Carey apply his labor theory of value to land? Did land have a monopoly value, because of its limited amount and differences of fertility or situation, over and above any cost of labor and capital in bringing land into use? No, said Carey, there is only one cause and measure of value. This is the cost of reproduction. There is no distinct category of land value. There is no distributive share properly called economic rent.

As this is a cardinal point, we must let Carey speak in his own words: ". . . of those portions of the earth which man converts into bows and arrows, canoes, ships, houses, books, cloth, or steam-engines, the value is determined by the cost of reproduction—that is, in all advancing communities, is less than the cost of production—and . . . the decline in the former below the latter is always most rapid when population and the consequent power of association increase most rapidly." This is Carey's theory of value, which he contends is universal in its application. Then he goes on to state what others hold to be the grand exception: "When, however, we look to those portions of it [land] which he uses for the purposes of cultivation, we find, according to all these writers [Malthus, Ricardo, Senior, Mill, etc.], a law directly the opposite of all this—the value of land being equal to the cost of producing it in its existing form, *plus* the value of a monopoly power increasing with the growth of numbers, and most rapidly when the growth of population and of the power of association is most rapid."

"Whether or not this really is so, is to be determined by an examination of the facts of the case, as exhibited in the value of land compared with the labor that would now be required for its reproduction in its existing form. Should that result in proving the former to be greater than the latter, then the doctrine of all these writers must be admitted to be correct; but, should it prove that land will nowhere exchange for as much labor as would be required for such reproduction, it will then have to be admitted that value is, in all and every case, but a measure of the amount of physical and mental effort required to overcome the obstacles standing in the way of the accomplishment of our desires. . . ." And he continues: we must then admit "that the price charged for the use of land is, like that charged for the use of all other . . . things, but compensation for the accumulations resulting from the labors of the past—that that price tends everywhere to diminish in its proportion to the product obtained by help of the machine— and, that there is but one system of laws for the government of all matter, let the form in which it exists be what it may."

Carey proceeds to cite examples, using rough figures to sharpen the lesson. The annual value of the land of Great Britain had recently been estimated by Sir Robert Peel at £47,800,000, which, at 4 per cent, would give a principal sum of £1,200,000,000. "Estimating the wages of laborers, miners, mechanics, and those by whom their labors are directed, at £50 per annum each, the land would . . . represent the labors of twenty-four millions of men for a single year; or of one million for twenty-four years." Carey then submits to his readers the supposition that the island was "reduced to the state in which it was found by Caesar; covered with impenetrable woods . . . and abounding in marshes and swamps, heaths and sandy wastes; and then estimate the quantity of labor that would be required to place it in its present position," with land cleared, enclosed, drained, and all of the facilities of transportation, mining, manufactures, school and court houses, "and the . . . tens of thousands of other improvements required for bringing into activity those powers for the use of which rent is paid. . . ." That restoration would need "the labor of millions of men for centuries, . . . although provided with all the machinery of modern times. . . ."

He multiplies instances. The farms of New York, with buildings, roads, and other improvements, are valued (1850) at some $1,100,000,000, equal to a million men working at a dollar a day for four years. "Were the land restored to the condition in which it stood in the days of Hendrick Hudson, and presented a free gift to an association of the greatest capitalists of Europe, with a bonus in money equal to the present value, their private fortunes and the bonus would be . . . exhausted before the existing improvements had, even to the extent of one-fifth, been executed."

His pronouncement upon these illustrations is: "The amount received as rent is interest upon the value of labor expended, *minus* the difference between the productive power" of New York soils "and that of the newer soils that can now be brought into activity. . . ." Property in land, Carey contends, obeys the same law with property of all other descriptions. The greatest cities, "with all their advantages of situation . . . would exchange for but a small portion of the labor that would be required to reproduce them, were their sites again reduced to the state in which they were found by the people by whom they were first commenced."

Determined always to have consistency, Carey scouted the idea of monopoly value from mere scarcity, aside from labor cost. He faced the problem frankly: "Here are two fields upon which has been bestowed an equal quantity of labor, the one of which will command twice the rent, and will sell for twice the price, of the other; and it may be asked—If value results exclusively from labor, how does it happen that the owner of the one is so much richer than the owner of the other?" His answer was that labor was applied to many fields, but only one proved to be extraordinarily rewarding. The value of this field was measured by the high cost of reproducing it, that is, discovering, in the course of farming operations, another field of similar fertility. Jenny Lind, the celebrated singer of his day, received hundreds of times as much for a concert as did a singer capable of good but not unique performance. An impressario must expend much effort with many candidates in seeking to produce another voice of such quality as Jenny Lind possessed. Probably he would not succeed, but that cost was responsible for the high value of the supreme voice.

This explanation of a unique or monopoly value is not convincing, and it is difficult to believe that it could have satisfied Carey himself. It would seem that Smith, Ricardo, McCulloch, and many more were correct in saying that value may result from usefulness plus scarcity, with no reference to labor cost. Monopoly or high differential value, they admitted, was a special case not obeying the general rule that labor was the cause of value. Actually, as appears in our discussion of the view of later economists, the seeming contradiction is removed if we attribute value to utility alone, more precisely to marginal utility. That is, value derives from the least satisfaction which regularly depends on possession or use of a good. Superior land or a particularly gifted artist or an extraordinarily fine diamond—all of which may happen without higher labor cost—are prized because of the special enjoyment they afford.

Carey was on firmer ground when he insisted on the conservation and increase of values by means of intimate association of producers and consumers. A concise way of putting it is: economy dictates the maximum creation of useful forms of matter with minimum cost of producing place utilities. A community profits by making, so far as possible, all that it requires for use. Costs of transportation should be avoided wherever feasible. Carey offered impressive illustrations of the advantages of this advice and of the evil effects of disobedience to this principle. Britain, in its colonial policy, refused to allow the people of its West India islands to convert their cane into anything beyond crude "muscovado" sugar (moist, yellow), which must then be sent to the home country, 3000 miles away, to be refined. The by-product, molasses, must be shipped elsewhere to be distilled into rum. This condemned the islands to agricultural pursuits, which meant, in that case, that most of the inhabitants were held in slavery. The workers were limited to the most rudimentary operations, all of the same sort. There was little place for the skill and ingenuity of the mechanic. Confined to gross production of raw material, with no variety of occupations and quickening exchanges in the community, the economy was stultified.

The same practice injured the American continental settlers. Said the House of Commons, in 1710, "the erecting of manufactories in the colonies had a tendency to lessen their dependence on Great Britain." Forty years later the setting up of any mill, or other engine, for splitting or rolling iron was prohibited. Only pig iron, the crudest product, was encouraged by being admitted to England duty free, there to be manufactured into usable forms, so the colonials were supplied by a double transportation. Britain went further and forbade commerce in certain manufactures within the colonies (beaver hats made in Connecticut, for example), and the number of hatters' apprentices was restricted by law. Artisans were prohibited under heavy penalties from leaving the mother country. Lord Chatham declared that he "would not allow the colonists to make even a hobnail for themselves."

The son of an Irish patriot, Henry Carey was naturally bitter at the economic subjection of Ireland by England. Except for a short period prior to the Act of Union (1800) Irish manufactures, by direct and indirect means, were virtually prevented. The purpose was to draw raw materials, including food, to England and Scotland, and compel the Irish to supply themselves with finished goods from Birmingham, Manchester, and Glasgow. "Deprived of all employment, except in the labor of agriculture, land became, of course, the great object of pursuit . . . and the people had now before them the choice between the occupation of land, *at any rent,* or *starvation.* The lord of the land was thus enabled to dictate his own terms. . . . 'Enormous rents, low wages, farms of an enormous extent, let by rapacious and indolent proprietors to monopolizing land-jobbers, to be re-let by intermediate oppressors, for five times their value, among the wretched starvers on potatoes and water,' led to a constant succession of outrages, followed by Insurrection Acts, Arms Acts, and Coercion Acts. . . ." When Carey wrote the dreadful Irish potato famine was fresh in memory. Because of a blight infecting this principal food crop, in the five years ending in 1851, some 1,000,000 inhabitants of Ireland died of starvation and 1,600,000 were forced to emigrate, chiefly to the United States. In the midst of her tragic hunger, Ireland was obliged to send meat and grain to England as tribute to absentee landlords. Finally the very landlords themselves were impoverished by dependence of the Irish population.

All that was needed to avoid this history of "slavery, depopulation, and death," Carey contended, was to allow Ireland to develop a varied economy, in which capital and wealth of many sorts would have been accumulated and produced. Ireland was not overpopulated in comparison with her latent, but largely forbidden, resources. Under the ruinous system forced upon Ireland, she was compelled to export her soil and her people.

Wherever a community—a locality or a country—is dependent on a distant market, because it does not have both farms and factories at home, much of its substance is drained away in costs of transportation and exactions of traders— middlemen, commission men, creditors, customs men, and a swarm of government officials collecting revenue and guarding against rebellion. We shall see Carey's deprecation of mere traffickers reappearing in Veblen. The metropolis, the great centralized depot of trade and industry, whether abroad or at home, is a vicious development, Carey declared. Better decentralization, with producers of many kinds in close association with each other and with consumers. This is a policy, strikingly enough, to which advanced countries, including England and the United States, have recently come. For in such countries as these, dispersion of industry and commerce in relatively small, partially self-contained towns and districts, was encouraged by the Great Depression of the nineteen-thirties and since World War II.

In order for association to prosper there must be a combination of different skills and callings. In such a community, commerce (cultural and economic and political, as distinguished from tribute to distant trade and exploiting traders) must make for alertness, education, opportunity, and self-discipline. Instead of the narrowness and numbness caused by confinement to one occupation, progress would follow. Though agreeing in the primacy of agriculture, Carey was as far as possible at odds with the economic counsel of Thomas Jefferson, who during much of his life contended that industry corrupted democracy. However, Carey believed, like Jefferson, in cherishing self-government and local responsibility. But, said Carey, these political and moral merits could not belong to people who were economically dependent on powers at a distance. This position has an immediate bearing on the problem of national versus state and local authority as illustrated in the 1964 Civil Rights law passed by Congress. Carey urged certain national uniformities. Only the national government was competent to enact certain economic and social protections and promotions. Indeed, Carey especially was known as a "national economist" or "economic nationalist." He believed, however, that relative self-sufficiency of local communities would facilitate, not hinder, willing obedience to wise over-all controls. The truth, for Carey, lay in the paradox perceived and acted upon by Stalin in binding together the many diverse peoples of the U.S.S.R. by encouraging each to develop its own local resources and pride. Unity through variety, even separatism, was his prescription. Similarly, Carey praised Colbert's policy of rendering the colonies of France as far as possible self-contained. While Adam Smith is generally considered the apostle of world trade, Carey never tired of pointing out that the illustrious Scots economist elevated local, domestic commerce to a higher position.

We may apply this great social principle which Carey preached to the United States of past years and of our own day. When cotton was king, the southern states cherished their "peculiar institution" of slavery precisely because their economy—single devotion to agriculture—was peculiar. This peculiarity produced the Civil War. Political and cultural connotations of the contest had their roots in economic variety in the North and economic sameness in the South. Now that the South, for almost a century since the Civil War, has been developing industry, commerce, and credit within the section, as Carey urged, it is better fitted to conform to desirable national standards of law and custom. This is not only because the South is now more like the remainder of the country in its economy, but also because, possessing greater internal economic competence, it is better able to share in national sentiments, and adopt them as its own. It may be suitable to add that the writer of these lines is a Southerner born and bred.

This discussion of Henry C. Carey's ardent preference for

internal exchanges between producers and consumers of many
faculties and demands within a community, and his exhibit of
the wastes and harm of transferring goods over long distances
to the benefit mainly of traders and transporters, brings us to
his most celebrated policy. As we have seen earlier, after an
initial phase of disagreement, he espoused his father's insistence
on governmental promotion of home industry through protective
tariffs. The principal argument for free international trade, from
before the time of Adam Smith, had been the benefits of
specialization. By devoting itself to the forms of production in
which it enjoyed an advantage, and exchanging with other
countries for what they produced with special economy, a
nation gained more at less cost than if it tried to supply itself
with all that it required. As Smith said, grapes could be grown
in England and tolerable wine, at a price, could be made from
them, but it was cheaper to send English hardware to Portugal
and fetch superior wines from there. Polar bears are best obtained from the Greenland seas, and citrus fruits from Florida
or California. Those holding to this recommendation went
further. Even if a country could produce two commodities, say
wool and wheat, more cheaply than another country, it might
be wise for the first country to confine itself to the commodity
in which it had the greater comparative advantage and export
that to secure the article in which it had a lesser advantage. The
country in question might get more wheat, say, by producing
only wool and exporting that, though all the time it could grow
wheat at lower absolute cost than could the country with which
it traded. Of course this presupposes uninterrupted intercourse,
or peace. To the extent that a nation must munition itself for
war, and dare not depend on others for military necessities, it
must nourish defense industries, and that would form an exception to the free trade rule.

To such argument of the economy of specialization Carey
opposed countervailing observations. What was lost in benefit
of climate, other natural resources, or customary skills, would
be more than made up in variety of pursuits. A community
producing many kinds of commodities—raw materials, foods,
manufactures—would have a livelier, more ingenious, more
stable economy than if it shut itself up to a few forms of output.
If it did the latter, its products were apt to be the crudest, least
valuable for their bulk, and therefore the most costly to trans-

port. Since most employers and workers produced the same things, they would have little to exchange with each other within the country. Lacking mutual stimulation, enterprise and inventiveness would sink, and circulation of money would slow down.

Planters and farmers should be brought into the nearest connection with demanders of their products. To sustain fertility of the soil requires that all waste materials be returned to the land. This need is violated if foodstuffs and raw materials are shipped abroad. Carey placed a stress on the use as fertilizer of human excrement from the cities and towns, a recommendation which was more appropriate in his day than since. Later the practice of carting off "night soil" to be spread on the fields was no longer possible as privies and cess pools were replaced by sewerage systems which carried this valuable refuse into the streams and ultimately into the ocean. The loss had to be compensated by use of artificial fertilizers or importation of guano. Carey was correct, however, in saying that much refuse that replaces nutrients in the earth is sacrificed if the materials go to other countries.

Farmers close to industrial communities find a ready market for their perishable products—vegetables, fruits, milk, and poultry. Staple crops, such as cereals, cotton, and tobacco are less liable to vacillation of price if there is domestic demand for them. The same is true of minerals. If the yield of the earth is to be exported, this should be in manufactured form. Woolen or cotton cloth represents much more than the fibers of which it is composed, for it contains the food, housing, all other consumption of the manufacturers, and the auxiliary materials and machinery required for its making, all of which have contributed to sustain a population of many employments.

The interaction between industry and agriculture is illustrated in the rural community in Massachusetts in which these lines are being written. When there were no manufacturing towns at hand, the farmers had to contrive many implements for themselves or resort at best to a mere blacksmith's shop. With no local markets for their products they left this stubborn soil for new lands in the West. Now, in return for their lumber, pulpwood, vegetables, fruits, milk, all sold nearby, they are conveniently supplied with modern equipment and repairs, electric power, education, and amusements. Labor, formerly much of the time idle on the isolated farms, is now in demand in factories reached in a matter of minutes. The newest farm houses are prefabricated with every improvement of plumbing and central heating by oil or propane gas. Boiling of maple sap to make syrup, once done on a petty scale for use of the farm family, is now reduced to a business; thirty cords of slabs, formerly almost waste of the sawmill, become fuel for making 900 gallons of syrup sold in the adjacent town at $6 a gallon.

The roads not long ago—specimens of them still exist in back portions of the neighborhood—were narrow, uneven dirt tracks through the forest. They were emblems of the cost of transportation, so taxing that they were little used. The subsistence farmers remained on their retired acres, often depending for "store goods" on the peddler bent under his pack, or bringing tinware and calico by wagon, and maybe trading eggs for these articles. The roads were a trial to man and beast because they ran nowhere except to scattered neighbors' houses; they invited to no markets, to no opportunities for employment. Now the roads are widened, graded, surfaced, traversed to and from town by cars and trucks. Farming, primitive a few decades ago, has become scientific, and more varied in crops. A man may work in a shoe or paper factory, a machine shop or food processing plant, and still get more from his land than formerly, for his family helps him raise thousands of broiling chickens, or cucumbers from a few acres bring cash from the pickle factory. The one-room schoolhouse, to which the children walked in all weathers, is abandoned for a modern consolidated school serving, by bus, the whole district.

This is one example, Carey would say, of the association of agriculture and industry in the local community, with active commerce between country and town. In order for decentralized manufactures to be established and prosper, Carey felt, it was necessary for government to offer protection by import duties on competing foreign products. An illustration, from the community just cited, is pertinent. Several nearby factories make hand tools. These are now threatened by Japanese and West German imports, not equal in quality, but sold at half the price of those locally produced. Carey contended that the civilizing value, in all departments of life, or the social income from nourishing native manufactures, is immeasurably greater than the small saving in price of the same sorts of wares brought from a distance.

With agriculture so augmented by mechanical and chemical improvements, with food producers near to consumers, there was no fear of the gloomy dictate of Malthus that population tended to exceed the means of subsistence. Combined effort led to larger, not more grudging, returns from land. So far from wanting to restrict population, Carey hoped that "the addition to our population by immigration will speedily rise to millions." "To substitute true Christianity for the detestable system known as the Malthusian, it is needed that we prove to the world that it is population that makes the food come from the rich soils, and that food tends to increase more rapidly than population. . . ." It was significant, Carey said many times, that Malthus's doctrine of diminishing returns from agriculture, and its sequel, Ricardo's principle of rising rents, both originated in England. For that country, bent on making itself "the workshop of the world," condemned distant peoples to unintelligent methods of food production, much idleness of labor, and expenditure of a high proportion of total effort in transporting food and bringing back manufactured goods. It was no wonder that purely agricultural peoples were poverty-stricken, unable to develop their social resources, and so did not command the increasing returns which a varied economy invited.

If manufacturing, instead of being centralized, was dispersed, and domesticated, both capital and labor on the land would get an increasing proportion of the product, and the landlord would receive an ever decreasing relative share.

For Further Reading

Carey, Henry Charles, *Principles of Political Economy* (Philadelphia: Carey, Lea & Blanchard, 3 vols., 1837–40).
———, *Principles of Social Science* (Philadelphia: J. B. Lippincott & Co., 3 vols., 1858–60).
———, *The Harmony of Interests, Agricultural, Manufacturing, and Commercial* (Philadelphia: H. C. Baird & Co., 1890). An excellent summary of Carey's views is in the conclusion, pp. 227–9.
Kaplan, A. D. H., *Henry C. Carey* (Baltimore: The Johns Hopkins Press, 1931).
Dictionary of American Biography, articles on the Careys, father and son, outline their ideas as well as their lives.

8

DESTINY FROM DEAN STREET

Karl Marx

Of all the economic thinkers included in this book, Karl Marx probably appears to Americans the most alien. His ideas and the movements resulting from them are apt to be viewed as sinister. The two chief countries whose governments profess allegiance to Marx's system—Russia and China—have fewer bonds with—indeed are regarded as inveterately hostile to—the western world. Marx wrote, and thought, chiefly in a language foreign to English, so that we know his works in translation if at all.

We may bring him a little closer by recalling that he was keenly aware of the United States. He was never here, though his *alter ego*, Friedrich Engels, visited this country, and Marx, with Engel's help, regularly contributed European reports to the *New York Tribune*. Many of these letters discussed the Civil War as seen by Europeans. America was acknowledged by Marx to form an exception to his forecast of how a fundamental social change would come about.* Marx transferred the headquarters of the International Workingmen's Association (the "First International") from Europe to New York. Consequently the early manuscript minutes of the International, partly in Marx's hand, are in New York. Numbers of Marx's colleagues emigrated to America in the middle of the last century and were the first to spread his doctrines here. One of his close

---

* A knowledgeable student, Earl Browder, has explored pertinent theoretical and practical issues in *Marx and America* (New York: Duell, Sloan and Pearce, 1958).

friends, Georg Weydemeyer, became a colonel in the United States Army, and Marx's correspondence with another, Friedrich Albert Sorge, was deposited by Sorge in the New York Public Library.

Three terms which constantly occur in Marx's writings have for Americans a distinctly foreign ring and have acquired objectionable connotations. One, taken as representing the Marxian method of thought, is "dialectic." This means simply logical argument, disputation, or debate. To some it carries the flavor of disingenuous or tricky reasoning, but this character does not belong to the word. Another term is "proletariat" or "proletarian," which seems not only strange but repulsive in the phrase "dictatorship of the proletariat." The word is from the Latin *proletarius*, meaning to the ancient Romans the lowest class, who contributed to the state nothing but offspring. Marx used it for workingmen, those who lived by their labor alone. Some think of it as implying rabble, but accurately it designates workers or the working class. The third expression is "bourgeois," which stands for burger, townsman, a member of the middle, commercial, or business class. These three words lose their unfamiliar or fearsome taint if we accept them as meaning simply argument, workers, business men. As he used them, they are so embedded in Marxian literature that it is easiest to continue to employ them in their original forms, but of themselves they convey no threat or dire intention.

Other features combine to make Marx uncongenial, to say the least, to Americans. Though he lived most of his life in England, and more than others entertained world or universal concepts, Marx was German through and through, and the behavior of Germans in two world wars has placed a stigma on what we regard as German culture. We think of Marx as angry, fierce, a mental picture traceable as much to his full black beard and piercing eyes as to anything in the man's philosophy. *The Red Prussian* is the title of one biography. He came himself of the middle (professional rather than commercial) class, and was highly educated. Some may harbor a lurking prejudice because, as passionate champion of the workers, he was treasonable to his own social group. We conceive of him as bitter, desperately serious with no saving sense of humor. He was certainly intense, suffered poverty throughout his adult life, could be harsh in his judgments even of persons who had helped him, but withal was not unbalanced or lacking in lighter moments. The Marx household, in spite of anxieties, managed to be a merry one. He was a favorite of the children in his London slum, and was remembered by his grandchildren as their playfellow. I mentioned to M. Longuet, Marx's grandson and himself a public man in France, that I visited Hampstead Heath where Marx took youngsters on outings. "Oh, yes," he responded with a smile, "grandfather used to let us ride the donkeys kept there for hire by Spanish boys. Once we went on a Sunday, and I complained when we found no donkeys. 'Why, son, don't you know,' my grandfather explained, 'on Sundays all the donkeys put on long black pants and go to church'!"

Marx was born May 5, 1818 at Trier (French Trèves) in the Rhine Province of Prussia, an ancient town founded by Augustus, with many Roman remains and the center of the Moselle wine industry. Both of his parents were descended from learned rabbis. His father was a lawyer and minor government official who, when Karl was five years old, embraced the Christian religion and the whole family was baptized as Protestants. We do not know whether or not this was dictated by policy, in order to keep his official post; it may have been, as with others, an act of personal preference. The choice had no effect on the convictions of the son, who was destined to be emphatically secular, though it may have forwarded his marriage into a Lutheran family. He wrote celebrated examinations of Christianity, but from a sociological and legal, not a theological, viewpoint.

Karl was a sturdy, active, bright boy, an apt student in the local schools, and was his mother's *Wunderkind*. At seventeen he entered the nearby University of Bonn. Here he was half-hearted in the study of law, wrote bad verses, and wasted time gambling, which drew grieved remonstrances from his father. After one year he transferred to the University of Berlin, where he abandoned the idea of becoming a lawyer and devoted himself to intensive reading in history and philosophy. He immersed himself in the system of thought of Hegel, who had recently died as professor of philosophy at Berlin. Marx's formal indoctrination was enlivened by discussions with other "Young Hegelians" of whom the brothers Bruno and Edgar Bauer, older than Karl, were the central figures. Hegel's conception was that culture—religion, art, government—develops through conflict. One position in belief and practice, which he called a *thesis*, is questioned and assailed by another, its *antithesis*. This assertion and negation are reconciled in a new form, a *synthesis*. The process is repeated. The synthesis in its turn is taken as a thesis, which is combated by an antithesis, and from the opposition emerges a fresh synthesis. With Hegel this dueling exists in the spheres of reasoning and emotion; it is mental, moral, juridical. The end result, semipermanent anyhow, is an absolute. In religion the absolute is Christianity; in government it is the monarchical state. This last ideal gave the Young Hegelians a practical bond, for they were passionately eager for the unification of Germany, then a loose confederation of states, the kingdom of Prussia being the most potent. Marx remained all his life, in spite of the sweep of his international plans, a patriotic German.

To understand Hegel's influence on Marx we must note the older philosopher offered a formula for the historical process, change through struggle. This was the dialectical perception—declaration, refutation, and a solution, followed by further action, reaction, and combination, until hopefully a satisfactory, stable situation would be reached, free of antagonisms. The pattern was dynamic, the new being born from the old.

But Marx gave this historical development a radically different motive power. He converted the formula of change from ideological into materialistic. For Marx the conflicts were not in the realm of thoughts or of the senses, but were between economic classes. Masters and slaves, feudal lords and serfs, capitalist employers and wage-workers in successive periods strove with each other. The contemporary contest was between the classes in the last pair. When the workers freed themselves from subjugation to profit-seeking employers, and converted private property in the means of production to common ownership, classes and consequently their contentions would disappear. There would be only one class, that of the workers, now become their own masters.

Marx kept conflict in full measure, but he found its roots not in the mind, or in religious yearnings, or aesthetic forms, or in political behavior. Rather the battles of history were between the oppressors and the oppressed, exploiters and the exploited. The class dominant at any stage exercised power

through control of the means of production, first through ownership of the workers themselves as chattel slaves, later by ownership of the land on which serfs must labor for a living, finally
by possession of instruments of production (factories, railroads,
ships, commercial capital, as well as land). In modern society
the workers, stripped of ownership of means of production,
with only their labor to offer, were obliged to secure access
to capital and land on terms dictated by the privileged
possessors.

Marx's materialism made expressions of culture—religion,
law, art, government—subordinate to the mode of production
prevailing at any period. They take their character from economic tensions. Thus the "higher life" of the intellect and the
spirit is a reflection of material conditions. Literature, painting,
architecture, music, theology, and systems of government are
not causes, but consequences. "Dialectical materialism" or
"materialist determinism" was rejected by most as dethroning
the mind, the will, the senses, above all, God. It was a more
obnoxious form of predestination, in which Marx would out-
Calvin Calvin. The Protestant theologian, fatalistic to be sure,
had the Almighty as the disposer of man's fortunes. Marx came
down to the means of winning bread and cheese, to hoe and
spade, cart, marketplace, and interest rate, water wheel and
steam engine. Heaven had sunk to earth. Striving had been
shorn of its nobler qualities, had become mere strife. Prayer,
worship, duty, altruism, truth—where were these in Marx's
world of production, exchange, and the distribution of wealth?
Granted that man is an animal, what had Marx done to man's
immortal soul?

As we shall see, Marx did not voice this diagnosis at first,
and he was never completely dogmatic in his economic interpretation of history. Deliberate intention, design, judgment,
wisdom, compassion, love of the beautiful and the true play
their part in social destinies. The direction of change may be
chosen to a degree, processes may be speeded or slower,
economic forces may be ameliorated by the sense of justice.
Conscious effort may influence the result for better or for
worse. The evolvement of human institutions and behavior is
infinitely complex, but the fundamental determinants are in
the processes of getting a living, of applying labor to nature.
Other influences are by comparison mere tinctures.

The Prussian king prevailed on the French authorities to destroy a Paris newspaper published by German exiles, the *Vorwärts,* claimed to be incendiary. Marx was among the contributors ordered expelled. He moved his family to Brussels, where he readily promised the police not to publish anything on Belgian politics. He was soon joined by Engels.

Friedrich Engels was two years younger than Marx, born in Barmen 28 November, 1820. When near his university degree at Elberfeld he left for a business apprenticeship in the consular office at Bremen and thereafter joined his father, a successful textile manufacturer with plants in Germany and Manchester, England. Though equipped in philosophy, Engels's forte was industrial history, informed by his practical participation in factory management. When Marx was still groping in the fogs of metaphysics, Engels was exploring and applying the actual facts of business conduct. That this anatomy of capitalism later became a preoccupation of Marx we surely owe to Engels' example and influence.

Engels was a plainer writer than Marx, able to put down quickly and briefly the lessons from abundant observation of the course of the Industrial Revolution, with no sacrifice of penetrating thought. Marx made an elaborate production of writing. He tortured himself and often his readers to be complete and thorough to the last detail. Rather than publish what did not satisfy his demand for perfection, he left much in fragments. Engels by comparison was direct and summary. What he did not say at one time he would come to afterward. In their memorable collaboration, which has forever linked their names, it was Engels who constantly urged Marx to have done, to commit to print and amend later on if he chose. When Engels's pleas for promptness were unavailing, he would supply a manuscript for Marx to adopt. As we shall see, after Marx's death Engels put together the bits and pieces left by his friend to make the second and third volumes of *Das Kapital.*

Engels was Marx's guardian angel. Himself original and gifted, and passionately devoted to human freedom, it is accurate to say that Marx was Engels's life work. Engels offered total friendship, sharing thoughts, maturing purposes, contributing with his pen, and, as soon as he was able, contributing also from his purse. Practical and dependable, he was a balance to Marx's moods. The minds and hearts of the two were so

merged as often to defy discrimination in the product. Marx
was the more profound and deserves pre-eminence, but without Engels he would have been less. Marx had one life, of
study, writing, and agitation. Engels, fortunately, had two, or
three—daily demands of business, correspondence and collaboration with Marx, and sports, particularly riding in the
hunt. Marx was always afraid his friend would break his neck
at ditches and walls. Manchester industrialists with whom
Engels associated likely had no notion that he was a revolutionary. Following youthful service in the German army, he
made military science an avocation and published works on the
subject that were admired by professional soldiers.

Marx and Engels were opposites in appearance. Marx, while
above middle height, was stocky, thick, with wavy, abundant
black hair and beard, graying in his later years. Engels was
taller, slenderer, and blond. Whereas Marx's eyes bored into
one, Engels's glance was bland, all friendliness. When Engels
was already a thinker and writer of capacity, he was taken to
be an ingenuous youth. All who have left recollections speak
of his unfailing kindliness of manner.

Short sketches of the careers—career, in the singular, is
accurate—of Marx and Engels at this point in the story usually
run forward to their production of the *Communist Manifesto,*
1848. But we must know the preliminaries of this epoch-mak-
ing performance. Their first joint effort was to break a lance
against writers in the Berlin *Allgemeine Literatur-Zeitung* who
clung to the Hegelian proposition that ideas make reality in
society. These essayists discredited any role of the masses in
their own liberation and pointedly attacked the historical materialism which Marx and Engels had already developed. The
latter replied that "To-day only crass political ignorance can
imagine that bourgeois life must be held together by the State.
The truth is that the State is held together by bourgeois life."
Their publisher changed the title of their book from *A Criticism
of Critical Criticism* to *The Holy Family,* which suited a mocking polemic against an opinionated elite. Engels preached similar doctrine in his *Condition of the Working Class in England
in 1844,* which not only portrayed the physical effects of industrial exploitation but looked to a proletarian-socialist
revolution. Then the two of them assailed German philosophy
again in a prodigious manuscript of eight hundred pages which

would have made arid reading had not the publisher declined it. No matter, the enthusiastic authors were straightening out their own notions. Marx whetted his mental edge in differences with his old friend Proudhon. In reply to Proudhon's *Philosophy of Poverty* Marx published his *Poverty of Philosophy,* 1847 (in French so Proudhon could read it). Here Marx systematically stated his materialist conception of history, or social evolution through struggles of economic classes. This evolution of human institutions reminds one of Darwin's explanation of evolution of natural organisms in *The Origin of Species* more than twenty years later.

Marx and Engels had been nursing along the scattered fragments of the League of the Just. The purpose was to win these intelligent, socially conscious workers from French utopian infatuation or from contentment with mere reform. By visits and addresses they were urged to enter into a proletarian movement for overthrow of the bourgeois owning class. This educational work combined with the widespread rising discontent in Europe, which was building up to the revolutions of 1848, to convert the League of the Just. It was not easy to persuade the League to adopt the program of Marx and Engels, for the workers were suspicious of the intellectuals' advice.

In the beginning of 1847 an emissary to Marx in Brussels and to Engels in Paris begged that they would join the League of the Just and formally assist in giving it a new organization and revolutionary drive. They consented; at a congress the League of the Just dropped conspiratorial methods, changed its name to the Communist League, and commissioned Marx and Engels to draw up a manifesto (Engels's term) of its aims, to be discussed at a second congress early in 1848. Engels was first to get busy on this assignment, choosing originally the device of twenty-five questions and answers. He wrote to Marx: "Think over the confession of faith a bit. I think it would be better to drop the catechism form and call the thing a communist manifesto. As a certain amount of history will have to be brought in I think the present form is unsuitable. I am bringing along what I have done here. It is in simple narrative form, but miserably edited and done in a terrible hurry."

Engels joined Marx at Ostend. The two went to London and from seperate drafts framed the celebrated document in January, 1848. The ideas of the authors were practically identical.

Marx seems to have been chiefly responsible for the final wording. It was printed in London and sent by the central executive to the branches a few days before the February revolution threw Europe into a convulsion. The *Communist Manifesto* was not published; it was known probably to no more than a hundred members of the League and had no agency in the national democratic upheavals that ensued. In fact it overrode mere national liberal reforms to proclaim a class war. The cry was "Workers of the World, unite."*

How came this compact document of thirty printed pages to be the acknowledged well-spring of communist and socialist movements throughout the world? A knowing writer (Gustav Mayer) finds its power in "the colossal urgency of its message; its style is highly-wrought" by "authors conscious of their historical mission." Another (Franz Mehring) has pitched on "the world outlook of its authors in a mirror whose glass could not have been clearer or its frame smaller." Because of its terseness in exposition, argument, and challenge, it may not be paraphrased, to say nothing of losing the spirited language.

The *Manifesto* begins with the historic changes wrought by struggles of classes. The extraordinary achievements of capitalist production are extolled (as later in *Das Kapital*), but this system is periodically stultified by commercial crises caused by too much production. Since capitalism has become international, labor must organize in the same fashion. The description of wages, tending toward the minimum of subsistence, is taken from Malthus and Ricardo. Communists will abolish only that "private" property which is really social in character, which has been filched from the workers in uncompensated labor-time.

The workers must first "win the battle of democracy," "raise the proletariat to the position of ruling class." The proletariat will then "use its political supremacy to wrest, by degrees, all capital from the bourgeoisie, to centralize all instruments of production in the hands of the state. . . ." First moves, differing from country to country, will be to abolish property in land and apply all rents to public purposes, centralize credit, communication, and transport in the state, establish a plan for improve-

---

* This famous motto had been offered in a Communist newspaper some months earlier; it may have been coined by Engels.

ment of agriculture. Lesser policies will be abolition of the right of inheritance, decentralization of industry so as gradually to remove the distinction between town and country, and provide free education for all children in public schools. Later more comprehensive changes will be accomplished. Then the public power will lose its political character, for there will be no more class antagonism, and government will be concerned merely with administration of the economy.

The next section (an echo of what Marx and Engels had recently been writing) shows the shortcomings of existing forms of socialism and communism as compared with the program for the revolutionary international proletariat which the *Manifesto* sets forth. In the beginning the communists will have varying immediate aims and alliances in different European countries, but will "everywhere support every revolutionary movement against the existing social and political order of things." Ultimately, since "working men have no country," nations as antagonistic units will disappear in a cooperative world.

"The Communists disdain to conceal their views and aims. They openly declare that their ends can be attained only by the forcible overthrow of all existing social conditions. Let the ruling classes tremble at a Communist revolution. The proletarians have nothing to lose but their chains. They have a world to win.

"Working men of all countries, unite!"

The grand feature of the *Communist Manifesto* is the presentation of social changes—past, present, and future—as inexorable. The process is described and documented. Wishes, selfish devices for avoidance, political maneuvers may temporarily delay but cannot cancel the progress which is defined. The capitalist class, not least by its own necessities, is doomed to give way to the proletariat which will usher in "the free development of each . . . for the free development of all."

No timetable of this mighty transformation is offered. We know otherwise that the authors, both under the age of thirty, moved by a generous enthusiam, foreshortened the process in their minds. It was to take far longer than they expected for the contradictions in capitalism to render the system unworkable. In western countries political ameliorations would prevent the workers from sinking into desperate destitution. Social and labor legislation and labor unions would help workers to share in increased production. In certain countries, notably Britain and the United States, as Marx and Engels specifically recognized, the transition to a cooperative economy might come gradually, without wholesale, sudden expropriation of capital. However, this protraction of the process, this greater endurance of private capitalism does not alter the force of the reasoning. If Marx and Engels looked for momentous upheavals earlier, the capitalist world could not have been more astonished by the Soviet revolution during World War I and the progressive sweep of communism in the fifty years following.

The authors of the *Manifesto* did well to discard the original scheme of a simple catechism to inform workers. Their thesis demanded historical review and ardent argument. The *Manifesto* requires knowledge for its understanding, but one admires the authors' skill in compressing much into small space without becoming cryptic or cloudy. This was fortunate for the spread of socialist ideas because Marx's major work, *Capital,* is long and involved.

In February, 1848, the monarchy of Louis Philippe was unseated in France and this touched off an epidemic of revolutions. King Leopold of Belgium succeeded in keeping his throne and threw foreign radicals out of the country. Marx was arrested and released only under order of expulsion. At the cordial invitation of Ferdinand Flocon, on behalf of the provisional government, Marx went to Paris to direct efforts of the Communist League from that favorable center. Successful risings in Vienna and Berlin in March, 1848 justified publication of a revolutionary organ at Cologne, capital of the Rhineland. The *Neue Rheinische Zeitung,* with Marx as editor, appeared during a troubled year, with an interval of forced suspension. When Marx had paid the paper's debts, he was obliged to pawn his wife's silver to eke out a living for his family, now increased to six, including the devoted "Lenchen" (Helene Demuth, their lifelong servant and friend). We do not record the details of twenty months of ceaseless, anxious activity, in which victory of counter-revolution in one country after another proved what Marx knew in his heart, that years of preparation must precede a workers' society. He was expelled from Germany, and returned to Paris only to be ordered by the royalist ministry to leave the capital. He and Engels managed to get to London (autumn of 1849), which became Marx's home for the remainder of his life.

For a while Marx edited from London the *Neue Rheinische Revue,* published in Hamburg. Its six numbers analyzed the defeat of the 1848 revolution in Germany, Hungary, Poland, Austria, and France. Marx and Engels still believed that force, not gradual reform, must usher in new societies. But for all that, this mid-century European spasm was the last they were to witness, and they settled with patience to the long task of more thorough preparation for a distant future.

Not so, however, with most of the political refugees, especially Germans, who had sought asylum in London. Bitter, insecure, and longing for the chance of return to their homeland, they deceived themselves with pitiable schemes for provoking new workers' rebellions. Marx and Engels and wiser ones who stood with them knew these hopes were illusory and said so. This produced a split in the Communist League, caused as much by the poverty and worry of all of them as by difference of policy. Marx and Engels divorced themselves from their resentful brethren. Though a sorrowful parting, this was fortunate, otherwise energies needed for hard study, thinking, and writing would have been dissipated in doomed filibustering projects. Personal kindnesses continued in testimony to old associations.

The Marx family, after a couple of forced moves, found shelter in two rooms at No. 28 Dean Street, Soho Square. Here they endured abominable suffering for six years. The squalid district was a pocket of exiles, one more depressed than another. The psychological gloom was unhealthful enough, but the crowding in shabby houses was worse. In the summer of 1854 an outbreak of cholera was attributed, doubtless mistakenly, to drains dug through the bone-pits of the victims of the bubonic plague of two centuries earlier. Existence, buoyed by high resolve, might have been tolerable with a few more shillings for the necessities of life. Engels had gone to Manchester to work for his father's firm. He gave Marx what spasmodic financial assistance he could snatch from support of himself, his companion Mary Burns, and Mary's needy Irish relatives. Marx's only earnings were from articles on European events supplied to the *New York Tribune,* one of whose editors, Charles A. Dana, a follower of Fourier, Marx knew from

Cologne days. Marx was supposed to get two pounds each for two letters a week, which would have been sustenance. But many of his contributions were not printed, others, he complained, were appropriated for unsigned editorials, and for none of these was he paid. When sales slackened, Dana reduced Marx to half pay. Anyhow, his receipts arrived irregularly and tardily. Sometimes he could not furnish his pieces, for he had not a penny to buy newspapers to inform himself or even paper on which to write. At one point he was compelled to suspend correspondence with the *Tribune* because he was frantically assembling proofs of forgeries of the Prussian prosecutor in the trial for high treason of eleven old communist comrades at Cologne. In sending off his pamphlet exposing the frauds, he wrote that "its author is practically an internee owing to the lack of adequate covering for his feet and his behind." Again, "My affairs have now reached the agreeable point at which I can no longer leave the house because my clothes are in pawn and can no longer eat meat because my credit is exhausted."

Sale of Frau Marx's silver and repeated visits to "uncle" in Soho with household items to pawn could not save the family from a diet at times of bread and potatoes. Marx and his loyal family bore this misery as long as he had the opiate of work, but recurrent illness laid him low. Worse befell in deaths of three of the children. A son, Guido, sickly from birth, succumbed after a year. An infant daughter lived no longer. Frau Marx at Easter, 1852, wrote in her diary, "our poor little Franziska fell ill with severe bronchitis. For three days the poor child struggled against death. . . . Her small lifeless body rested in our little back room whilst we all went together into the front room and when night came we made up beds on the floor. The three surviving children lay with us and we cried for the poor little angel who now rested so cold and lifeless in the next room." They had no money. "I went to a French fugitive who lives near us and who had visited us shortly before. He received me with . . . sympathy and gave me two pounds and with that money the coffin in which my child could rest peacefully was paid for. It had no cradle when it was born and even the last little shell was denied it long enough." The family was harder hit, just three years later, by the loss of nine-year-old Edgar, a talented boy and only son, endearing even in his fatal illness.

While Marx went regularly to the British Museum library to pore all day over economic works and reports of government investigations, his wife had not this relief from home cares. Occasionally there were passages between husband and wife, as was inevitable, but without her unfailing concern for him the world would be poorer. It is a long lane that has no turning; finally late in 1856 the family was able, on the strength of small legacies from Frau Marx's relatives, to rent a little house, No. 9 Grafton Terrace, Maitland Park, not far from Hampstead Heath, which was their favorite outing place. They redeemed household goods from the pawnshop and spread themselves in what seemed spacious quarters "compared with the holes we have previously had to live in." The grateful relief proved temporary, and soon the damask napkins and other possessions of any value were tripping back to be pledged for loans at the sign of the three brass balls.

Marx refused to take work at the hands of any bourgeois employer, calling this a matter of principle. He labored endlessly, as writer, teacher, and contriver, to advance the prospect of the workers, all of course for love, but the price of his obstinacy was too much misery for those nearest him and for himself. He knew and said repeatedly that all must live for many years into the future in a private capitalist world. Why, then, must he be a purist in his personal economy? The eccentricity of genius is the usual—and specious—answer.

The two friends, Marx and Engels, were hopeful of a continuing income for Karl from articles to be contributed to an American encyclopedia. Engels would do the military ones, Marx those on politics and history; maybe they could collect a little staff of refugees, have an office, and make a thing of it. They deluded themselves. They found out that, as since, such work pays Grub Street wages—in their case less than a penny a line. In his plight, Marx's hopes were always ready to be raised, though he was sadly used to having them dashed. He let himself believe that the commercial crisis of 1857, originating in America and spreading to England and the Continent, would prove severe enough to invite popular rebellion. He made meticulous notes of its progress, even taking pathetic satisfaction when the *Tribune* reduced his articles from two per week to one, as a sign of bad times. He labored with renewed zeal on his *Critique of Political Economy,* published through the good offices of Lassalle in Berlin in 1859. The book, too abstract to register an early success, did get him forward toward his greater work, *Capital*, of eight years later. But that was all for the time being, and the economic crisis cured itself without the social results which Marx envisaged.

Marx visited an uncle in Holland, got some financial help from him, and proceeded to Germany, his entry permitted by a restricted amnesty. In Berlin the flaming Lassalle was prosperous through the patronage ("kept man" some called his situation) of Countess Sophie von Hatzfeldt, whose protracted lawsuit against her husband Lassalle had at length brought to a successful conclusion. Lassalle proposed joint editorship of a new revolutionary journal, but the time was not ripe for this castle in Spain. Marx did arrange for *Die Presse* of Vienna to take his articles regularly, but in fact this paper printed and paid for only a small part of what Marx sent. The *New York Tribune* cut him off entirely.

In 1862 creditors besieged Marx's house, bailiffs levied on his furniture. He was ready to take his older daughters out of school, find places for them as governesses, declare himself bankrupt, and retreat to worse lodgings. A reluctant application for a job with a railway company had been turned down because Marx's handwriting was so execrable. Rescue came in the nick of time. Engels, in spite of his own troubles (the death of Mary Burns and the cotton famine that threatened his business in Manchester) contributed a hundred pounds. Soon Marx inherited something from his mother and more (nearly a thousand pounds) from his old comrade Wilhelm Wolff. This last enabled him to work with comparative peace of mind on *Das Kapital,* the first volume of which he dedicated to Wolff.

Throughout the American Civil War Marx was confident that the Union would be victorious over Southern slavery and secession. Engels, viewing Northern military ineptitude and tardy arousal, prophesied defeat. Marx, unlike Engels, had never been in the United States, but he always had an accurate estimate of economic potential here, especially after the gold discoveries in California. He was sure that the industrial and political resources of the North would come to bear and be successful. Here he saw the bourgeoisie overcoming what amounted to feudalism.

Karl Marx is chiefly known for the *Communist Manifesto,*

the International Workingmen's Association, and *Das Kapital*. The "First International" grew out of a large meeting at St. Martin's Hall, London, September 28, 1864, to welcome a delegation of French workers. The Great Exhibition (Prince Albert, Victoria's consort, its royal patron) had established fraternal relations between English unionists and their fellows across the channel. Formation of an International Workers' Committee gave Marx the opportunity to draw up a declaration of principles and plan of organization. Labor unions in various countries had made headway. Particularly the British workers, by firm insistence, had prevented Lord Palmerston from favoring the Confederacy, fighting for perpetuation of slavery, in the American Civil War. This demonstrated the political power of labor. Capitalism, especially under the British free trade slogan, was developing internationally. British workers declared to their French confrères that labor must do likewise. British manufacturers vitiated hard-won gains of British unions by importing workers from France where unions were comparatively backward. Marx, breaking his rule of many years now, felt justified in diverting himself from his studies for *Das Kapital* to guide a promising movement, at a propitious moment, to promote combined action of the proletarians in all countries.

Marx framed the trenchant Inaugural Address to the working class. He declared (and supported his contention with figures in the case of Britain) that the conspicuous prosperity of international capital was at the expense of the workers. At the same time, two achievements of the workers in Britain were significant for the future. First, the ten-hours law in factories manifested the capacity of labor, through political pressure, to check capitalist greed, to set aside the operation of supply and demand. Second, cooperatively owned manufactures and other enterprises proved that the private capitalist was not necessary to production. Marx's historical review closed with the old exhortation, "Workers of the World, unite!"

The International held annual congresses (60 or 70 delegates from the main European countries) and between times the General Council in London directed policy and rallied support for strikers. In some respects the International Workingmen's Association was an early anticipation of the International Labor Organization established as a part of the League of Nations after World War I. Of course the means of improving and

evening labor standards as between countries had to be different in the two organizations; the ILO is not class-conscious,
does not muster political pressure.

Marx gave constant zeal to the First International, especially to the supervisory work of the General Council, for he
often did not appear at the annual congresses. Such an organization was besought to welcome affiliation of all kinds of
factional labor groups. Marx warded off several that were pet
promotions of individual revolutionaries but which would dis-
tract from or bring discredit upon the objects of the main body.
This was a delicate task, for the labor movements in France,
Germany, Italy, Spain, Belgium, Poland, and Switzerland were
in varying stages of development, all of them less mature than
in Britain, and autonomy of the national groups was the
established general principle.

Marx had been at work on his *magnum opus, Das Kapital,*
since 1861, though with interruptions from illness and demands of the International. Materials had been gathered for
the second and third volumes, parts of which had been written
while the remainder was in memoranda, but only Volume I was
completed in 1866 and published in German at Hamburg by
Otto Meissner late in 1867. This is the only volume which
Marx himself finished. For this reason and because of its
subject matter it is from Volume I that the prodigious influence
of the work has sprung. If ever an effort claimed thorough
enquiry, painstaking exposition, and vigorous argument, this
book embodies those qualities. Though the whole aim was to be
scientific, rather than ideological, and in spite of the abstract
reasoning of much of it, this is a passionate appeal. Without
that spirit its impact would have been limited.

Naturally, as the herald of a new era in human society, the
work has been accorded not only enthusiasm and almost slavish
obedience, but has been subjected to terrified abuse and rigorous
scholarly criticism. We could notice flaws and fallacies exposed
by academic scrutiny.* However, these defects, while undoubted, are really beside the point and do not touch Marx's
message. The book is less theoretical than it is historical. Marx
observed, felt, and wrote in the period when the Industrial

---

* See Joan Robinson, *An Essay on Marxian Economics* (London:
Macmillan, 1960).

Revolution had manifested the surprising accomplishments and, by the same token, the inhumanities of capitalism. It is a report on an epoch, the results of which—physical, financial, social, and moral—were plain by Marx's time.

Das Kapital is usefully contrasted with the thought of Adam Smith and David Ricardo and their immediate disciples. They were dazzled, if one may apply that word to such sober, sensible viewers, by the prospects and power of industrial capitalism, then in its beginnings. It was enough for them to define the benefits of division of labor, the promise of individual initiative, and practice of competition in a market economy. They sought for laws controlling a system assumed to be permanent. The evolution of capitalism had not become evident. Consequently their analysis was substantially static.

Giving his verdict almost a century after Smith and two generations after Ricardo, Marx enjoyed a perspective which they did not possess. For Marx the wheel had turned. He saw a sociological process, one form of production rising, reaching its zenith, declining, and then succeeded by another. He described a fundamental historical principle activating this whole scene of changes from ancient to modern time. Forces which for Smith and Ricardo were absolute, or nearly so, for Marx were relative.

Marx's momentous advance over Smith and Ricardo is not to be praised without the realization that he himself was their pupil. The world takes Marx as the prime radical. Actually he was a classicist. Nobody gave the thought of previous masters of capitalist political economy more assiduous and respectful examination. Especially in the rigor of his formulation did he pattern after David Ricardo. He regarded himself as making anything but an emotional plea. The strength of his work, in his own mind, was its searching scientific character. In his experience with contemporary reformers he had had enough of idealists—Fourier, St. Simon, Owen, even Proudhon, not to speak of lesser experimenters with eccentric and unlikely projects. He wanted not to excite or convert, but to lay bare the underlying principles of social development and let this steely demonstration carry its lesson.

That much said, we, a hundred years after Marx, may estimate his inspiration better than he could do it. From the first, bred in (Hegelian) historical method, of quick moral sympathies, a personal sufferer in the popular behalf, he was enormously indignant at the wrongs systematically visited upon the masses of the people. Thus revolted, but true to industrious German scholarly method, he was bent on substantiating his social thesis. But the economic reasoning which he applied was subordinate to his moral purpose. The grandeur of his advocacy—remembering that he advocated nothing, merely dissected and explained—is in the human rightness of his impulse. He saw the workers ground down by forces which elevated the few to despotic power, and he protested.

In this light, though Marx would have been the last to seek to escape censure on grounds of strict theory, to find fault here and there with his doctrinal presentation is to calculate without the host. We may verify this judgment by appeal to the results of his work. Does anyone suppose that more than a few leaders of the millions of people who have followed his advice are moved by the correctness in all respects of Marx's theory? The masses of communists, to the extent that they know more than Marx's name, have been inspired by his indictment of exploitation and his promise of liberation of the common people. They take him surely not as a professor, but as a prophet, not as a master of economic analysis, but as a messiah. Marx himself said, in impatience with doctrinaires, "Whatever else I am, I am not a Marxist."

A commodity, an article of capitalist commerce, possesses use-value, but that is subordinate, in the capitalist economy, to its value in exchange, or market value. The basis of value is labor—the concept taken by Marx from Smith and Ricardo. The peculiar merit of a commodity, from the capitalist point of view, is that it contains more labor than the worker was compensated for. It contains unpaid labor, or surplus labor. Say the wage worker in six hours produces the equivalent of the food, clothing, and houseroom which he receives for his labor. But he is not permitted by the capitalist employer to stop after six hours. By changes in the modes and institutions of production, the worker has been divested of ownership of raw materials, tools, and access to the market. He has nothing but his labor to sell. Therefore in order to live he must accept the dictates of the capitalist employer who now owns materials and tools and can enter the market. The employer, in his position of power, compels the worker to remain at his task additional hours. In this extra time the worker contributes, without benefit to himself, surplus-labor. This extracted surplus-labor is the source of income to the owner of the means of production, whether he be the profit-taking industrialist or financier or the landlord claiming rent.

Only a part of these shares is consumed by the expropriators in their own living. What remains is added to the capital accumulation, extends capitalist operation, and amplifies production and trade. Competition between capitalists favors the more fortunate and the more competent. These introduce the most efficient means of production, increasingly concentrate ownership and control in their own hands, and drive their disadvantaged fellows into the ranks of the proletariat.

Capital is of two sorts, fixed (buildings and machinery) and variable (mainly what is paid out in wages). Constant or fixed capital reproduces itself, but does not alter in value. It is variable or circulating capital which is used to extract surplus labor and is the instrument for producing and accumulating surplus value. If the proportions of fixed and circulating capital did not change, increased production, employment, and wages would enable the workers to improve their standard of living. Their status would not alter, they would still be dependent on employers, just as a slave who is better fed remains a slave. But what Marx calls the organic composition of capital changes. In the process of capital accumulation, fixed capital increases at the expense of circulating capital. With greater efficiency of plant and of workers, and relatively less circulating capital available, the demand for workers shrinks. Not only is this happening, but concentration of equipment in fewer hands has the same effect.

The result is creation of an industrial reserve army of the unemployed. Part of this reserve of workers will be summoned back to production in brisk times, but the existence of surplus workers forms a constant threat to those who are employed, dragging down their wages, admonishing them to be amenable to employers' demands. Many in the reserve army, especially in hard times, are chronically unemployed and are degraded into pauperism, dependent on charity or public maintenance.

This general tendency toward enrichment of the few and impoverishment of the many is broken or punctuated by capitalist crises, recurrent periods of stimulated production followed by contraction. The slump is caused by too much production compared to the capacity for consumption. Call it overproduction or underconsumption, the result is the same. The workers, the mass of consumers, systematically paid for only a part of their output, are unable to buy what they have produced. The commercial crisis is the endemic disease of capitalism, now quiescent, now active, but always lurking and threatening.

Three treatments for the disease, when it breaks out, are familiar. One, which is the prescription of classical political economy, is to do nothing, allow production to fall off while raw materials are wasted, machinery remains idle, obsolescence takes its toll, skills grow rusty, and swelling numbers of the unemployed become destitute. In this process of retrenchment or liquidation, fictitious values are reduced or canceled, and the capitalist practice of appropriating surplus-labor may be resumed, at first on a lower plane.

Another expedient is to open new markets, either by invading what rivals have enjoyed or by imperialist adventure, finding cheaper raw materials and cheaper labor in less developed parts of the globe.

The third method, swiftest and most ruthless, is that of war, which destroys machinery, materials, and population at a reckless rate. This resort to war perpetuates, even accelerates profits to capitalists, transfers immediate costs to the organized community as a whole, and buries its greatest loss in graveyards.

But all of these exits from capitalist depression are temporary, for they minister to symptoms, not causes. The capitalist appetite for exploitation revives only to become more voracious than before. Finally the unrelenting expropriation of labor will build to a dreadful climax, when the capitalist mode of production is no longer possible for the capitalists themselves, not to speak of the workers who have been starved and driven to desperation. In this catastrophe the workers, ironically helped by discipline instilled in them by capitalist masters, will revolt. They will seize the reins of government, take over the means of production (which are functionally social, only legally private in ownership) and conduct the economy for the benefit of producers. Whereas the few formerly expropriated the many, now the many expropriate the few. Government, which before existed as the executive committee of the owning class, will become merely the means of economic administration in a classless society.

We must stress again the earlier reminder that a secret of success of the book is its prevailing scientific detachment. In spite of its origin and Marx's fierce commitment to the cause of the workers, evidence of this fact is often poignantly present. Many literate persons are surprised at the answer to the question, Where does one look for the most lyrical appreciation of the accomplishments of capitalism? It is in this first volume of Marx's *Das Kapital*. Marx does not descend to scolding, much less to vituperation. The work is a description, not a diatribe; its conclusion is a forecast, not a forensic.

Such was Marx's historical review, theoretical analysis, and sociological forecast in Volume I of *Das Kapital*. We do not attempt to summarize volumes II and III. They remained a mass of disjointed manuscript during Marx's lifetime, and were carpentered, so far as possible salvaged, by Engels, to be published, respectively, in 1885 and 1894. Volume II concerns the circulation of capital, or the processes by which the capitalist, having availed himself of surplus-labor, realizes his profit in the market. Volume III explores the distribution of capitalist gains between the various groups of capitalist claimants. These volumes are necessarily inferior in construction and less dynamic as compared with the first. They contain nuggets of insight rather than a continuous vein of precious metal and are relatively little known.

In its later years the International had troubles external and internal. Governments, exaggerating the power of the organization, persecuted its national branches after the fall of the Paris Commune in 1871. The General Council, combating this hostility, was blamed by sections of the membership for being dictatorial. Anarchist and conspiratorial factions gathered about Mikhail Bakunin, whose expulsion from the International did not close the rift. At the insistence of Marx and Engels, headquarters of the General Council were moved to New York in 1872. Here, divorced from the active European scene, the International soon expired—but not before it had set an example of world labor cooperation to be followed later in multiplying ways.

Marx's last decade was cheered by the presence of Engels, who moved to London; by translation of the first volume of

Capital into numerous languages, and its increasing influence, especially in Russia; and by some easing of the family finances. On the other hand his health suffered from continuing over-work. The death of his wife from cancer in 1881 left him broken in body and spirit. Visits to warmer climates to relieve him of attacks of bronchitis and pleurisy were unavailing. He died in his sleep March 14, 1883. Engels spoke briefly and simply at his private burial in Highgate Cemetery: "Marx was above all a revolutionary, and his great aim in life was to co-operate . . . in the overthrow of capitalist society and the State institutions which it has created, to co-operate in the emancipation of the modern proletariat, to whom he was the first to give a consciousness of its class position and its class needs. . . ." Engels survived Marx by a dozen years during which he succeeded to his friend's place as center of the workers' militant movement.

For Further Reading

Marx, Karl, *Capital, A Critique of Political Economy,* Vol. I, Capitalist Production, 1867 (Chicago: Charles H. Kerr & Co., 1919).

————, and Friedrich Engels, *Basic Writings on Politics and Philosophy.* Edited by Lewis S. Feuer (Garden City, N.Y.: Doubleday & Co., Inc., 1959).

Aveling, Edward B., *The Student's Marx* (New York: Charles Scrib-ner's Sons, 1902).

Cole, G. D. H., *What Marx Really Meant* (New York: Alfred A. Knopf, Inc., 1937).

Spargo, John, *Karl Marx, his Life and Work* (New York: Huebsch, 1910).

Mehring, Franz, *Karl Marx, the Story of his Life* (New York: Covici, Friede, 1935).

Reminiscences of Marx and Engels (Moscow: Foreign Languages Pub-lishing House, n.d.).

9

PROGRESS AND POVERTY

Henry George

Henry George, like other economists whose careers we are reviewing, reflected in his writings his environment and experiences. He had read next to nothing in the literature of the subject when his central economic idea popped into his head. It was born of physical observation. The title of his most famous book, *Progress and Poverty,* is an exact description of what he saw. This was poverty in the populous cities of New York and Philadelphia contrasting with the progress he witnessed on the rapidly settling Pacific coast. Once the answer to the riddle—why progress entails poverty—seized on him, he turned to the books to test his explanation, though no contrary doctrine could have dislodged his intense conviction, confirmed by what he viewed around him. He discovered to his satisfaction that learned, zealous writers a century earlier had entertained the same thought. Self-taught, he now read the standard authors to buttress and elaborate his contention until he became familiar with main works that supported or dissented from his belief.

Lack of formal education, given the facts of Henry George's life, left him with limitations, but these were minor as compared with the positive benefits of a mind uncluttered by previous reasoning of others. This sounds disrespectful of the body of economic philosophy, as though it could be an encumbrance. But do not forget that the truly original economists were inspired by events more than by what they heard in classrooms or found in libraries. Their first task was to refute received opinion, though study enriched their understanding and gave solidity to their own exposition.

Henry George was born September 2, 1839 in the heart of

Philadelphia, the eldest son in a large family. His father's people were English, his mother's Scotch. His father had a small publishing and bookselling business in Episcopal church literature and was later a custom house clerk. His mother had kept a school. The household contrived to make ends meet in modest comfort. Henry's deeply religious home, not only church-going but devoted to family prayers, influenced his otherwise boisterous boyhood. The King James Bible, its language as well as its precepts, became his possession and gave beauty of form as well as moral tone to what he was later to write. Numerous economists, by no means all, stated their principles with clarity (Adam Smith, Malthus, List, for example), but few had Henry George's native artistry with words. His long newspaper practice, as we shall see, taught him to be simple and direct, and his feeling lent an eloquence which won hosts of apostles.

Vigorous, self-willed, and restless, young Henry was a trial to a succession of schoolmasters, but he battened on books from the Apprentices Library (Emerson, history, the romantic *Scottish Chiefs*), liked popular science lectures at the Franklin Institute, and rejoined in a "debating society." This last was as much given to black cigars and fisticuffs as to the discussion of public issues. His parents could not object when at less than fourteen he quit school for good to wrap parcels and run errands in a crockery shop at $2 a week. But not for long, for before he was fifteen he embarked with a friendly captain as ship's boy on a sailing vessel, the *Hindoo,* bound with lumber for Australia.

He took to novel duties with zest and found time to record the ship's doings in a spirited diary now preserved, with his old sea chest, in the New York Public Library. A high point of the long voyage, for young Henry, was a month at anchor in Hobson's Bay, Melbourne, where the crew rebelled to join the rush to Australia's gold fields. The boy, who was to know better another treasure frontier (California) set down his impressions of the frantic port and town, with its outfitters' auctions and booted hopefuls destined for riches or disappointment. A different scene greeted him when the ship breasted onward to Calcutta, where ancient destitution spoke in the corpses floating in the long reach of the Hooghly River, with no attention except from devouring crows. He never forgot this sight of human misery.

After fourteen months the *Hindoo* returned, and the captain advised his ship's boy to seek a job ashore. Henry's father wisely apprenticed him in a print shop. Here, long before his time was out, he could set type with the speed and accuracy of a journeyman. Irked by his trifling learner's wage, he quarreled with his foreman and was dismissed. This was 1857, in the midst of depression, when thousands of more experienced workers in Philadelphia were unemployed. Henry went on a coal barge to Boston, and, home again, was reduced to scabbing in a struck printery while the chance lasted. Out of pocket and out of humor, he disputed his parents' support of slavery, which they defended as legal and Biblical. It was time for him to try his luck at a distance.

Philadelphia friends had settled in Oregon Territory, and beckoned him thither with the prospect of journeyman's wages on a newspaper. But penniless, how was he to get there? Then loomed, in the Philadelphia Navy Yard, the steamer *Shubrick,* fitting out for lighthouse service on the Pacific coast. Earnest pleas with his congressman and a little overstating of his credentials finally rewarded Henry George with a berth as steward. A damaging storm off Hatteras, yellow fever among the crew at Montevideo, a dispiriting passage through the Straits of Magellan were surmounted, but on reaching the Golden Gate the catch was that Henry George had engaged to remain with the *Shubrick* for a full year, seven months more. James George, a cousin and bookkeeper in a San Francisco store, took Henry home for shore leave. What with Henry's feigning illness, and the captain's failure to retrieve him, the lighthouse tender sailed off, recording the steward as "Run away."

Henry George ran farther. San Francisco's gold rush prosperity had succumbed to depression, but new strikes along the Frazer River in British Columbia promised better. Henry and his Cousin James worked their way up the coast to tend a miners' store at Victoria. But soon the diggings gave out, customers too, and Henry borrowed money to get back to San Francisco. When things looked worse, winter coming on, an old printer friend got him a job and Henry lived at the What Cheer House, a temperance hotel where the best cheer for him was in the proprietor's library. Much that Henry George later showed he had read must have been in this pleasant interval. It did not last long for, again unemployed, he struck out for

Placerville gold. He never got there, but hoboed around, catching work on farms, sleeping in barns.

Drifting back to San Francisco, fortune smiled on him. The *California Home Journal,* a literary weekly, West Coast style, took him on and soon he was foreman printer at $5 a day. He came to believe the glowing tales he set in type, fell in love with the new country, and postponed any plan to return to his old home in Philadelphia. Better so, thought his family, for in California he would escape the Civil War. He could not escape unemployment. But when the *Home Journal* let him go, he with a few friends published the *Daily Evening Journal* on a shoestring. While this prospect faded another venture became imminent. This was marriage to Annie Fox, an orphan to whom he had been engaged for a year. Her guardian prudently forbade the match, since Henry George had only ardor to substitute for means of support. The young couple had shared *The Household Book of Verse,* and resolved to start their lilting household on fifty cents, all the bridegroom had. A borrowed suit and a few borrowed dollars pieced out for the runaway marriage. Love had found a way—a poor way but abundant love as the years were to prove.

For a couple of years the reward of rashness was success. The Georges moved to Sacramento, where Henry set type on the *Union.* His pay of $40 a week, a pleasant little house, and soon a son, Henry George, Jr., crowned their happiness. There was money left over for a trifling speculation in mining stocks. But the dramatic purpose of good fortune was to usher in bad. Henry, as earlier, quarreled with his boss and the family returned to bitter years in San Francisco. Stopgap jobs at the printer's font, peddling clothes wringers, home sewing taken in by Annie, trips to the pawnshop that could not pay the rent. Finally income was reduced to 25 cents a day from a pitiable printshop enterprise. The birth of a second son made misery complete. The doctor ordered, "Don't stop to wash the child; he is starving. Feed him."

The father rushed into the rainy streets. "I . . . made up my mind," he told afterward, "to get money from the first man whose appearance might indicate that he had it to give. I stopped . . . a stranger—and told him I wanted $5. . . . I told him that my wife was confined and that I had nothing to give her to eat. He gave me the money. If he had not, I think that I was desperate enough to have killed him."

When later Henry George wrote a book about poverty he knew whereof he spoke.

If art is born in anguish, Stephen Foster writing melodies in Bowery flophouses or Poe making verses in that Fordham cottage gave no better examples than Henry George composing essays with hunger for inspiration. Most men would have thought of surrender instead of syntax. But he practiced his craftsmanship and ere long the *Californian* magazine numbered our hero, along with a couple more unknowns, Mark Twain and Bret Harte, among its contributors. In the shock of Lincoln's assassination George offered a "stirring article" (the editor's words) to the newspaper where he was substitute printer. His enraged rhetoric brought him an assignment by the *Alta California* to report San Francisco's mourning.

Not without too-familiar dark intervals, our story brightens. George was asked to join the staff of a new paper, the San Francisco *Daily Times,* where he was alternately printer, reporter, and editorial writer until, on the resignation of Noah Brooks, Henry George was made managing editor. This was June 1867, George was twenty-eight. He espoused Radical Republican correction of lingering recalcitrance in the states lately in rebellion, but he also upheld reduction of protective tariffs, which was no part of the Radicals' program. Free trade, as Professor Barker points out, was a basic tenet of Henry George before he arrived at land reform. This is significant, for, as we shall see, his whole philosophy as it developed was one of economic liberty.

At his editorial desk, in the thick of controversy over California's present and future, George assailed private monopolies. He attacked the transcontinental railroad and telegraph monopolies. But especially he blasted monopoly of land. California had been founded in speculation, but that was by little people, typically the Gold Rush miners. Now landgrabbers on a huge scale would make sure that all development, by labor, industry, and agriculture, must pay them tribute. George demanded that land owned by the City of San Francisco remain public. Another forecast of his later advocacy was for a shorter work day and higher wages for labor. He warned that the new railroad link might import to the West Coast the social pressures of the older settled portions of the country.

He came to personal grips with the telegraph monopoly of the Western Union. Leaving his post with the *Times,* he was sent to Philadelphia and New York by a new paper, the *Herald,* which required the national and world news dispatches enjoyed exclusively by San Francisco papers belonging to the Associated Press. Without this coverage the *Herald* could not compete. George met with blank refusal from the AP dispatchers and exorbitant rates for telegraphing news that he gathered himself. His vigorous protests in influential quarters fetched him exactly nothing. Contemptuous treatment of his exertions for a free press hardened his resolve against economic privilege.

In this mood he was oppressed, in New York City, by "the shocking contrast between monstrous wealth and debasing want," and he vowed to himself to seek out the remedy. Back in California, editing a little paper in Oakland, the answer to the riddle, why wealth had want for a twin, sprang into his mind. Riding into the foothills one day, he paused to admire the view of San Francisco Bay and asked a passing teamster "what land was worth there." The teamster "pointed to some cows grazing off so far that they looked like mice and said: 'I don't know exactly, but there is a man over there who will sell land for a thousand dollars an acre.' Like a flash it came upon me that there was the reason of advancing poverty with advancing wealth. With the growth of population, land grows in value, and the men who work it must pay for the privilege. I turned back amidst quiet thought, to the perception that then came to me and has been with me ever since."

Was this for Henry George "the moment of truth?" Recently he had dipped into John Stuart Mill's *Principles of Political Economy* and had exchanged letters with Mill. The Englishman's book explained the doctrine of land rent, but whether the Californian read this part or drew his own conclusion from it is uncertain. Current land policy controversy on the Pacific Coast may have prepared George's thought. A man may forget much that influenced him in reaching his deepest conviction. On the other hand, Henry George, not bookish at this stage (in economics anyhow), but sensitive to social wrongs and a keen observer, may well have experienced his apocalyptic vision. In any event that was his story and we may credit his honesty.

George shifted to management and part ownership of another paper, a Democratic party organ in Sacramento under sponsorship of his friend Governor Haight. This sheet flourished because George had finally won his fight against the news monopoly; he was West Coast agent for a rival news service made possible by a telegraph company competing with the Western Union. In editorials he smote the giant corporations, railroad and other, and the land engrossers that were draining the earnings of independent enterprisers, farmers, and workers. When the Central Pacific stopped George's clamor by clandestinely buying the paper, George put his ejectment to brilliant use.

He published a substantial pamphlet, *Our Land and Land Policy* (1871) which was a close approach to the central idea elaborately pressed eight years later in *Progress and Poverty*. Aside from other merits, the little work showed industrious assemblage of data and drew upon wider reading than George had done before. The frontispiece was a map of California exhibiting, in color, the land grants to railroads following, in wide bands, the lines that had been constructed. The picture, he said accurately, "is absolutely startling—a commentary on the railroad land-grant policy of Congress to the force of which no words can add. Observe the proportion which these reservations bear to the total area of the State [more than half], and observe at the same time . . . how the railroad reservations cover nearly all the great central valleys, and leave but the mountains, and you may get an idea of how these reservations are cursing the State."

The better parts of California, eligible for agriculture and settlement, had been preempted by these and other prodigious land monopolies which he enumerated. Already, even in a sparse population, men who needed to apply their labor to natural resources were depressed and exploited by artificially high rents and selling prices of land. "The value of land is the power which its ownership gives to appropriate the product of labour, and, as a sequence, where rents (the share of the land-owner) are high, wages (the share of the labourer) are low. . . . In a new country the value of labour is at first at its maximum, the value of land at its minimum. As population grows and land becomes monopolised and increases in value, the value of labour steadily decreases." And further, "The prices of land . . . to-day are not warranted by our present population, but are sustained by speculation founded upon the certainty of the greater population which is coming."

The only just title to land, growing out of a man's right to his own effort, is limited to the amount of land he works. The mere owner of land, by exacting a part of the product of the worker, to that degree owns, enslaves, the worker, and will eventually reduce him to a subsistence return for his labor. Capital and enterprise—the other active elements in production—will similarly be obliged to render tribute to possessors of land.

Henry George's proposal was that further land grants be stopped forthwith, and that government be supported by taxes on land values, since these values were created by the community.

Followed then more journalism, as editor and part owner of two San Francisco newspapers. George was vigorous in reform, too sanguine of continued success, and when the postwar depression hit California in 1875 he lost valuable properties. Fortunately a new Democratic governor, whom he had helped to elect, out of admiration for George gave him a political plum. The office of state inspector of gas meters hardly seemed in a writing man's line, but actually the sinecure (as it soon proved to be) was intended to free him for preparation of a book that commanded all of his energies. Not quite all, for in a few lectures, at the University of California and elsewhere, he repeated opinions from his manuscript and formulated ideas which were then incorporated in his book. Discussions in the Land Reform League of California, the first to promote the ideas of Henry George, must have helped him to anticipate and answer objections to his argument.

His full statement, when completed, was the product of his California environment, in contrast to eastern large cities. Other influences were his own upbringing and vicissitudes of fortune, and naturally in *Progress and Poverty* reappeared, usually in improved form, propositions which he had advanced in editorials over the years. Diligent reading of English economists and historical works made notable contribution, as did the advice of sympathetic friends. We are readily able to discern the natural history, as it were, of the volume. Yet it was not a thesis issuing from a particular geographical or sociological quarter. It was anything but a parochial study. He gave it a general application, a universality of reasoning without which it could never have won its wide acceptance, not to say devoted support. His moral emphasis, reformist zeal, and his crusading spirit worked in this behalf. Moving passages—which might occur anywhere in the text—appealed not simply to intellectual agreement, but to heart and conscience. Later on, in the hands of too many, political economy was to become overly technical, narrow, almost irrelevant to social welfare. George made economic forces crisscross with others to accomplish the good life.

For this reason some would call him reformer before he was economist. This betrays a demerit in the critic, not in the author. The habits and policies of the community, in the philosophical view, are not to be compartmented or understood as divided. In discussing most of the economists included in the present volume we see that, in addition to acute analysis, they wrote with fervor, melted the particular into the whole, and believed they were serving the public advantage. A mason is a necessary and worthy workman, but he is not an architect.

It is pertinent to remember George's method of composition during three years of unremitting work, 1876–1879, on *Progress and Poverty*. During this period the family lived in comfortable houses near San Francisco Bay, where the author, in walks along the shore, smoothed kinks out of his mind. In a dressing gown he did his reading early in the day, prone on his sofa, often beginning with a book of poetry. This relaxed start helped the easy unfolding of his ideas on paper. He wrote with a gold penpoint in more senses than one. While his rhetorical paragraphs have been especially admired, the simplicity of his language, page after page of pointed reasoning, is more remarkable. This was the art that conceals art.

The book was written during a period of deep economic depression. Though George's primary object was "to seek the law which associates poverty and progress, and increases want with advancing wealth," he believed that "in the explanation of this paradox we shall find the explanation of . . . recurring seasons of industrial and commercial paralysis. . . ." He began by discrediting principal accepted doctrines which, if valid, would have militated against his solution. He reviewed the most influential texts, chiefly of the classical school. He first attacked the wage fund theory which held that workers are paid from capital. More specifically, in the words of McCulloch, "That portion of the capital . . . of a country which the employers of labor . . . are willing to pay out in the purchase of labor . . . forms the only source from which . . . the wages of labor can be derived." Hence the average wage at any time was the result of dividing the wage fund by the number of workers. This dogma, developed in primitive forms from Smith and Malthus, became explicit in Ricardo and was categorically repeated by Ricardo's disciples, notably John Stuart Mill.

In rigid expression this pronouncement dominated economic thought for fifty years, subjecting the present and future to the past, confining the most creative element in production (labor) to the inclinations of capitalists. Wages could not rise unless the wage fund was increased or the number of workers was reduced. The first condition (more wage capital through savings) was beyond the power of workers. The second condition (restraints on population) was cruel if dependent on disease, poverty, and premature deaths, and was unlikely if dependent on workers' prudence through late marriages and continence in wedlock. This fatalistic prospect ruled out improvement in the lot of the masses of workers through labor unions and factory legislation. The capitalistic structure, presumed to be limited by its own inevitable laws, allowed no room for institutional changes.

However, shortly before George wrote, the authority of the wage fund had been undermined by English writers—by Longe, taught by his practical observations as a factory inspector, and by Thornton, on grounds of theory. And John Stuart Mill, the classical advocate, had partially recanted. In America, Francis A. Walker had put the mechanistic doctrine further on its way to complete abandonment. But Henry George developed his own demonstration that "wages, instead of being drawn from capital, are in reality drawn from the product of the labor for which they are paid." Wages are furnished from continuous production; workers in effect, by means of exchanges of their goods and services, employ each other. Profits and wages are not antithetical, like buckets in a well where if one goes up the other must go down. Instead, they are sympathetic, rising and falling together. The controlling fund, if there be one, is the magnitude of production. "The payment of wages . . . always implies the previous rendering of labor. . . . As the laborer who works for an employer does not get his wages until he has performed the work, his case is similar to that of the depositor in a bank who cannot draw money out until he has put money in."

In preparatory stages of production, as in plowing for a crop, labor is adding value to the stock of wealth which supplies consumption. He went on to explore roundabout production with its complicated intermediate exchanges, and concluded: "where labor is rendered before wages are paid, the advance of capital is really made by labor, and is from the employed to the employer, not from the employer to the employed." And finally, "The series of exchanges which unite production and consumption may be likened to a curved pipe filled with water. If a quantity of water is poured in at one end, a like quantity is released at the other. It is not identically the same water, but is its equivalent. And so they who do the work of production put in as they take out—they receive in subsistence and wages [only] the produce of their labor."

George then probed deeper to invalidate the Malthusian theory of population which, as he said, lay back of the wage fund doctrine. He examined conditions in the most crowded countries—India, China, and Ireland—and declared that not niggardliness of nature but unjust, stupid human institutions caused the numbers of people to press on the means of subsistence. Wherever "vice and misery check increase by limiting marriages or shortening the term of human life, there is not a single case in which the vice and misery can be traced to an actual increase in the number of mouths over the power of the accompanying hands to feed them; but in every case the vice and misery are shown to spring either from unsocial ignorance and rapacity, unjust laws or destructive warfare." He found that in fact the reproductive force in the vegetable and animal kingdoms rather than in man proves the power of subsistence to increase faster than population.

He drew on the demonstrations of Henry C. Carey to show the power of men in association to multiply production. "I assert that in any given state of civilization a greater number of people can collectively be better provided for than a smaller." "Of all living things, man is the only one who can give play to the reproductive forces, more powerful than his own, which supply him with food. Beast, insect, bird, and fish take only what they find. Their increase is at the expense of their food, and when they have reached the existing limits of food, their food must increase before they can increase. . . . Both the jay-hawk and the man eat chickens, but the more jay-hawks the fewer chickens, while the more men the more chickens." The law of diminishing returns in agriculture—that Nemesis of chastisement and vengeance which haunted all the classical economists—did not oppress him. Science, technology, "the numberless economies resulting from a larger population" enable "the power of the human factor" to compensate, more than compensate, "for the decline in the power of the natural factor."

In social and natural forces all is relative. We must not, in our surmises, be led into extremes. Though there be a *tendency* for population to outrun the food supply, this does not raise the specter of starvation. Water will freeze at 32 degrees, but this does not mean that, at lower temperature, a lake will solidify to the bottom.

Actually, it is in sparse and primitive populations that men go hungry. It is not because of "the pressure of population that the Digger Indians live on grasshoppers, or the aboriginal inhabitants of Australia eat the worms found in rotten wood." "Whence is it," he reminded, "that capital overflows for remunerative investment? Is it not from densely populated countries to sparsely populated countries?"

Disease, vice, destitution, ignorance are the fruits of maldistribution of wealth. In the most poverty-stricken countries a "merciless banditti . . . of landlords, among whom the soil has been divided as their absolute possession" stripped the laborer of all but rags on his back and roots to munch. If predatory arrangements did not raise some to surplus and depress more to misery, the energies of society would provide sufficiency for all. It was exploitation that destroyed Ireland. "Even during the [potato] famine, grain and meat and butter and cheese were carted for exportation along roads lined with the starving and past trenches into which the dead were piled."

We may leave George's refutation of Malthus with one of the passages of opinion, interspersed in the text, which reads like blank verse: "the Malthusian doctrine parries the demand for reform, and shelters selfishness from question and from conscience by the interposition of an inevitable necessity. It furnishes a philosophy by which Dives as he feasts can shut out the image of Lazarus who faints with hunger at his door; by which wealth may complacently button up its pocket when poverty asks an arms, and the rich Christian bend on Sundays in a nicely upholstered pew to implore the good gifts of the All Father without any feeling of responsibility for the squalid misery that is festering but a square away. For poverty, want, and starvation are by this theory not chargeable either to individual greed or to social maladjustments; they are the inevitable results of universal laws, with which, if it were not impious, it were as hopeless to quarrel as with the law of gravitation."

We have taken a long running start for our leap. What did Henry George assign as the cause of poverty going step by step with progress?

It was the private ownership of land and other natural resources. Since land is limited in amount, private owners exact rent from the users of it. Rent is measured by the difference in productiveness (of agricultural land) or the advantage of location (of urban land) as compared with marginal land, or land which is barely worth the expenditure of labor and capital. This, of course, is Ricardo's explanation of rent, which George took over completely. With growth of population the demand for land increases. As resort must be had to poorer land or land less well situated—as the margin of use is driven lower—rents rise. This means that the same force which benefits one claimant in the distribution of wealth—the landlord—deprives other claimants—capitalists and workers. The effect of the private ownership of land (and the exaction of rent) is like the driving of a wedge into the end of a log. One part is elevated while the other is depressed. Poverty is the counterpart of progress. Said Henry George: "If one man can command the land upon which others must labor, he can appropriate the produce of their labor as the price of his permission to labor. . . . The one receives without producing; the others produce without receiving."

Why does the landlord receive without producing? Because nature furnishes or made the land, and society made it valuable. The landlord, the owner of bare land, as contrasted with the capitalist and worker, is merely passive. He cashes in on his legal title to a resource to which capital and labor are obliged to apply their efforts. His title, though legal, is not morally or economically justified. Private ownership must rest upon a man's right to his own body, his own powers. What he exerts himself to bring into existence is his, to do with as he chooses.

It was often put to Henry George that landowners have given their wealth for the land they hold, or have inherited land from another who purchased it. His answer was that the present owner's title is as good and no better than that of the owner before him, and that if land titles are traced back far enough they are found to rest upon force or fraud, or in many cases monopolization of more land than the first claimant could work. If it be said that present owners should not be dispossessed because society has for ages acquiesced in their rights, it may be reminded that society has expropriated owners in other instances where the form of private property was disapproved. Piracy used to be common and was tolerated. Queen Elizabeth maintained royal pirates, whom she knighted, such as Drake and Hawkins. But later pirate ships were confiscated and the pirates were hanged. Slave-holding was long legal and even honorific, but was abolished in one country after another, sometimes with compensation, in the United States without compensation.

We must distinguish sharply between capital and land. Capital is brought into existence by human effort, and may be multiplied in amount. Land is the free gift of nature, and may not be increased. We speak familiarly of "real estate," often meaning land and improvements. The two are in different economic categories. Land, mere extent of the earth's surface, or mineral deposits unworked, have cost no man's labor. Land yields a return, not because of anything the owner has done, but because others must apply their labor and capital to it. This return, rent, with the development of society will generally rise. Capital, on the other hand—buildings, railroads, subways, etc.—are the products of human exertion. If demand for capital goods expands, more capital will be offered, and hence the yield of capital does not automatically go up. Whatever the owner of land has put on the land or into it—home, barn, factory, or fertilizer, drainage tile, or terracing—is properly his, for without his effort or the effort of the person from whom he acquired it, the improvements would not exist. But a landlord, considered simply as the claimant to a gift of nature, has no such legitimate title.

What we call "land value" is really the value of society, the facilities furnished by roads, streets, wharves, business establishments, schools, and the protections supplied by police, firemen, sewers, water systems, and courts. It is true that the individual landowner, if he has built a home or factory on the land, has by so much contributed to the value of the land, or he has added something to its desirability because he is a member of the community. But his individual addition, as capitalist, to the value of his land is so small, as compared with the contribution of the community as a whole, that, practically, society is justified in ignoring it.

The social origin of land values will be clearer if we take an actual locality as an illustration. The New York City subway system extends in a northeasterly direction some fifteen miles to 179th Street and Hillside Avenue in a section on Long Island called Jamaica. Thousands of commuters from the outlying counties want to park their cars and take the subway into the city. The first parking lots are some seven or eight blocks from the subway entrance. The lots are perfect examples of bare ground—no improvements except maybe a topping of cinders and a shanty for the attendant. The lots farthest from the subway charge 35 cents a day for parking, those a little nearer 45 cents, and so the charge increases to 65 and 75 cents and, next to the subway entrance, $1.00. What the parking lot owners are selling is manifestly the subway. The subway was constructed by the city, the public; the private owners of land near it receive what Henry George called an "unearned increment."

His proposal was to tax away economic rents, since these are the product of the community. It would not be necessary to nationalize land. Take the rent, the yield of land, in tax, and the land would have no selling value in the hands of private owners. It could not be sold, since nobody will give a price for the right to pay taxes. Then other taxes—income taxes, excise taxes, import duties, general property taxes—could be dispensed with. That is, public revenue would be collected from land value created by the public, and taxes which penalize active producers of wealth would be lifted.

If the rent of the landowner is taxed, will he simply shift the burden to his tenant by raising the rent? No, a tax on land rests upon the owner. Why? Because the rent is the difference of advantage between the land in question and marginal land that pays no rent. Rent cannot be attributed to any other cause. If the landlord could raise the rent to compensate him for an increase in tax, he would have raised the rent long ago without that excuse. The landlord is receiving all the rent his land will bring. If his tax is increased, the increase falls on him. This is a merit in a land tax. We know who pays it, as contrasted with many taxes the incidence, or final resting place of which, is uncertain.

As the landowner makes no contribution to production, taxing away his income will not discourage effort. Nor will a tax equal to rent make the land less useful. The occupier will now pay his rent to the public treasury instead of to the landlord, and in doing so will be relieved of the taxes he is at present paying on his labor, capital, and enterprise. Under the prevailing system, workers, capitalists, and enterprisers are supporting the public services—schools, defense and the rest— and are supporting an army of landlords besides.

A particular gain from the land tax, stressed by Henry George, is that it will raise the margin of production. This is because much land is now withheld from use while the owner waits for further increase in its value. This applies especially to cities. Often land is underused, holding obsolete or small buildings which yield just enough in revenue to the owner to permit him to pay present land taxes. If such land—vacant or devoted to trifling, temporizing purposes—be taxed for its full economic rent, the owner would at once improve it so he could meet the tax. The margin of use, in most cities, is now far more distant than it need be if intervening sites were put to appropriate use. The artificially low margin has the effect, of course, of raising land rents all along the line.

What of farmers? Could they afford to operate under a tax falling solely on land? George believed that they would not be at a disadvantage; their land, apart from improvements and equipment—barns, fences, stock, and implements—has comparatively little value, since society furnishes them relatively few services. Under the system proposed, farmers would not pay on their capital, or bear the burden of the miscellaneous taxes now levied.

Shortly after publication (1880 in the regular printing), *Progress and Poverty* reached a huge circulation, entered a rapid succession of editions, and was translated into other languages. From obscurity the author soon became a national and world figure. In a period prolific in proposals for reform in economic and social life, his book was among the most conspicuous. He wrote other works—notably *Social Problems* and *Protection or*

Free Trade—but after his panacea became the subject of widespread controversy he was primarily propagandist and leader of an organized movement. He lectured throughout the United States and repeatedly crusaded in England, Scotland, Ireland, and Australia. Having moved his home to New York City, he was twice the candidate of tax reform and labor groups for the mayoralty (in 1886 when he was second in a close election, and again in 1897). He died suddenly of apoplexy in the last campaign.

What was Henry George's relation to the other chief, and more enduring, reform movement of his time—socialism? Though his idealism and talents as a champion of human betterment added impetus to the socialism of the Fabians in Britain, he was the foe of Marxism. George was an individualist, not a collectivist. He was a defender of private capitalism as of the rights of workers, a believer in *laissez faire* and the beneficence of "natural" economic laws. If the one crying injustice of private receipt of land rent was removed, he was sure of harmonious progress without poverty. While he was less dogmatic than some have supposed, he did not admit, what socialists proclaimed, that there are unearned increments from capital investment as well as from land ownership. Industrialists, who as a class have been mortal enemies of socialism, were among George's chief supporters. Workers, to whom George appealed also, have found socialism a superior hope.

For Further Reading

George, Henry, *Progress and Poverty,* 1879. (Fiftieth Anniversary Edition (New York: Schalkenbach Foundation, 1929).

———, *Protection or Free Trade,* vol. 4 in *The Complete Works of Henry George* (Garden City, N.Y.: Doubleday, Page & Co., 1911).

———, *Significant Paragraphs from . . . Progress and Poverty,* Introduction by John Dewey (New York: Doubleday & Co., Inc., 1929).

Barker, Charles A., *Henry George* (New York: Oxford University Press, Inc., 1955). Most recent, fullest, scholarly life.

Post, Louis F., *The Prophet of San Francisco* (New York: Vanguard Press, Inc., 1930). Reminiscences of a close associate.

Geiger, George R., *The Philosophy of Henry George.* Introduction by John Dewey (New York: The Macmillan Co., 1933). Thoroughly informed discussion.

10

TIGHTROPE

Alfred Marshall

Most of the economists discussed in this book had a novel point of view, squinted at man's bread and butter relationships from a special angle. Colbert, rejecting feudal and town-guild stagnation, made the central government the engine of economic progress. Adam Smith protested against this mercantilism in favor of individual freedom. Malthus got hold of the particular problem of population growth and what it portended for social improvement. Ricardo, besides graving deeper and correcting lines that Smith had drawn, developed the principles on which the economic product is shared between land, capital, and labor. Robert Owen was a reforming utopian socialist. He sought by conscious effort to better the economic environment which was degrading humankind. Friedrich List, owing to the situation in his native Germany and in America where he lived for a time, was a throw-back to the mercantilists. He insisted on the nation as an economic entity rather than trusting to the individual. Henry C. Carey, much like List, moved by the buoyancy of young America, celebrated increasing returns, not the pessimism of the European classicists.

Karl Marx gave wider sweep to the historical method used by List and Carey. His was a philosophy of history, with the masses of workers claiming his burning solicitude. He decried the mechanics of Smith and Ricardo and substituted the creative will of the cooperative community. Henry George, on the other hand, was an apostle of individual initiative, which could have its just rewards only when the parasitical receipts of private landlords were abolished.

Now we come to the prime representative of the neoclassicists, Alfred Marshall. He refined and supplemented the work of Smith, Malthus, Ricardo, and others of their school. With nicety and penetration he adapted century-old concepts to business and social conditions of his day. As several of his talented students have put it, he was a toolmaker, the perfecter, and frequently the inventor of instruments of economic analysis. Unlike the others who have been mentioned above, he did not propose a new system, or indeed important structural changes in the incentives and modes of his time. Rather, he accepted what he found but devised improved means of understanding prevailing practices. This does not imply that he was merely a technician. On the contrary, he deplored poverty; the wish of his life was to see opportunity opened to all. He did not exercise himself as in a gymnasium but applied his knowledge to the problems of labor, commerce, currency, public finance, and the other concerns of society.

To illustrate by a metaphor, Marshall explored a cave—its vaults, passages, stalactite, and stalagmite formations—but he did not set forth the great geologic upheaval which created the cavern. He was an artist of delicate detail, not the painter of a mural. He was an expert on the putting green, not with the wooden driver on the fairway. Much less did he stray into the rough. This figure recalls the story of the American business man who became a golf enthusiast too late in life to make progress with his game. His infatuation, however, was complete, and he promised himself that when he could retire he would equip himself with the best irons and play over the celebrated course at St. Andrews, Scotland. He realized his ambition. Excited and nervous, he was worse than usual. It took him all day to get around the difficult eighteen holes. As he came up to the clubhouse late in the afternoon, tired but happy, he said apologetically to the little Scotsman who had been his caddy, "Well, I guess this has been pretty dull for you, going around with me, because you have all champion players here." "No, sir," was the reply, "I've been going over this course, man and boy, for forty years, and you've showed me parts of it today I never saw before!" Marshall did not get himself into positions where he must make futile or desperate shots.

But enough of preliminary matters. Alfred Marshall was

born in 1842 in Clapham, London, His Marshall descent was from a long line of clergymen and schoolmasters. His father was a cashier in the Bank of England; he was not born with a silver spoon in his mouth, but with a rod in his hand, for he was a tyrant in his family, lording it over his poor wife and his puny son Alfred. He begged a place for Alfred in the Merchant Taylors' School, where the boy learned Latin and Greek with less enthusiasm than he early showed for mathematics. On top of this diet, his masterful parent imposed long hours, reaching late into the night, at Hebrew. It was James Mill with little John Stuart over again, with the same criminal disregard of the boy's need for youthful companionship and play. Fortunately, Alfred was rescued from this regimen during the summer by an aunt in the country, who supplied him with gun, boat, and even a pony.

Thus the victim survived to be entitled to a scholarship at St. John's College, Oxford, where his father meant he should go on to take holy orders. But Alfred had had enough of dead languages, and, with a loan from a rich uncle, entered St. John's College, Cambridge. Here he could put the classics on the shelf while he indulged freely his passion for mathematics. Conscientious, he wasted not a moment of his time. But already the true economist, he made it a rule to break off study of demanding mathematics after short intervals of intense application. To rest his mind he read "light literature," including (in the original, of course) Aeschylus' *Agamenon!* "Never work when you are tired" was a motto with him through life. That was all right for an Alfred Marshall, but most of us would give a more liberal interpretation to fatigue.

In taking his degree, 1865, Marshall was Second Wrangler in the mathematics tripos when Lord Rayleigh, afterward the celebrated physicist and Nobel Prize winner, was First. As an undergraduate Marshall intended to follow his father's wish that he enter the church; maybe he would be a foreign missionary, then a favorite aim of serious-minded collegians. By stages he abandoned these ideas, though he preserved always a religious attitude toward life. In a discussion club he became intimate with Henry Sidgwick and F. D. Maurice, both of whom believed in works more than in dogmatic faith. Teaching mathematics the while, Marshall went from one absorption to another—first atomic physics, then metaphysics (with a stay in Germany to study Kant), followed by psychology, ethics, and so to political economy. Ethics had made him question the inequalities in opportunity which he saw about him, John Stuart Mill's *Political Economy* sharpened his curiosity. In his vacations, he recorded, "I visited the poorest quarters of several cities . . ., looking at the faces of the poorest people . . . I resolved to make as thorough a study as I could of Political Economy." He bought a small portrait of a man with a hopeless, down-and-out look. "I set it up above the chimney-piece in my room in college and thenceforward called it my patron saint, and devoted myself to trying how to fit men like that for heaven. Meantime, I got a good deal interested in the semi-mathematical side of pure Economics, and was afraid of becoming a mere thinker. But a glance at my patron saint seemed to call me back to the right path."

This incident, illustrating Marshall's sincere humanitarian concern, contrasts with the far more spontaneous and passionate devotion of his contemporary, Karl Marx. One does not dwell on the difference to Marshall's discredit. Marx and Marshall, in temperament, in personal history, and in immediate surroundings, lived in separate worlds. Marx needed no painter's likeness of it to spur him to the destruction of poverty. He had the real thing—in his slum, in his street, in his home! Marx the revolutionary had a deep and furious resolve, while Marshall, the academician, had ever a kindling kindness. Emotionally Marx was like a primary color, unmixed. Marshall by comparison was of pastel shade. An anecdote of Charles Lamb is a propos. A visitor who mixed salt with his tobacco to make his pipe mild found Lamb smoking a black briar stuffed with the strongest weed. "Mr. Lamb," he inquired, "how can you do that?" Lamb's reply was, "I toiled after it, Sir, as some men toil after virtue."

Marx was a refugee, expelled from his homeland, a man without a country. Marshall was on his native heath; indeed he lived for fifty years in the cultural enclave of Cambridge University. Marx was extramural, Marshall intramural. With Marx, Hegel (as he applied Hegel) was an intellectual and moral obsession. With Marshall, Hegel was an author he had read with attention. Marx was a wild thistle, Marshall grew in a garden border. Their difference (not in scholarship, for both were assiduous students) was in intensity of purpose. We could go on with such contrasts. But the greatest, which will appear as we proceed, was that Marshall pictured an economy balanced by opposing forces, or counterpoised, constantly adjusting itself through subtle variations, while Marx saw all as a moving panorama, one stage but the preparation for the next. In this sense Marshall's system was static, Marx's dynamic.

Marshall was appointed to a lectureship in St. John's, Cambridge (his own College) in 1868. As with Adam Smith at Glasgow more than a century earlier, his bailiwick was nominally moral science, but actually it was political economy which he taught there for nine years. During this time he published practically nothing. The gestation period with Marshall was exceptionally long. It was only by the penetration and finish of his work when it did appear that he escaped being called repetitious of Jevons, who was prompter to print. When Marshall was well known and could command indulgence of his publisher he in some instances impounded proof sheets for years without returning them, the type kept standing all the while. In the present day this would be impossible because no matter what the jewels of thought of a professor, printers are apt to cost more! In 1875 in a four-month tour of the United States Marshall's special inquiry was into this country's protective tariff, then entering its heyday as a result of the Civil War. As an English economist, imbued with his own nation's historic free trade teachings, he wanted "to study the problem of Protection on the spot"—that is as practiced and defended by the principal dissenter country. He came with some sympathy for the American contention that a new country required positive legislative encouragement for development of its industrial capacities. He recognized that Britain had been too ready to preach that what was good for her—open markets for her manufactures—suited the book of nations less mature economically.

Marshall visited factories in the chief American cities, and in Philadelphia, the center of protectionist advocacy, he got an earful. "One of my most vivid recollections," he later told the Economic Section of the British Association, "is that of Mr. Carey's splendid anger, as he exclaimed that foreign commerce [which Carey deplored] had made even the railways of America run from east to west, rather than from north to south." (This was Henry C. Carey, then 82 years old; see Chapter 7). Marshall's reasoned conclusion was that protection may have been beneficial for America prior to the Civil War but that were he an American at the time of his visit, he "should unhesitatingly vote for Free Trade." Nor, later, did he see any merit in Simon N. Patten's protectionist position.

In spite of his complaints, sometimes justified, of ill health, Marshall had a resistant constitution. His frame was slight but erect. His facial expression, judging from photographs, was ingenuous but intent, what Keynes described as the look of "an intelligent angel." He was fond of fun, with a quick sense of humor, and versatile in conversation.

At the age of 35 he married Mary Paley, a great-granddaughter of Archdeacon Paley who had been a convert to the population doctrine of Malthus. His wife had been his pupil, was later lecturer in economics in Newnham College, and his first book, *Economics of Industry* (1879), was written in collaboration with her. Though she had a more than wifely participation in his scholarly work, Marshall had inherited from his overbearing father a conception of woman's role which persuaded him to oppose the admission of women to Cambridge degrees. He helped to defeat the proposal. If this seems narrow in one of his intelligence and social awareness, we may recall that about the same time, in the eighteen-nineties, a smilar prejudice existed in America. A future president of Bryn Mawr College, when she applied for graduate study in Johns Hopkins University, was allowed to attend the lectures if she would sit behind a screen in the balcony.

After his marriage Marshall left Cambridge to be Professor of Political Economy and Principal of the newly established University College, Bristol. In keeping with the aims of popular education, he gave a series of evening lectures on Henry George's *Progress and Poverty*, which had just appeared. It was not a case of ice meeting fire, but it was something like that. Again we have the contrast between the academic analyzer, with a cordial desire for social welfare, and the ardent reformer (non-academic in George's case) who is able to support his contention with economic learning also. At Bristol Marshall's health broke down (kidney stone) and he went with his wife for a year's recuperation in Italy. He said later that he "lost ten of the best years of his life—from 37 to 47—through illness," but that was an exaggeration. Actually, he was always strong enough to spend summers walking through the Alps with a knapsack of books and more books sent ahead. He never charged at the heights, but (and this was his intellectual method also) took them by gradual ascents.

At the lamented death of young Arnold Toynbee, the famous Dr. Jowett, Master of Balliol College, Oxford, invited Marshall to take Toynbee's place as Fellow and Lecturer in Political Economy. His pupils were the candidates for the Indian Civil Service; thus Marshall was a successor to the assignment of Malthus at Haileybury. After a successful year at Oxford he went back to Cambridge as Professor of Political Economy. This was in 1885. Until he resigned his chair in 1908 at the age of 66, he not only established the eminence of Cambridge in economic studies but through his books and his pupils, he became acknowledged dean in his subject in academic circles in many countries. What Mill had been in the English-speaking world, through his *Principles of Political Economy*, Marshall now was through his *Principles of Economics*. The present writer is old enough to remember when Marshall's chief treatise was the standard text, or perhaps I should say the standard of texts. Other treatments, mostly not so detailed, had their special flavors, but they were apt to take much from Marshall which their users likely did not identify as his.

In fact, this creates a difficulty in speaking of Alfred Marshall's contributions to economic concepts and analysis. "Where is the problem?" one may ask. "We have Marshall's works. Look in them for what he thought. He always scrupulously acknowledged the prior publication of an idea by another if he knew of it. The remainder must be his own." That is true, but his formulations and phraseology became so much the language of the science that, in reading him now, one does not recognize his originality. As was remarked of Shakespeare, "his plays are full of quotations."

His style is so graceful and, as he said of Mill's, "so easeful as to incite his readers to overmuch rapidity." A generalization is offered, elaborated, exceptions to it are faithfully noted, and one glides into related observations so that the whole exposition and argument is of a piece. His thinking was of fine texture, exceedingly discriminating. The reader is struck by his suggestiveness. He made his points vivid with apt illustrations from many quarters, especially citing familiarly from actual industrial practice. In this he reminds one of Adam Smith, who interlarded his analyses with allusions to commercial usages. Marshall recommended as "a first duty for economists sitting at the feet of business men, and learning from them." He did not mean that economists should approve all the actions of the market-place, far from it. He worked at a time when business was assuming intricate forms, when British industry, commerce, and finance had stretched tentacles throughout the world. His attention to business is reflected in his use of the word "economics" rather than the older term "political economy." He centered on the private economy more than on the public sphere. He shared Mill's "attempt to combine many of the essential principles of Socialism with an unswerving devotion to individuality and a hatred to mechanical regulations of life." He did not agree with the old cry of *laissez faire*, "Let Government keep up its police, but in other matters fold its hands and go to sleep."

His prescription was for government to assume responsibility for those benefits only—such as planning cities, insuring a pure milk supply—which free private enterprise could not furnish at all or not so effectively. He observed that "Government has now many new large and subtle resources for finding out where it can do more harm than good." The technical advantages of collectivism were outweighed, he thought, by the lack of inventiveness. He condemned the dead hand of bureaucracy. "A Government," he remarked, "could print a good edition of Shakespeare's works, but it could not get them written. . . . I am urging that every new extension of governmental work in branches of production which need ceaseless creation and initiative is to be regarded as *prima facie* anti-social, because it retards the growth of that knowledge and those ideas which are incomparably the most important form of collective wealth." He believed that the successes of public projects depended on private discoveries. "The carcase of municipal electric works belongs to the officials; the genius belongs to free enterprise."

The collectivism which Marshall, the exponent of business, distrusted was a compound of utopian communities, municipal undertakings, and proposals of the English Fabians. He had early read *Das Kapital* of Marx, but that did not figure in his immediate criticisms. He actively approved of voluntary cooperation, being president of the Co-operative Congress in 1889. Reasons for the further intervention of government in the economy, many of which Marshall noted, have increased since his day. Mounting large-scale production, concentration of control in industry and finance, the severest depression in all history, a second and greater world war, not to speak of the example of communism in many countries and semisocialism in Marshall's own Britain are causes and evidences which he did not witness.

Perhaps if he were alive today he would agree that organized research, in science and in other fields, yields results equal or superior to those he believed could be accomplished only by the individual investigator working with or without a profit motive. The great laboratories of business enterprises use team work. The development of atomic energy could not have been achieved under other than public auspices, though employing, of course, a host of scientists from the universities and from industry.* Further, insecurities of life, beyond the capacity of individuals to provide against, especially recurrent mass unemployment, have reached proportions requiring governmental efforts at prevention and amelioration. "Depressed areas," whether depleted mining districts of Wales or the poverty-stricken Appalachian region of America, demand many-sided forms of rescue to which nothing less than national resources seem competent. In the forty years since Marshall died the hope of coping with major social evils mainly through private action has obviously retreated. Thus even the most advanced of his characteristic remedies—cooperatives, labor unions, development of social-mindedness in business men—have had to be powerfully supplemented by the state. We accept the fact of a "mixed economy"—partly public, partly private, and the two intertwined—as Marshall two generations ago would not willingly have done.

Alfred Marshall was among the earilest to use mathematics (that is, beyond mere arithmetic) and especially diagrams, in economic analysis and demonstration. His mathematical gift and training, however, did not make him what is called today a "mathematical economist." On the contrary, he considered that the mathematician was not fitted to keep in mind (as indeed who is?) the innumerable forces, historical, psychological,

---

* A. C. Pigou, who knew Marshall better than others, thought these developments would not have persuaded him to favor superseding private by public enterprise. (*Alfred Marshall and Current Thought,* published in 1953, pp. 62–3).

political, which impinge on economic behavior. In his earliest review (1872), of Jevons's *Theory of Political Economy,* he said: "We owe several valuable suggestions to the many investigations in which skilled mathematicians . . . have applied their favourite method to the treatment of economical problems. But all that has been important in their reasonings and results has, with scarcely an exception, been capable of being described in ordinary language. . . ." On the other hand, diagrams, or graphic representation, equally terse, could be understood by all readers. "The book [of Jevons] would be improved if the mathematics were omitted, but the diagrams retained."

Marshall, for these reasons and because he did not want to appear obscure to business men whom he hoped to influence, was apt to relegate his formulas and diagrams to footnotes, where the reader could take them or leave them. However, he constructed what his pupil Keynes called "elegant diagrams" in teaching his advanced students. Keynes, incidentally, did not follow his master's advice to use mathematics only for his own purposes in reaching his conclusions, and not to make a parade of these analyses in print. Not a little as a consequence of Keynes's example, employment of mathematics (and of complicated diagrams, too) in economic exposition has grown in favor. The circle of those to whom symbols, in preference to words, are intelligible, widens. The current pursuit of mathematics as a necessary tool in the natural sciences (following the blaze of the Soviet Union's Sputnik) has encouraged this equipment. Aside from the number who are thus instructed, the deeper question (to which Marshall pointed) is whether this method of reasoning and statement is best adapted to encompass the multifold complications of economic (social) problems.

Thus Marshall, more expert in mathematics than 99 out of 100 economists, wrote to his former pupil, the distinguished statistician A. L. Bowley, "In my view every economic fact, whether or not it is of such a nature as to be expressed in numbers, stands in relation as cause and effect to many other facts: and since it *never* happens that all of them can be expressed in numbers, the application of exact mathematical methods to those which can is nearly always waste of time. . . ." Mathematical assumptions of symmetry did not yield economic results. He would warn the economist against what he regarded as "mathematical toys. I think the economic, as distinguished from the mathematical, student is hurt by being invited to spend his time on them, before he has made a sufficiently realistic study of those statistics to know roughly, without calculation, on which side of the target the center of the shots lies. He assumes there is no wind. I believe that a Boer marksman [this was during the Boer War], who takes account of the wind, will by instinct get nearer the truth than he by mathematics." He went on to observe that "in economics other things are not equal."

In addition to mathematics and diagrams, and acute analysis expressed in the English language, an important component of Marshall's treatment was always economic history. He had given much (he himself confessed disproportionate) time to historical investigations, but in reduced dimension they inform all of his writing. His historical awareness enabled him to approach earlier doctrines in their setting and prompted him to value the enduring truths in them rather than to quarrel with their shortcomings. He had little sympathy with the purely theoretical, often dogmatic disputations that were the preoccupation of many academic economists, his contemporaries.

His historical sense fed and was fed by his absorbing interest in the actual modes and motives of manufacturers, workers, and merchants. Their doings, of the economic significance of which they might have little or no appreciation, were the raw materials of Marshall's reasoning.

A word about Marshall's habits of life before we come to economic ideas which we associate with him. When he and his wife returned to Cambridge from Bristol they built a house, "Balliol Croft," on the edge of the town. Marshall spent most of his time in his book-filled study. It was here that two afternoons a week he gave assistance to individual students whether they attended his lectures or not. This personal instruction in conversations had the greatest influence on pupils with a special turn for his subject. He was assiduous in reading and writing comments on their papers. He gave of himself in these intimate ways more than in his lectures, which were few, maybe forty-five in a whole year, or three a week for two terms. His lectures were informal, without notes usually and suggestive rather than systematic. Sometimes an event in the news would furnish him a text for the day. He continued to give a general or principles course, which many professors of his distinction

would have left to junior associates. His advanced c
a week, was on some special topic. He was fond of invi
leaders, cooperators, and visiting economists to his home, and
regularly included a few undergraduates and younger colleagues
to meet them. In this pleasant routine, exciting only in his
scholarly inquiries, he lived out his days. Of course other
economists who were teachers led a quiet life. Of those treated
here, Smith and Malthus were much in Marshall's pattern,
except for the storms that broke over Malthus's head because
of his population sacrilege. Marshall provoked few controversies.

Alfred Marshall contributed more than others toward establishing economics as a discipline, not only by his writings and
teaching, but in an organizational way. He took the lead in
founding in 1890 what became the Royal Economic Society.
In this he was certainly influenced by the formation of the
American Economic Association a few years earlier; he cultivated and always prized friendships and correspondence with
American economists. Secondly, he succeeded, with effort, in
getting economics recognized in Cambridge University as a distinct subject of study, instead of being included as a subordinate
part of the moral sciences. This was in 1903, and in sixty years
since, partly precisely because economics has claimed separate
concentration, many now see the benefits of renewing some
alliance with neighboring fields which Marshall, curriculum-
wise, excluded.

Marshall arrived at his fundamental concepts of economics
early, while still in his late twenties, in the years 1867–71. The
works of Ricardo and Mill he knew, but the reading of treatises
of a Frenchman and a German, Cournot and von Thünen, who
employed a mathematical approach, added a new dimension to
his thought. It was the notion that we value goods and services
in bits and pieces, not as a stock or totality, but depending upon
the satisfaction we derive over a period of time. As Marshall
put it, our estimates of desirability "relate not so much to
aggregate quantities, as to increments of quantities, and that . . .
the demand for a thing is a continuous function, of which the
'marginal' increment is, in stable equilibrium, balanced against
the corresponding increment of its cost of production." The
marginal unit is that which a consumer is just persuaded to
purchase or a supplier to offer. Marshall at first used the word
"terminal," then when Jevons's book employed "final," Marshall

adopted that, but later preferred "marginal." In his hands and those of Austrian economists this became one of the most familiar concepts in economic analysis.

Marginal (utility, say) seems to be better than final or last utility because it does not imply least possible utility, but the least utility applicable to a particular person, with his wants and means of satisfying them, at a particular time. Marginal utility for the same person may alter. As indicated above, the idea of margin described not only consumption or demand, but production or supply. We speak of marginal cost of production.

We have said that Marshall was a generous man, wishing to find good rather than evil, and the true instead of the false. Through this faculty he became a great conciliator between two principal schools of thought on the crucial question, How is value determined? Members of the school of Smith, Malthus, Ricardo, down through J. S. Mill, in a period of insufficient production, were exponents of a "pain economy." They were impressed by toil, trouble, sacrifice—in a word, by costs. The simplest, rudimentary cost was that of labor. So they said value is proportionate to labor. Marx lifted this definition off the page of the treatise and made it a battle cry.

Then along came the neoclassicists (Austrians, Jevons, etc.) who preferred a competitive society based on private property in the means of production and the incentive of private profit. But if labor created all value, how justify rent, interest, and profit? Probably their swing to utility as the whole explanation of value was not purposely in answer to Marx. By their time production had been amplified, and labor unions and factory legislation symbolized improvement in the standard of living. The consumer and his choices entered into calculation. The science of psychology was making progress. Thus subjective elements, degrees of pleasure, received emphasis, instead of the old obsession with degrees of pain.

Marshall, with his respect for thought in the past and his desire to incorporate new views, combined the two, cost and utility. Said Marshall, "We might as reasonably dispute whether it is the upper or the under blade of a pair of scissors that cuts a piece of paper, as whether value is governed by utility or cost of production." He went on to elaborate, and ended, "we may say that, *as a general rule*, the shorter the period which we are considering, the greater must be the share of our attention which is given to the influence of demand on value; and the longer the period, the more important will be the influence of cost of production on value."

This quotation illustrates the prominence Marshall gave to the element of time, which he called "the centre of the chief difficulty of almost every economic problem . . . what is a short period for one problem, is a long period for another." Time, continuous time, was important because, with each force acting on all others and all others on it, adjustments are constantly taking place. The character of these adjustments is largely a matter of duration.

Equilibrium of demand and supply illustrated the mutual tensions, or counteracting forces which Marshall outlined. He made particular contribution to the behavior of demand at the margin. He emphasized the role of substitution of a slightly less desirable commodity in the face of rising price. Of more importance, he introduced the term (though not the concept) of elasticity of demand. He showed elaborately how demand for an article or a service will often vary out of proportion to a change in price, responding with alacrity or lethargically.

Again, Marshall went into detail on the relative economies of small-scale and large-scale enterprises, especially those subject to the principle of increasing returns. As Pigou testified, "Marshall's ideal engine of progress was the small business, with its 'captain of industry' always pressing forward with initiative and enterprise in constructive work." He distinguished in an illuminating way "external" and "internal" economies. Among external, "The head of a large business can reserve all his strength for the broadest and most fundamental problems of his trade." The enterpriser on a small scale, absorbed in day-to-day operation, may not know of opportunities of invention and movements in the market even were he able to profit by them. "On the other hand the small employer," Marshall observed, "has advantages of his own. The master's eye is everywhere; there is no shirking by his foremen or workmen, no divided responsibility. . . ."

He pointed accurately to the limits of large-scale undertakings, in which, in spite of efforts to spur initiative in subordinate managers, the vast organization is apt to become unwieldly and gains, technically inviting, are canceled in fact.

The term "quasi-rent" was introduced by Marshall to describe an increased return to capital goods due to their temporary scarcity. Manufacturers possessing the machines needed to produce a textile which has suddenly become fashionable would enjoy an advantage similar to that of the owner of superior land. However, his differential income, unlike that of the landlord, must be temporary, because more machines would be produced, whereas the amount of land could not be increased. Like true rent, quasi-rent results from price; it does not cause price. Quasi-rent is closely related to the gain from semimonopoly or from complete monopoly over a short period. This way of looking at a favored or privileged element in production applies not only to capital, but to enterprise and labor. Those with unique skill, even if not inborn, but diligently acquired, will enjoy a special rentlike advantage of income. This again is a sort of monopoly and yields a producer's surplus. The whole idea is that of a differential above the margin where the normal cost of production is least advantageous.

Marshall's *Principles of Economics*, his chief treatise, was published in 1890, enjoyed an immediate warm reception, and went through eight editions and one reprint in his lifetime. His *Industry and Trade* (1919) less systematic, is an assemblage of monographs concerning, as Keynes said, "the forms of individualistic capitalism as this had established itself in Western Europe at about the year 1900, of how they came to pass, and of how far they served the public interest." Almost at the end of his life he collected residual fragments, some written long before, in *Money, Credit and Commerce* (1923). Between times he had published journal articles, pamphlets, letters to the London *Times*, and introductions to books of others, to a considerable number. After his death Keynes collected and edited *Official Papers by Alfred Marshall* (1926), giving his preparatory memoranda and evidence before commissions on trade depression, the poor, Indian currency, taxes, and other subjects on which his counsel was eagerly sought.

For Further Reading

Marshall, Alfred, *Principles of Economics* (London: Macmillan & Co., 1890).

Keynes, John Maynard, *Essays in Biography* (New York: Harcourt, Brace & World, 1933). Pp. 150–266 contain the best summary of Marshall's life and contributions, on which the present sketch has relied heavily. This essay had been included in the same author-editor's *Memorials of Alfred Marshall* (London: Macmillan & Co., 1925, pp. 1–65); this volume also has shorter reminiscences by F. Y. Edgeworth, C. R. Fay, E. A. Benians, A. C. Pigou; has over a hundred pages of letters of Marshall which throw light on his life and ideas.

Pigou, A. C., *Alfred Marshall and Current Thought* (London: Macmillan & Co., 1953). An estimate of Marshall's system a generation after his death.

Davenport, H. J., *The Economics of Alfred Marshall* (Ithaca, N.Y.: Cornell University Press, 1935). Pp. 1–35 place Marshall in his setting, in doctrine and in period.

11

AMUSED BYSTANDER

Thorstein Veblen

Thorstein Veblen (1857–1929) is included in this portrait gallery for sufficient reasons. He may have been, in the latter half of his life, the best known, to the literate, even the general American public, of academic economists. His reputation was due to his derisive criticism of social institutions and manners. He was solemnly shocking. Sardonic is not the word for his wit, for that implies heartlessness. Rather he was sarcastic and scornful; his thrusts were replete in irony. He seized attention by means of, not in spite of, his show of learning. He was far from the buffoon, in both motive and method. Though Veblen was more recondite, involved, and scholarly, his closest parallel as commentator on morals and habits was perhaps his contemporary, George Bernard Shaw.

He shared the serious purpose of the other economists here presented, but he was unique in his faculty of pricking complacency. No other was playful, certainly not in Veblen's sophisticated fashion. All the influential economists were necessarily critics, though they were also formulators of principles. Veblen was primarily a critic. To be such he needed and possessed profound knowledge, but what he contributed was not so much original ideas and policies as color, emphasis, and flavor. Veblen was an economic italic in his time.

His period was signalized by the lush, weedlike upspringing of American finance capitalism, and it was the antisocial aspects of this growth which he chiefly satirized. He was the foe of exploitation as contrasted with productive effort. This was the strain which ran through all his work, whether he was provoked by corporate combinations, currency controversy, economic depression following 1893, or the events of World War I and its aftermath. He indicted predatory, parasitic business, in all its manifestations and accessories, as it subtracted from serviceable industry and thus sabotaged, as he believed, the common welfare.

It seems not to have been noted, even by Veblen himself, that in this distaste he was following Henry C. Carey, who earlier constantly contrasted the mere trafficker, buying in the cheapest market and selling in the dearest, with the underlying producers of goods and services. Veblen highlighted pecuniary manipulation to a degree that Carey did not, because the abuses of this practice were not so developed in Carey's day, and Veblen supplied a sting with which Carey was not gifted. But if we are to look for an anticipator of Veblen in economic analysis, aside from the Socialists, he was Carey. Much else besides deprecation of economic waste and diversion of effort were similar in the two writers, including a high appreciation of the value of association and of technological advance. The reader is referred back to the chapter on Carey, and, better, to those of Carey's works which suggest other common elements.

In the flush of Veblen's celebrity, especially for his *Theory of the Leisure Class* (1899) and his *Theory of Business Enterprise* (1904), it was regularly asked, apprehensively, "Is Veblen a Socialist?" The answer is that substantially he was, though he declined to put a tag to his beliefs. Generally socialists applauded his publications; after the Bolshevik revolution he praised the Soviet system for abolition of private property and substitution of production for use, not profit. He may have been more effective as a socialist auxiliary than if he had marched in the ranks, as it were.

While he was born and always lived in America, he had the advantage of a cultural detachment that made for a candid view of the scene in this country. He was the sixth of twelve children of Norwegian farm parents who emigrated to Wisconsin and settled on eighty frontier acres among fellow countrymen. The close-knit community cherished Norwegian habits and language, and until Thorstein was approaching manhood he spoke little English. He always cultivated Norwegian traditions, was devoted to the sagas and translated one of them. Thus his background and upbringing was one of homely industry, and he early acquired suspicion of land-jobbers and credit sharpers who preyed on the immigrants, his own family included. When Thorstein was eight, the Veblens moved to a much larger holding in Minnesota where his father, Thomas, soon turned the wild prairie to fruitful production. Thomas was sensible, ingenious, and deliberate, while his wife was quick and spirited. Thorstein (if we may believe that children inherit qualities directly from their parents) may have received his thorough, slow manner from his father and his mental agility from his mother.

In local schools Thorstein attracted attention as a likely candidate for the Lutheran ministry. His father strained family resources to enter him at the age of seventeen (1874) in the preparatory department of Carleton College. When he graduated from Carleton he had earned the reputation of an "odd ball." Acknowledged to be brilliant, he was contradictory in behavior, by turns shy and assertive, silent and disputatious, as easy as a cactus to be friends with. Missionary-earnest in aim, the courses in the college stressed religion and moral philosophy, with pretensions in the classics, less in the physical sciences, little in English literature, and total neglect of biology and American history. Economics (Bishop Francis Wayland's textbook) was baptized in orthodoxy.

Yet in economics, which was to become the rallying-point of Veblen's thought, he had the benefit of random instruction from the gifted young John Bates Clark, more willing than other members of the faculty to depart from authoritarian patterns. In after years Veblen jested at the conventional, individualistic system of Clark, yet Clark, so different in temperament, never ceased to aid the ugly duckling he had helped hatch at Carleton. The same personal confidence was to persist between the mercurial Veblen and others, sponsors and colleagues, who were poles removed from him in convictions. In Carleton, as later in other institutions, Veblen educated himself by unprescribed reading that nursed originality which the unsympathetic called perverseness. He was always a heretic in a believing world. A saving grace was the dry humor with which he twisted axioms. Veblen, aloof from others, found a congenial spirit at Carleton in Ellen Rolfe, daughter of a wealthy business man, who moved in her own thoughts of literature and philosophy. So ill-assorted in backgrounds, Ellen and Thorstein made a pair intellectually, and they were married some years later.

Veblen taught for a year in an academy (mathematics, a subject he detested), and with slender savings went to Johns Hopkins University to study philosophy and political economy. Unlike most others, he did not find the atmosphere of this first of the great American graduate schools stimulating and soon transferred to Yale. At New Haven his chief teachers were Noah Porter, the president (moral philosophy) and William Graham Sumner (sociology). Though these two lights were hostile to each other—Porter anti-Darwin, and Sumner notable for applying the concept of evolution in the social sciences—both contributed to Veblen ideas which, cast in his own idiom, were to reappear in his works. In his reading at Yale, amplified by his command of German (self-taught) Veblen ranged widely in history, anthropology, psychology, political science, and theology. As economist, philosopher, and social critic he was to draw familiarly on all these fields.

When Veblen received his doctorate from Yale (1884), with excellent recommendations for scholarship in hand, he sought a teaching position. Relatives and friends exerted themselves in his behalf in various institutions in the Midwest, but to no avail. In all but possession of the Ph.D. degree Veblen appeared unacceptable. He was an agnostic at a time when religious faith—or at least profession and observance—was almost a prerequisite for academic preferment. He was an economic dissenter when authority was on the side of private business enterprise and *laissez faire*. His rough dress, something between the garb of a woodsman and a tramp, and his slow speech and abstracted manner were not prepossessing in the eyes of a college president or department head.

The result was that Veblen returned to his boyhood Norwegian community in Minnesota, much as his contemporary, Simon Patten, after university education in Germany, retreated to his father's Illinois farm because no opportunity offered for his talents. In 1888 Veblen married Ellen Rolfe and they lived at Ellen's home at Stacyville, Iowa, she furnishing spiritual and material support. Thorstein excused his long idleness by feigning slow recuperation from a vague illness contracted in the East. He loafed, camped in the woods, indulged his fancy for amateur botany. Yet he and his wife read assiduously, including the books of protest—Henry George's *Progress and Poverty*, Edward Bellamy's *Looking Backward* and *Equality*—voicing the current social discontent. Agricultural and industrial depression was punctuated by strikes of railroad workers and miners, scandals involving business promoters who bribed members of Congress, the Haymarket bombing in Chicago and the hanging of accused anarchists, and the Populist Party lifting "a banner under which the hosts of reform can rally." Though Veblen seemed to show no inclination to commence a career or connect himself with the practicalities of life, the turmoil of the times was slanting his mind.

Economists secure in their university chairs—Newcomb, Francis A. Walker, Taussig, Laughlin, Ely, and more—were unshaken in their devotion to private capitalism. They deplored the recklessness of labor outbreaks, defended traditional competition which was transforming into corporate combination, scolded socialists of any ilk as ungodly. Two exceptions to the stalwarts of the old school were John Bates Clark and Lester F. Ward, who were more limber. A "cultural lag" has rarely been better illustrated than in the writers and teachers of the popular economics textbooks of this period in America. The forces making for collectivism where not unrecognized were misread. Business combination, if not berated, was excused as furnishing more scope to superior captains of industry and finance whose operations were benevolent in the result. Combinations of workers, on the other hand, were misguided and dangerous. True, formation of the American Economic Association in 1885 by more forward-looking, generally younger men, promised revision of obsolete views, but progress was circumspect. Veblen, as we shall see, was far in the lead, so much so that he was a prophet crying in a wilderness.

Veblen's exasperated family saw no chance for him except to return to university study. In the fall of 1891 he presented himself at Cornell as applicant for an advanced degree, though he already had the most advanced degree obtainable. Professor J. Laurence Laughlin was sufficiently impressed to secure for him a special fellowship that would keep him in bread and cheese, and he buckled down to American (especially constitutional) history.

This was the beginning of a series of connections in different institutions where Veblen got a toehold. Veblen was received pretty much on sufferance, confined to appointments that were temporary or minor or both. His off-beat opinions were partly responsible, as they should not have been, for his relegation to subordinate posts. His caustic mode of expressing his criticisms did not help. His rough clothing, chosen for utility only, with a big safety pin here and there substituting for a button, attracted unfavorable notice. He became famous for his strictures on "conspicuous consumption." He himself practiced conspicuous non-consumption. He was a snob in reverse. He made a merit of simple, not to say primitive, housekeeping arrangements. Once he bought a disused chicken house, took it apart, carted it off to a woodsy lot and erected for himself a shack which suited him but appeared to others to give a roof over his head and little more. When at one university he lived in a tent in a friend's basement, with access through a window. He took his idiosyncracies into his classroom to the despair of most of his students and all administrators who depended on conformity to regulations in attendance, record-keeping, and the like.

Seated before the class, Veblen looked into his lap, mumbled to himself in a scarcely audible voice observations which, if heard, were often disconnected and vexing to all but a few students able to fill gaps for themselves. He passed everybody in his classes with the same middling mark. In addition he irked his academic superiors and sponsors more than once by his extramarital adventures. In spite of, or maybe because of, his outré personality and physical appearance, he attracted women who frequently wanted to prolong an association which Veblen had ceased to relish. As counterpart of casual side-romances, he separated intermittently from his current wife, or she from him. Devoted friends overlooked his persistent oddities, valued him for his talents, took care of him as an orphan of the storm, and some who were able at different times contributed a good part of whatever salary his university paid him.

During all this, for some thirty years, he evidenced as much scholarly industry as those who fared better in official recognition, and more independence and originality of mind than most. Though subordinated in academic rank, he made his own prestige in spite of neglect and slights. By no means all his colleagues spoke and acted to his prejudice. The ardent loyalty shown him by some in the inner circle is remembered to their credit. A man is what he is, or Veblen was what he was, and there is no use in lamenting that he refused to conform to convention even in trifles where he could have added to his own comfort and prosperity with no sacrifices of principle. Whether his influence, wide in any event, suffered from his perversity may be a question. An incidental evidence of interest in Veblen almost forty years after his death came to this writer's notice recently in using a catalog file-drawer, under the letter V, in the New York Public Library. The many cards listing works by and about Veblen are notably soiled, from thumbing, as compared with others in that drawer. This forms a rough index, perhaps, to Veblen's popularity.

When Professor Laughlin became head of the economics department in the new University of Chicago, he took Veblen along with him on a fellowship. This was in 1892, when the Populist Party was blasting "robber barons" for corporate oppression of farmers and industrial workers. The pertinence of these charges was demonstarted in the treatment of strikers at the Homestead plant of the Carnegie Steel Company near Pittsburgh. H. C. Frick, in Carnegie's absence in Europe, called in Pinkerton guards. When the battling was over, a dozen men lay dead. In the Coeur d'Alène (silver mining) district of Idaho, federal troops maintained martial law following clashes between union men and strike-breakers. That same summer in the coal region of Tennessee, unionists protested against the practice of leasing convicts to the operators. When the legislature obstinately favored the corporations, the unionists released convicts by hundreds, then fought the militia. These bloody struggles were on the eve of the national economic depression commencing in 1893.

The next year Chicago was the rallying point of marches of thousands of the unemployed to Washington ("Coxey's Army" being the best known), demanding paper money to finance public works for the jobless. While influential economists, including most of those at Chicago, denounced this movement, Veblen saw in it a revolutionary conception of the role of productive capital. If private owners, proclaiming their right to do with their property as they chose, could not serve the needs of society, then masses of people, abandoned to misery, would appeal to government for redress. The same year Chicago was the scene of the Pullman strike. The sympathetic American Railway Union, led by Eugene V. Debs, tied up a score of lines centering in Chicago until the strike was broken by a

sweeping injunction and United States troops sent in by President Cleveland. George Pullman, widely advertised as a
benevolent employer, rejected all appeals for arbitration. Debs
was jailed for a year.

The depression of 1893, confused as were its causes, had
a different impact on America from those that had preceded.
The older response to hard times was dumbly submissive,
described in the patient adage, "what cannot be cured must
be endured." Now the sufferers, though bewildered, were vocal.
The defiance had the spirit of "what cannot be endured must
be cured." Developing American capitalism had reached a
crisis. Veblen was impressed by the "cumulative organic change
in the constitution of the industrial community." That is to
say, " 'industrial integration' has gone far enough to obtrude
itself as a vital fact upon the consciousness of an appreciable
fraction of the common people of the country." The public
good must be paramount to private rights or to class claims.

Veblen could not accept gracefully the auspices of the University of Chicago. It was founded by John D. Rockefeller,
whose predatory business practices were viewed by the
University administration, if blameable at all, as abundantly
excused by his magnificent benefaction to education. President
Harper, in clerical and academic robes, embodied the masterful
methods of the captain of industry. Perhaps Harper's autocratic
drive was serviceable in organizing the large institution, literally
from the ground up, but Veblen did not admire the oligarchical
management and strong religious flavor which resulted. Though
on a small stipend, without rank except after a while as reader
or tutor, Veblen undertook many types of work on the campus.
He edited, at first unofficially, *The Journal of Political Economy*,
wrote articles and reviews for it, translated for publication by
the University a German treatise on finance, taught a course
on socialism, even wrote speeches for the President. In subtle
ways he was critical of economic orthodoxy; in the confident
pronouncements of professors at Chicago and elsewhere he
found sufficient opportunities for dissent. However, he profited
positively from suggestions of his colleagues, as soon appeared
in his writings. He disregarded the discussions, then rife, on
boundary lines between the so-called disciplines in the social
sciences. The more eager of his students valued the freedom
with which he habitually crossed intellectual frontiers. He com-

bined economics, government, law, psychology, anthropology, sociology, art, the natural sciences, literature, what have you. His familiar allusions were by no means shallow; they helped to give meaning to the particular topic in hand.

In papers before the Graduate Club of the university Veblen dismissed assumed principles and pictured economic action. He insisted, in Dorfman's words, "that economics must be studied from the standpoint of the economic interest, not the pecuniary interest, that the economic processes, not their pecuniary corrollaries in human action, are the important consideration for the community." Realistically he wanted to be done with "the metaphysics of normality."

It was while at Chicago (promoted at length to the rank of instructor) that Veblen brought out his most famous book, *The Theory of the Leisure Class*. The publisher made him revise it several times for clarity of language, and in addition, it seems, required Veblen to guarantee him against loss. It is difficult to say whether readers have appreciated the book chiefly as a satire on manners or, to quote the subtitle, as "an economic study of the evolution of institutions." Is it popular because it is a spoof or because it is, beneath the raillery, a bitter accusation of the power structure in capitalist society? If the first, that is, if readers are titillated by the derisive banter, their pleasure is the greater because his sarcasm takes the form of scientific pronouncement. He seems to be ponderously sober, in dead earnest, presenting evidence proceeding from scholarly research, expressed in the language of a dissertation. Veblen appears as a clown, not rigged out in baggy pantaloons, oversize shoes, red wig, and chalked face, but neatly dressed as becomes a serious lecturer to students. He preserves a deadpan gravity.

Many enjoy the sallies against the foibles of the idle rich, but they value Veblen's book for its underlying distinction between the predatory and the productive classes. It is an Americanized Marxism, updated, reduced to selective condemnations instead of being imbued, as Marx was, with revolutionary ardor. The class struggle, in Veblen's hands, becomes a pantomime, a costume piece of posturings by shallow, privileged persons, contrasting with the unpretentious conduct of the useful majority in society.

The *Theory of the Leisure Class*, like most of Veblen's work, is a study of a culture, and thus draws on anthropology, social history, psychology, and other lore with which he had made himself familiar. He follows an economic path, but the scenery on all sides is delightfully varied. Much of the attraction of the discussion is owing to the surprising light in which Veblen views commonplace conduct which the reader has never imagined had any profound sociological significance. An author may have thanks for acquainting me with previously unknown material, but that involves work on my part. I am immediately grateful if he takes what I already know and reveals in it what I never suspected. He caters to my self-esteem because quickly I am no longer a pupil being instructed. Once I begin to squint at familiar behavior from the author's angle, I myself become an author, or a companion of the author, for additional illustrations pop into my mind from my own experience. If I belong, as I probably do, to the humdrum majority in the community, I am flattered to find the minority, whom I have considered my betters, held up to ridicule. By the same token I am pictured as praiseworthy compared to the presumptuous and the privileged. "Blessed are the poor in spirit," who are shown " a rod for the fool's back." "Subtilty to the simple" is peculiarly comforting.

Savage peoples in a peaceable state, without individual ownership of property, enjoyed competent execution of useful tasks. This is what Veblen celebrates as "the instinct of workmanship." But with progress from primitive savagery to barbarism, war and the hunting of large game became the business of men, and women were confined to the daily drudgery of the camp, such as preparing food, bearing burdens, scraping skins for clothing, and so forth. The hunters and warriors became, by comparison, a leisure class. To be sure, their employments were dangerous and were in great part beneficial for the tribe, but the occupations involving exploit came to be considered worthy, while other callings, less spectacular, were classed as unworthy. Those who were "habituated to the infliction of injury by force and stratagem" were honored, were regarded as superior, while those consigned to "menial work" were looked upon—and looked upon themselves—as inferior.

As this scheme of life develops, "The men of the upper classes are not only exempt, but by prescriptive custom they are debarred, from all industrial occupations. The range of employments open to them is rigidly defined," limited to "government, warfare, religious observances, and sports. . . . To the lower grades of the leisure class certain other employments are open," but they are subsidiary to the noble pursuits of the top class—such, for example, as manufacture of weapons, making of war canoes, training hunting hawks, or preparing sacred apparatus. Certain women of high rank are excused from "the more vulgar kinds of manual labour." But most women, like the slaves, were for utility, not ornament.

The barbarian distinction between exploit and drudgery is carried over into modern life, where honor and elegance attach to military, political, and priestly performance, not to providing bread and cheese, hewing wood and drawing water. The activities that denote prowess depend on the commonplace, arduous efforts of others. It is the underlying mass of workers who support the personages esteemed precisely because thay do not create wealth, but seize upon or by other means possess themselves of it. Forms of address used toward chieftains and gods imply worship of the aggressive and the formidable, what Veblen calls "the conventional exaltation of the strong hand." The ox and the dove do not appear in heraldic devices, which show instead a "predilection . . . for the more rapacious beasts and birds of prey." The "high office of slaughter, as an expression of the slayer's prepotence, casts a glamour of worth . . . over all the tools and accessories of the act. Arms are honourable, and the use of them, even in seeking the life of the meanest creatures of the fields, becomes a honorific employment. At the same time, employment in industry becomes correspondingly odious, and . . . the handling of the . . . implements of industry falls beneath the dignity of able-bodied men."

In the evolution of society, wealth which confers respect becomes less and less the trophy of war or raids and increasingly the gains from industrial aggression. Ownership of wealth, which at first was admired as the evidence of efficiency, becomes itself the mark of reputability. The wealth may be acquired by one's own efforts or by inheritance; indeed, the more passive the receiver, the greater the distinction from the possession. It is acquisition of goods which determines status. The striving for possessions as proof of status is competitive. "Keeping up with the Joneses" is not enough; each one is committed to "a restless straining to place a wider and ever-widening pecuniary interval between himself and this average standard." Veblen says that "So long as the comparison is distinctly unfavourable to himself, the normal . . . individual will live in chronic dissatisfaction with his present lot."

This picture of an unceasing race for riches "to . . . gain the esteem and envy of one's fellow-men" may be an exaggerated generalization characteristic of Veblen. Are there no persons, or income groups, that are contented with their worldly goods? If you have read Bobbie Burns' "The Cotter's Saturday Night" or Longfellow's "The Village Blacksmith" you have examples of lowly folk who are satisfied with their lot. Obedience to what Veblen himself calls "the instinct of workmanship" gives them genuine composure. A modest sufficiency preserves their self-respect. In spite of Veblen's stress on anxiety for display, many other elements besides material goods contribute to our feeling of well-being. Veblen does allow that "among people with strong religious convictions" moral worth may be substituted for pecuniary success. But even these, he contends, are not exceptions to the rule, for they in effect call on a supernatural power to witness their superiority. This appears to be forced reasoning. You may recall the advice given to Robinson Crusoe by his father, that the middle station in life, without the effort to lord it over others, is the happiest. Veblen was prone to make a point at the expense of pressing the argument too far. He tried to correct the balance, from time to time, by admitting cases that denied his flat assertions. But the thoughtful reader dissents from this merely technical accuracy, and is apt to object that Veblen is drawing a caricature, not a faithful portrait. His habit of inflating his propositions to shock the reader into agreement was at the cost of lowering his reputattion as a trustworthy interpreter of modern culture. Many who find him stimulating reflect that he must be taken with more than a grain of salt. He has suffered in comparison with others who were less highly colored.

If abstention from labor is the mark of wealth and entitles one to social admiration, an extra merit comes from being surrounded by attendants who themselves do nothing useful but simply pamper the exalted master or mistress. They illustrate "vicarious leisure." The "lady in waiting" and the lackey of the royal personage fill functions which are nominally menial, but since these duties do not in fact soil the hands of the flunkies, they reflect more honor on the one served. Also something is left over to gratify the pride of the members of the retinue. The more supernumeraries a potentate commands the worthier is he of being extolled. Not many years ago an American constitutional adviser to the Chinese government was assigned nine servants for his residence. The whole duty of one of these was to sit in a booth at the entrance to the garden and rise and bow when the distinguished guest came and went.

Veblen mentions Polynesian chiefs who would prefer to starve rather than carry food from the table to their own mouths. Certain super-elegant Chinese grandees, we know, allowed their finger-nails to grow to a length that made it obviously impossible for them to grasp any object with their hands—this as a proof of conspicuous leisure. Binding the feet of upper-class girl children until at maturity they became mere knobs on which to toddle had the same purpose of exhibiting incompetence. Veblen, dwelling on his favorite topic of extravagant waste in women's dress, wrote a regular little dissertation on the tight corset which so squeezed the innards that females of delicate breeding had little room for breathing and less for digestion. These wasp-waisted ones were translucent and at the slightest provocation sank to the ground in the "vapors." Their grotesque deformity proclaimed that their lordly husbands had no lack of housekeepers. Elaborate head-dresses, on gala occasions, of ladies of the French court several centuries ago were examples of conspicuous consumption and conspicuous leisure. One such construction required the talents of an hydraulic engineer, for mounted in the powdered pile of tresses was a waterfall. (With the addition of a little soap this would have produced, however, the undoubted utility of a shampoo!)

Of course the most exalted of all beings are the gods, who are held to want for nothing. In crudest contemplation they dwell in palaces of jasper environed by streets of gold and have very saints for servitors. This is the ultimate in exemption from pecuniary cares. Naturally members of the priestly class, in order to honor divine masters, must wear costly vestments, and churches must be elaborate in decoration. The whole idea is to equate the worshipful and the rich.

Waste of time, effort, and substance is in conflict with the instinct of workmanship or the common sense of productive efficiency. Even the show-off who flourishes his extravagance in order to win popular approval may feel compelled to pretend

to some element of usefulness in his expenditure. Thus lavish
entertainments may be advertized as for the benefit of a worthy
charity, though the net proceeds going to the needy may bear
only a small proportion to the total cost. The real object is
display, for which a modicum of social service is only the formal
excuse. Economy, or the wise fitting of means to ends, is hard
to banish utterly, though indulgence in futile luxury comes close
to accomplishing it. An example that would have been ready
to Veblen's hand happened shortly after his death, in the great
depression of the nineteen-thirties. A visitor to the distressed
district of Scott's Run in West Virginia found the children of
unemployed coal miners playing with high-priced toys. These
had been donated in surplus quantity to the White House
Christmas tree, and the President, according to custom, passed
them on to deprived youngsters. There is every reason for
furnishing holiday joy, but one reflected that *de luxe* playthings
were strewn more plentifully than food.

Sometimes Veblen's supposed scientific seriousness let him in
for gibes. He laid it out that "the well-to-do classes in . . . communities in which the dolicho-blond element predominates"
have a special liking for expansive lawns. The reason is advanced
that "this racial element has once been for a time a pastoral
people inhabiting a region with a humid climate." The natural
way to keep the grass down would be to put cows on the park-
land. But useful cows suggest thrift, so the owner has his
greensward cropped by "some . . . inadequate substitute, such
as deer, antelopes, or . . . such exotic beast." H. L. Mencken,
in a mocking review, suggested that if Veblen walked about
a pasture he would discover a better reason for omitting Bossie.

The reader may be taken with Veblen's ridicule and foolery
to the extent that he is unprepared for the caustic judgment
pronounced against the leisured, pecuniary class. It derives from
the predatory barbarism in which "clannishness, massiveness,
ferocity, unscupulousness, and tenacity of purpose . . . counted
toward the accumulation . . . of wealth." Later these traits of
"bold aggression . . . and a free resort to fraud . . . gave place
to shrewd practise and chicanery" as the best means to wealth.
"The ideal pecuniary man is like the ideal delinquent in his
unscrupulous conversion of goods and persons to his own ends,
and in a callous disregard of the feelings and wishes of others
and of the remote effects of his actions. . . ." The pecuniary

class is "the invidious or self-regarding," while the industrial class is "the non-invidious or economical," the first devoted to "personal . . . status," the second to "mechanical efficiency, or use. . . . The aristocratic and the bourgeois virtues—that is to say the destructive and the pecuniary traits—should be found chiefly among the upper classes, and the industrial virtues— that is to say the peaceable traits—chiefly among the classes given to mechanical industry."

This is true in a general way, but since the industrious individual must have pecuniary incentives in order to survive, wherever the pecuniary culture prevails, acquisitiveness is an object of the lowly. Unmitigated dominance of the pecuniary temperament would in time result "were it not for the fact that pecuniary efficiency is on the whole incompatible with industrial efficiency. . . . But the 'economic man,' whose only interest is the self-regarding one . . . is useless for the purposes of modern industry." Fortunately, the "interest in work differentiates the workman from the criminal on the one hand, and from the captain of industry on the other." Not completely, Veblen repeats, for by "the precept and example of the leisure class," the body of the people cultivate aristocratic traits to some degree.

Exploitation of the workers, though harsh enough, is not the worst disservice of the pecuniary masters. "The pecuniary struggle produces an underfed class, of large proportions. This underfeeding consists in a deficiency of the necessaries of life. . . . The strain of self-assertion against odds takes up the whole energy of the individual; he bends his efforts to compass his own invidious ends alone, and becomes continually more narrowly self-seeking. The industrial traits in this way tend to obsolescence through disuse." By grinding the faces of the poor (Veblen uses the milder expression, "by withdrawing as much as may be of the means of life from the lower classes"), the leisure class creates its own image in debased form. "The result is an assimilation of the lower classes to the type of human nature that belongs primarily to the upper classes only."

Veblen offers here no advice for lower-class revolt. The picture of oppression of workers by owners of the means of production had been more vividly drawn by Marx, Engels, and others. These were keenly aware, too, that the workers were prone to repay exploitation with envy rather than with defiance. It was precisely to overcome this insidious emulation that Marx, typically, dramatized the complete class antagonism in society, and called on workers to throw off their chains. Veblen may be thought of as a Marxist with a difference, or at one remove. Veblen was critic more than crusader. Compared with the socialists, as with the orthodox classicists, Veblen comprehended cultural shadings which the others arbitrarily neglected. Thus it is necessary to read Veblen's deepest preachments between the lines.

In *The Theory of the Leisure Class*, indulging his turn for paradox, Veblen contradicted in part the basic economic concept of saving. The more pretentious classes in society, he was saying, made a merit of waste. He contended that those less fortunate emulated, so far as they were able, the squanderings of the rich. Thus the individual, instead of striving to make his goods and his time go as far as possible in satisfying his material wants, was ready to stint himself in lesser or greater degree in order to provoke false admiration in his fellows. Veblen clothed sober-sided endeavor with foibles, vanity, frailties. He was not the first to introduce psychological elements in the economic calculus, for subjective valuations had been explored by Jevons and the Austrians. But others had kept all within the bounds of reasoned conduct, closely related to scarcity and limitations of the price system. Veblen, drawing on anthropology, pictured irrational motives. Before Veblen came along with his penchant for perversity, men's political, aesthetic, religious, and amorous doings might be unaccountable, but economic responses were considered, by comparison, to be deliberate and guided by intelligence. Veblen showed in his playful fashion that, in our bread and butter dealings also, we are only poor weak mortals, subjects for the philosopher's compassion.

While he analyzed actions of individuals, he was ever presenting collective social behavior. Of course this viewpoint was as old as the first economic writers, and the community as a whole had been elevated to principal place by such advocates as Owen and Marx. But here again the purposeful had crowded out the erratic and the discordant, which Veblen injected in quantity. The community did not try to apportion its resources thriftily but rejoiced in being spendthrift.

Veblen, in his seriocomical manner, did something to humanize the economic process. From the many fields with which he was conversant—ethnology, biology, psychology,

sociology, anthropology, even craniology—he added new dimensions to the economic man. From years of wide reading he
regurgitated in his essays. For the theoretical and the abstract
he substituted the historical and the instutional. His slant was
that of evolution, largely evolution of habits. He was a social
behaviorist. Tolerant and amused, he did not have his knife
out for every benign tumor.

This much said in homage, the reader should be warned that
not all of Veblen's writing is sparkling or stimulating. He could
be dull, leaden, and lengthy. Sometimes the mountain labored
and brought forth a mouse. He was unsystematic and repetitious.
His reasoning and illustrations could be far-fetched. Though
generous of spirit, with a mind reaching out for new impressions,
he offered—as what original writer has not done?—variations
on a few favorite themes.

We need not follow Veblen's academic wanderings, from
Chicago to Stanford University, thence to the University of
Missouri, briefly to the Food Administration during World
War I, then as an editor of the *The Dial* in New York, and
after that to the New School for Social Research. Everywhere
his famous course on "Economic Factors in Civilization"
attached able students to him, but his irregular romances failed
to endear him to college presidents. Between appointments he
had periods of unemployment; these would have been shorter
but for the handicap of his personal peculiarities. All the while,
however, secure or "on the wind," as he put it, he was writing
books, articles, and projecting further investigations. It is fruit-
less to recite mere titles. Most of what he wrote, unless on
some development of the day, was on the theme of producers
versus appropriators, to the discredit of the latter. He never
received from his professional colleagues the formal recognition,
say the presidency of the American Economic Association,
which many considered his due. It made no difference to Veblen,
who went his way unconcerned.

He spent his last years, in ill health, in California, in shacks
which only he could have found comfortable. He died of heart
failure and, by his wishes, his ashes were scattered over Pacific
waters. We do not conclude on this doleful note but go back
a decade to a group of his essays which reach into the present
and beyond.

In his pieces for the *Dial*, Veblen used a simpler, freer style than earlier, going directly to the point without the luggage of learning. Also there was less of the critic and more of the creator, which gave impact to his writing. Particularly memorable were the articles appearing in the magazine in 1919 and later collected under the title *The Engineers and the Price System*. The contrast was his favorite one between producers and predators, between business behavior and socially useful performance, or what Professor Riesman has called "workmanship versus wastemanship." But now he did not content himself with sharp observations; he made timely proposals.

Ever before his eyes were the lessons of the First World War, the Bolshevik Revolution in Russia, and the pressure in America for what was called reconstruction. The war, demanding mounting production, had given temporary primacy to efficient output in all fields for a great national purpose. Designs of private gain and the practice of business as usual, though they stubbornly obtruded, were discredited in public sanction. New incentives took over. In important areas—notably transportation —competition was adjourned for coordination under government auspices. Hitherto untried controls over prices and wages were introduced. Planning dismissed to a degree the old reliance on the profit motive. The necessity of competence diverted attention from the money-makers and focused on the technicians who could actually turn out goods and supply services. The economy became for the nonce consciously collective instead of individualist.

The Bolshevik Revolution had stunned capitalist countries and, since it took Russia out of the war, provoked the Allies— the United States included—into angry retaliation in military support of the Whites. The native counter-revolutionaries struggled to reinstate the old regime of the Czar, but it may be guessed that the forsaken Allies struck back more with the wish to punish than with any hope of reversing the event. Expropriation of private owners and soviet organizations to command the means of production, however blasted by others, fell in with Veblen's long preconception. The needs of the community were to be met immediately, not by roundabout capitalist methods.

The cataclysm of war and the horrid happenings in Russia issued in a fleeting resolve to give the world a fresh start. President Wilson's ideal in the League of Nations, political rather than economic, was rudely subverted by his colleagues at the Versailles peace table. Domestic proposals in America ranged from the timid to the extravagant. The menace of Russia's example led to repression of all suspected, even remotely, of imitation. American socialist headquarters, publications, and meetings were ruthlessly raided, and foreign workers were deported. In this atmosphere of fright most academic people were cowed. Compared to the heroism of the war, their programs for the future were unimpressive. Postwar depression, which might have led to firmer resolve, though acute, was brief. Soon the country relapsed into the "normalcy" of Harding.

Veblen attacked this complacency. He showed no fear of being called radical because he castigated the sabotage of production by captains of industry bent on profits, by labor unions striking for their members' selfish ends, by government imposing protective tariffs in restraint of trade. Improved technology had expanded the capacity for output beyond the limits of the market economy. The term "enterpriser" was a misnomer. This functionary had abandoned his earlier contribution to production. He devoted himself to financial maneuvers, leaving industrial management to technicians whose duties he did not bother to understand. It was these production engineers who made up "the indispensable General Staff of the industrial system," without whose "immediate and unremitting guidance . . . the industrial system will not work. It is a mechanically organized structure of technical processes designed, installed, and conducted" by these experts. "Without them and their constant attention the industrial equipment, the mechanical appliances of industry, will foot up to just so much junk. The material welfare of the community is unreservedly bound up with the due working of this industrial system and therefore with its unreserved control by the engineers, who alone are competent to manage it." The individual enterpriser, shorn though he was of serviceable functions, had given way to "the syndicated investment bankers" who continued "to control the industrial experts and limit their discretion, arbitrarily, for their own commercial gain, regardless of the needs of the community."

Veblen foresaw an end to the antagonism between financial manipulation for profit and the actual operation of the means of production. War experience had taught younger technologists to be no longer awestruck lieutenants of captains of finance;

"they are beginning to understand that commercial expediency has nothing better to contribute to the engineer's work than so much lag, leak, and friction . . . So the next question which the engineers are due to ask regarding this timeworn fabric of ownership, finance, sabotage, credit, and unearned income is likely to be: Why cumbers it the ground?"

Technological specialists, a minute fraction of the whole population of the country, by a strike could "swiftly bring a collapse of the old order and sweep the . . . fabric of finance and absentee sabotage into the discard for good and all." Veblen did not scruple to envisage, in Soviet lingo, a "Council of Technological Workers' and Soldiers' Deputies" that would conduct production for abundance "according to the state of the industrial arts . . . at their best."

Veblen did not enter into the momentous question of how the productive plant could be taken over by the engineers without social disruption. It would amount to a revolution, but he contented himself with observing that the time for it was not yet. "Bolshevism is not a present menace to the Vested Interests in America," provided the protectors of these vested interests did not by their hysterical measures of repression "make Bolshevism seem the lesser evil."

More than a dozen years later, when the Great Depression of the nineteen-thirties convicted the directors of the American economy of grievous incompetence, Veblen's forecast of a soviet of technicians to take over production seemed nearer realization. Howard Scott, an engineer with publicist talents, and close associates calling themselves "Technocracy," contrasted the capacities of industrial energy with the restraints of monetary management. Plentiful production for which the potential existed would sink prices and render old debts, based on higher costs, unpayable. In the hands of Technocracy the slide-rule seemed more formidable than the soap box had ever been. Though Technocrats disavowed Veblen's inspiration, his *Engineers and the Price System* justly sprang into a new popularity. The flurry of discussion magnified his reputation after the notoriety of Technocracy had faded.

For Further Reading

Veblen, Thorstein, *The Theory of the Leisure Class, an Economic Study of Institutions.* Numerous editions; that of Modern Library, Inc.,

New York, 1934, has an excellent foreword by Stuart Chase.
————, *The Engineers and the Price System*. (10th printing, New York: Viking Press, 1954).
————, *The Portable Veblen*. Edited by Max Lerner (New York: The Viking Press, 1950). Selections from a variety of Veblen's writings.
Dorfman, Joseph, *Thorstein Veblen and his America*. (5th printing, New York: The Viking Press, 1947). This famous critical biography presents Veblen A to Z.
Riesman, David, *Thorstein Veblen, a Critical Interpretation*. (New York: Charles Scribner's Sons, 1953).

12

REVISION PRO BONO PUBLICO

John Maynard Keynes

Keynes was the most influential economist of the twentieth century if we omit Lenin, who moved in a different and wider orbit. As compared with Lenin, Keynes was technical and limited in method, not radical—much less revolutionary—in motive. After World War I the commanding problem was, How remake society? Could mankind continue under capitalism, or must the premises and procedures of that system be abandoned in favor of communism? These terms—capitalism and communism—must be taken in broad meaning. Capitalism was practiced in advanced countries only, in western Europe, in North America, in developed areas of Latin America, in Australia, New Zealand, and South Africa. Yet capitalism penetrated, through imperialism and colonialism, to exploit the continents of Asia and Africa wherever commerce could reach. Communism was confined geographically to Russia, but its potential was far greater, for it aimed to topple capitalism in old strongholds and in due time embrace unawakened peoples.

Keynes, among economists, became the foremost champion of capitalism. We would be mistaken to prefer rigid conservatives, like von Hayek and von Mises, for this role, or, moving into the political sphere, Churchill. For Keynes saw that capitalism could hold the line only by yielding at critical points, by curing its fatal defects. Dogmatic resistance would not do. Capitalism, to endure, must be reformed, must introduce elements of deliberate social planning. He had extra incentive in the Great Depression which gripped capitalist countries in the nineteen-thirties while the Soviet economy continued to expand.

Keynes's chief significance was that he took the lead of academic economists in recognizing that capitalism could no longer prosper under old rules, that orthodoxy must be revised or be discredited.

As we shall see, he was not alone, or the boldest, in this resolve. Paradoxically, his impact was greater because he wrapped his reforms in sophisticated theoretical analysis. Instead of frontal attack on acknowledged evils, which would have been viewed by intellectuals as worthy but familiar declamation, he used indirection. His contrived terminology, mathematical formulas, and intricate demonstrations recommended his argument as profound. Obscurity here and there positively helped. How with this forty-foot-pole of recondite reasoning did he manage to lever practical public policy? How came it that the scratch of Keynes's pen in his closet soon reverberated in the world's council chambers? We shall discover answers as we sketch his brilliant career.

Keynes was born June 5, 1883 into a cultivated, comfortable home. His father, John Neville Keynes, was a Cambridge University don destined to his own distinction in logic, political economy, and administrative service. His mother, Florence, was active in civic welfare enterprises and later became mayoress of the town.

After local schooling he won a scholarship, at fourteen, to Eton. Here his rapid physical growth was matched by expanding mental curiosity, so that in two senses he stood head and shoulders above most of his fellows. His ready acceptance of responsibility and friendly trust in him made Maynard the natural spokesman of the boys in any rubs with the masters. The one fly in the ointment was uncertain health. Throughout life, though with cautions by himself and those near him, his driving nervous energies overtaxed his constitution with prematurely fatal effect. At Eton he took up hobbies and extra-curricular activities which became permanent enthusiasms—book collecting, journalism, dramatics, and more. He accepted his many school prizes with modest pride. His final achievements were election to a scholarship in King's College, Cambridge, in mathematics and classics, and he stood first in the Higher Certificate Examination.

He entered King's at nineteen (October 1902). This College was the fount of his education, his closest friendships, and forever after a focus of his affections. He remained identified with King's to the last, and as don and manager of the foundation's investments (bursar) he gave back even more than he had received. As one reads the record of his undergraduate years, he wonders when Maynard studied, that is in the conventional allotment of time to scholarly tasks. He did get his lessons with ample success, yet a lion's share of hours and zeal went into what was called simply "The Society," and into other congenial groups such as the "Discussion Society" and the "Midnight Society." Society figured largely; Keynes became secretary and later president of the Union Society, more comprehensive and of a different sort, for it was an apprentice parliament, debating public issues.

"The Society," of dons and students, select and secret, cultivating the "utmost intimacy" of the members, claimed Keynes's chief loyalty. Here were nurtured lifelong friendship, particularly with Lytton Strachey and Leonard Woolf. The purpose of exchanges was the deadly pursuit of truth, though relieved, happily, by lively sallies in conversation. But the too-close association and exclusiveness led to excessive introspection, adolescent dissection of personalities, and immature arrogance toward outsiders. With much that was better we may blame this tight fraternity for encouraging in Keynes an unbecoming conceit—tempted but not excused by his acknowledged gifts. Following undergraduate days his amiable and unselfish qualities were tinctured by occasional rudeness toward those of slower minds. He was an aristocrat in intellect and sentiment, equal to and always demanding first quality in letters, arts, and public affairs, but he had an undoubted "propensity"—to use his own word in another connection—for self-esteem. In the highest levels of negotiation, in which he later figured with such effect, he fortunately dropped this unlovely failing.

Keynes's concentration in college studies was on mathematics. His record was excellent but well below top performance. Not until his last year in King's did he turn to economics. Then he had the best instruction, for he attended the lectures of Alfred Marshall and enjoyed the friendly coaching of A. C. Pigou at weekly breakfasts. He read "masses of economics," with special enthusiasm for William Stanley Jevons's "Investigations into Currency and Finance." "I find Economics increasingly satisfactory," he recorded, "and I think I am rather good at it. I

want to manage a railway or organize a Trust. . . . It is so
easy and fascinating to master the principles of these things."
Marshall wished Maynard to prepare for the Economics Tripos,
then recently inaugurated at Cambridge at Marshall's urging,
but Keynes preferred to qualify in the civil service examination.
Though Marshall was the commanding figure in his field and
Keynes acknowledged the merits of his *Principles of Economics*,
appreciation ran from professor to pupil rather than the other
way around. In after years the optimism of Marshall's nicely
poised system was to be damaged or destroyed by Keynes's
demonstration that balance of forces might be achieved at less
than full employment—a fatal thrust. Pigou soon succeeded
Marshall; with his emphasis on welfare he was more to Keynes's
liking, and the names of the two are linked, though Pigou
remained skeptical on features of Keynes's doctrines.*

Maynard's family and friends were anxious at the off-hand
way in which he studied for the demanding examinations which,
hopefully, would usher him into a government post. The tests
were a trial of endurance, extending (with blessed intermis-
sions) over more than three weeks. Maynard and his mother
moved to London for the ordeal. Had Keynes not diverted
himself so frequently beforehand and during the inquisition,
he might have rated first. He came out a poor second and,
employment in the Treasury being pre-empted by his successful
rival, he chose to enter the India Office.

Not long before this he had toyed with the idea of fitting
himself for the bar, and, the preliminary fee paid by his father,
he ate a few dinners at the Inner Temple. G. M. Trevelyan
had encouraged him toward the law, which could lead on to
a career in politics; this should be Maynard's destiny instead
of "rushing into the tomb of the civil service." It took Keynes
nearly two years to agree that he was buried amidst "government by dotardry," and he resigned (June 1908) from the
India Office. Yet stale bureaucracy had not hampered him, for
he had come to know Indian problems, had won the lasting

---

* Near the end of Pigou's life the writer of these lines ventured to
introduce himself and two children to the tall grey ghost prowling the
stairs and walks of King's College. Aloof anyhow, Pigou invited no
conversation. Doubtless a show of deference in total strangers was
distasteful to him, as Harrod testifies (*Life of Keynes,* p. 144) it was
apt to be. His apparel was as casual as his air was abstracted, which
somewhat diminished the feeling that one was shaking hands with
history.

esteem of superiors, and had devoted his abundant spare time to intensive study of the theory of statistical probability. His dissertation on this subject did not win him, as he hoped, a fellowship at King's. But, both Marshall and Pigou active in his behalf, Keynes was appointed a lecturer in economics.

This was a grateful return to familiar associations. Keynes from the first was an engaging teacher in the principles of economics, money and banking, and operation of the foreign exchanges, with excursions into labor problems. He had a faculty for illustrating theory by reference to practice. As yet his exposition was orthodox, in the tradition of Marshall. He was soon made a fellow of King's. His lecture schedule was light by American standards; he used his spare time for reviews, articles, and laborious prolonged revision of his work on probability. This last, which became a wide-ranging theory of knowledge, was not published until 1921. He resumed his old vacation visits to Scotland, Switzerland, the Pyrenees, and elsewhere for mountain climbing, not to speak of house parties nearer home with bosom friends.

In 1913 important appointments came to Keynes; he published his *Indian Currency and Finance*, was made a member of a Royal Commission on that problem, was appointed secretary of the Royal Economic Society and editor of its journal, and became active in management of King's investments to the conspicuous benefit of the college.

His errands in London permitted him to renew intimacy with old Cambridge friends and others composing what was known as "the Bloomsbury set" of painters and writers. Keynes was drawn into their interests in the arts; he enjoyed their talents without adopting their affectations. Later on he was to give wide public impetus to drama, music, and ballet.

The next year brought outbreak of the First World War and Keynes's entrance into the Treasury. Soon he was head of the division responsible for the major area of external finance, especially inter-Allied loans. The war by rapid stages rendered the gold standard unworkable, and Keynes foresaw the eventual demise of that regulator of world currency, commerce, credit, and prices. For the time being he struggled to postpone bank suspension and control the mighty forces compelling inflation. We may not tell that story but must leap forward to place Keynes at the treaty table at Versailles.

Here, as principal British Treasury representative in devising the terms of peace, he was quickly in disagreement with the heads of victorious governments—Lloyd George, Clemenceau, and Woodrow Wilson. In differing degrees their prescription was vindictive punishment for Germany, heedless of economic and political results for reconstruction of Europe. Keynes's *Economic Consequences of the Peace* (1919) made him suddenly famous. His polemic branded the settlement as wicked folly and offered acid sketches of the Big Three chieftains, which were questioned for their loyalty and taste but not for their accuracy. Keynes's main point was that Germany, shorn of colonies and part of her home territory and merchant marine, could not muster the extravagant reparations, if at all, without ruin to the export trade of the countries she must indemnify through two generations. He showed that Germany could not pay the costs of the war without wreaking vengeance on her judges. Allied statesmen entertained the naïve notion that Germany could buckle to it, cut wages and other expenses of production, tax her people heavily and fork over as the penalty for her crimes. They seemed to be unaware of the transfer problem. Britain, France, and the others could not afford to be paid. Germany must soon exhaust her gold, could obtain more only by excluding allies to that extent from world markets, and then must pay in ships and coal and steel. This last expedient would bring cries of anguish from deprived enterprisers and workers in industrial centers of creditor countries. If Germany, in the heart of the Continent, sank under her excessive load of reparations, she would pull down Europe with her. The peace was born of war rage and scorned elementary wisdom. The project was worse than hopeless, promised tragedy for all concerned. An irony of war is that the victors, themselves depleted, must for their own salvation lift the vanquished from prostration.

Of course Keynes was the target of resentful critics. But his indictment of the Versailles treaty was documented in subsequent events—spiraling German inflation, disintegration of the Weimar Republic, paring down and then cancelation of reparations, the rise to power of Hitler, and the Second World War. Keynes followed his celebrated *Economic Consequences* with other books on the peace conference, *A Revision of the Treaty* (1922), *Essays in Biography* (1933), and *Dr. Melchior* (1949). He was active in the interwar years in journalism; he contributed main articles to the *Manchester Guardian* supplements covering "Reconstruction in Europe," wrote for the *Sunday Times* (London), and *New York World*. His articles were syndicated in principal newspapers of Europe, and, as board member, he gave assiduous counsel in the editorial policies of *The Nation* (later *New Statesman and Nation*). In his journal pieces he explored national and international problems in finance, commerce, labor, and politics.

He opposed Britain's return to the gold standard in 1925. He increasingly argued that the ancient regulator of currency and credit had been rendered obsolete, certainly in its simple form, and that currencies and the exchanges must be managed. Discretion, wits, policy must supplant the awkward, not to say dangerous, tyranny of gold, so ill distributed in the world following the war. This was a signal instance of Keynes's reliance on candid contrivance in economic relationships. Certain principles were fundamental and over a period were to be obeyed. But in the short run, which was his usual preoccupation, crises were to be met by deliberate adjustments though they departed from established rules. He cherished *laissez faire*, competition, individualist response to the profit motive, but was never backward in devising and urging measures of national, even international, control to forestall or repair misfortunes. In this respect he was a liberal, and, from time to time, the active supporter and adviser of the Liberal Party. As compared with the socialist planning of the Labor Party, whose accession to power he deplored, his prescriptions were indirect, often problematical in operation.

In viewing Keynes's schemes for promoting stability and progress one is reminded of the mock mechanical devices of the cartoonist Rube Goldberg. Instead of going upstairs and turning the faucets a householder would rig a series of gadgets to draw his bath. An alarm clock would spill seed in the parrot's cage; when the bird hopped from his perch the force pulled a cord which released a spring which banged a door which— supply more intermediate effects—would admit water to the tub in the desired mixture of hot and cold. As applied to Keynes's expedients, this illustration is an exaggeration, but the roundabout, inferential, frequently conjectural character is in point. In instances Keynes's ingenious arrangements of cause and result raise the question whether the game is worth the candle. Would it not be simpler and surer, if "natural" forces were to be overridden anyhow, to achieve the object without fuss? However that may be, Keynes in his more elaborate methods preferred to pay at least lip service to orthodoxy, pending return, hopefully, to traditional ways.

In 1925 Maynard Keynes married Lydia Lopokova, a principal ballerina of Diaghilev's (Russian) company, which had performed in London for a period of years with appreciation and then promotion by Keynes. Cambridge eyebrows were lifted until Lydia's simplicity and charm banished confusion of her delightful art with the "chorus line." She had earlier become a favorite in the Bloomsbury circles in which Keynes moved. Lydia Keynes, with her intelligence, spontaneity, and wit made her husband's life joyous. When his health became precarious she was his guardian, so far as possible, against his overexertion.

We come now to Keynes's principal theoretical works. In estimating the originality of the "Keynesian economics" we must remember that certain concepts and modes of analysis now familiar were introduced by him. We are tempted to call them traditional, forgetting that we owe them to Keynes. On the other hand, since he was insufficiently acquainted with some portions of previously held doctrine—and who is not?—he supposed that he was pioneering in a number of areas which had been explored before him. To a degree he suffered from "the tyranny of the unread." Also many who are absorbed in the "Keynesian revolution" fail to revert to earlier writers who expressed basically similar or closely related ideas.

The chief region of thought and proposals which Keynes seems to have neglected was the socialism of Marx and Engels. Aside from the celebrity and influence of their writings, this omission is strange because Keynes knew the English Fabians, modifiers of Marxism. Even more pertinent, the Bolshevik Revolution and the launch of the Soviets into Communism was the most startling economic development of Keynes's lifetime. Besides, his wife was Russian and he visited Leningrad, but he showed little perception of the momentous lesson of the Russian departure. Another blind spot of this learned scholar appears to have been the preachments of the nationalist economists, especially the Americans spanning more than a century from Alexander Hamilton to Simon N. Patten. We shall speak of anticipations of Keynes's thought and advocacy in both the Marxists (and other socialists) and the nationalist school.

Keynes's *Treatise on Money* (1930) and *General Theory of Employment, Interest and Money* (1936), were both published in the crisis of economic collapse, during the Great Depression. Idleness of men, materials, and machines, drop of prices and profits, disappearance of credit, derangement of currencies and commerce were in consternating contrast to capacity for production demonstrated shortly before. How explain this sudden rending of the capitalist fabric? How could prosperity be restored and kept on a course of progress? Keynes rejected the remedy of liquidation, which, reluctantly, was favored by adherents of *laissez faire* economics. For him the cure of deflation, centering especially on reduction of wages, must be worse than the disease. Bluestone (vitriol) will correct a case of poison ivy—by taking off the skin! Traditionalists said that if panic had been brought on by overspending, thrift must come to the rescue.

Keynes reversed this dour advice. Emphasis should be upon spending; consumption—not tightening the belt—would sustain prices, the prospect of profit, and therefore enterprise and fresh investment. Production was limited not by supply of capital resources, but by demand for goods and services. He showed elaborately how depression of wages would diminish consumption and thus scuttle incentive to resumption of output. Unfortunately, in the capitalist organization of society, saving and investment were in the hands of different persons, separate sectors of the economy. On occasion the actions of the two did not coincide. If investment exceeded saving, the result was swollen prosperity. If saving outran capital outlay, the consequence was depression with all its distressing manifestations.

It is easy to see why Keynes was preoccupied with consumption. Millions of people, unable to find work, could not buy goods which were in surplus supply. Warehouses and granaries were overflowing. Food and fibers were deliberately destroyed while masses of the unemployed went hungry and poorly clothed. Growing cotton and corn were ploughed under, meat animals were slaughtered for soap, coffee was dumped into the ocean, potatoes and fruits were allowed to rot in the fields. Children could not go to school because they lacked shoes. And why? Because we had too many shoes. The paradox: society was poor because it was rich. This imbecile state must drive anyone—not just a thoughtful Cambridge economist—to ask, Why can't we use what we have?

Thus impelled, Keynes worked out a theory of consumption to explain the stultifying breakdown. Consumption—or, rather, the demand for consumer goods—was his starting-point. This led him into his solution of the riddle of economic fluctuations, the succession of good times and bad times. An individual family has a "propensity to consume." This novel expression has a particular meaning, simple enough, but it must be understood. A family is in the habit of devoting a certain proportion of its income to buying goods and services, and the remainder it ordinarily saves. Perhaps there is no remainder, maybe the family uses the whole of its income for food, clothing, houseroom, fuel, education, recreation, etc. If independent income is exceedingly low or nonexistent, the family consumes more than current income by using savings, or going into debt, or receiving charity. It is the generally observed fact that as income of the family increases, a larger proportion of the income is not devoted to consumption but is left over for saving. A family with, say, an income of a hundred thousand dollars a year already possesses what it wishes for a full life, not only necessities and comforts, but luxuries, and can put large amounts into savings.

The propensity of the individual family to consume, the proportion of its income which it customarily consumes, according to size of income, applies more or less to all families in the community. Thus we may speak of aggregate propensity to consume. This is an average, true for any particular time, or in the short run. But we must introduce certain qualifications or refinements. The community's propensity to consume will not be altered by more income corresponding to higher prices or by lower income accompanied by lower prices. If living costs more or less, under the conditions, the proportion of income spent on consumption will not change. If the community spent five-sixths of its income on consumption before the increase in income and prices, or before a fall in income and prices, it will continue, in the short run anyhow, to divide its income between consumption and saving in the habitual way. Changes in propensity to consume do not follow from changes in money income and prices but from changes in real income—that is, changes in the amount of consumption goods money will buy.

Another refinement is of more importance. We spoke above

of a given level of income of a single family, and of that family's propensity to consume at that income, or the proportion of its income which it will devote to consumption. Suppose the individual family's income rises (real income, or more money coming in while prices remain the same). What proportion of its *additional* income will be used for consumption? What part of the *extra* or *new* income of $100 or $1000 will go for consumption? Remembering that families with larger real incomes assign a smaller proportion of income to consumption, it is plain that the part of the fresh increment of income spent for living costs will be less than was true of the last $100 or $1000 of old income.

The proportion of *additional* income used for consumption, we may say, marks the *marginal* propensity to consume. The marginal propensity to consume becomes clearer if we contrast it with the average propensity to consume. We have seen that the average falls as real income rises. But the marginal propensity to consume (the proportion of extra income which is consumed) falls faster than the average. Maybe five-sixths of former income went for consumption. But only four-sixths or two-thirds of the extra income goes for consumption. Of course, added in, this two-thirds of the last increment of income spent for consumption pulls down the average a little, but only a little, because the additional income is small as compared with the bulk of the family's income. But a line or curve representing marginal propensity to consume will tend to flatten as compared to a line defining the average propensity to consume. Make the additions to income many enough or large enough and the line standing for marginal propensity to consume will turn downward.

It is obvious that marginal propensity to consume applies to a changing or dynamic situation, not to a static condition of income. It gives us a moving picture, not a snapshot. However, these changes in propensity to consume due to changes in real income of families are going on all the time. At any one moment they melt into the community's propensity to consume. If we want to speak of how the community behaves if it gets more or less real income, we must have in mind marginal propensity to consume, for only this gives us a picture of change.

Now what of saving? For Keynes, saving is simply not consuming, not using up for purposes of living. If part of income is not used up in food, clothing, recreation, and other needs, what becomes of it? It is used to increase production. It goes to sustain workers who are getting out raw materials, building factories, roads, and other means of creating fresh income. Thus saving (not consuming) is equal to investment. Keynes in earlier writing had assumed the possibility of a disparity between the two—saving and investment—but later, in the *General Theory,* he correctly made them identical. His idea of the exact correspondence of saving and investment involves his definition of investment, which is an addition to the community's income. One who merely buys existing stocks and bonds is transferring claims on income, but he is not serving to create new income. The same applies to one who buys land for the sake of receiving the rent. He is living, to that extent, from what is already being produced. The point becomes clearer when we remember that money is a mere medium of exchange. Money is not capital. Money may be used to bring capital into existence—may put men and materials and machinery to work. Or it may be used to acquire, for purposes of consumption, goods and services already available. Again, true saving is investment, and only investment, leading to added output.

We do not need to halt over the motives of persons for saving, or, more accurately, not consuming. They want to enjoy the same satisfaction, or a greater satisfaction, at some time in the future, or to afford this benefit to those who inherit from them. Just as an individual or a family has a propensity to consume, so the individual or family has a propensity to save, or not to consume. And so, thinking of the entire community, we have a social or "aggregate" propensity to save (not consume). We may speak of the average propensity to save, or of the marginal propensity to save. These two, as with the propensity to consume, are different. The *marginal* propensity to save is the proportion of additional income which we are inclined to save.

Employing this feature of aggregate marginal propensity to save, we come upon a happy circumstance. If we devote work, materials, and equipment to additional production (make new capital outlays which do not merely take the place of old capital outlays which have been exhausted or become obsolete), society enjoys not only additional consumption, but gets back the whole of the capital outlay. Investment multiplies itself.

How? Take the case of the enterpriser who built the first cotton seed oil mill. Cotton seed had previously gone to waste, but now it would be crushed to get useful goods—cooking and salad oil, a main constituent for oleomargarine, the hulls become cattle feed, and many by-products result. This is true investment, creation of additional utilities. How the enterpriser secures the needed means of paying for bricks and mortar and machinery and workmen to erect the factory does not matter. He may use money already in his possession or he may borrow it.

In bringing the factory into existence he pays out $1,000,000. This investment is immediate income to suppliers of materials and to construction workers. Those receiving this new income have a desire to consume, say, two-thirds of it. This is the marginal propensity to consume. They will pay out two-thirds of $1,000,000 to butcher, baker, and candlestick maker, or some $667,000, and the remaining $333,000 is saved (not consumed). The process continues. The butcher, baker, and others, obeying the same marginal propensity to consume, devote to living expenses two-thirds of their new income, or $445,000, and save $222,000. In the next stage consumption is $296,000 (that is, two-thirds of $445,000) and saving is the remainder, or $148,000. Of course the increments to consumption and saving after a while run out. If you wish to do the arithmetic, you will see that when the effect of the investment of $1,000,000 is completed, the community will have a factory worth this amount, plus having enjoyed $3,000,000 of additional income, which has taken the form of $2,000,000 of consumption goods and services, and $1,000,000 of new saving.

This process of increase of income (consumption and saving) Keynes called the "multiplier" effect of new investment. The propulsive force of new investment diminishes in result, as when a stone is tossed into a still lake the first wave circle, immediately surrounding the place where the stone dropped, is pronounced, the next wave circle, more distant, is less pronounced, and finally no further wave circle is visible. In the case supposed (a marginal propensity to consume two-thirds of new income), the multiplier is three. The original investment multiplies itself three times. If the community wants to consume a higher proportion of its additional income, say nine-tenths, then the multiplier will be ten. In other words, the higher the proportion of new income devoted to consumption the better. This is obvious. The purpose of production is consumption.

The same principle, unfortunately, works in reverse. Suppose a decline in investment (the oil mill is not built, the clay pit does not yield bricks, iron ore does not become machinery, workmen are not employed in construction). Now investment, income, and consequently consumption and saving shrink, in multiples.

What has been said brings us to the question of employment. In any economy employment (the means of living) is foremost. Every society should afford opportunity to all who are able and willing to work to derive a livelihood from their efforts. In a capitalist economy the mass of the population is dependent on wages offered by owners of the means of production. These employers, in turn, are motivated by the desire—indeed the need—for profit. They operate under a system of prices—of labor (wages), of capital (interest), and of natural resources (rent), all related to the prices of commodities. Since there is no over-all control or plan, the price-profit-wage mechanism often functions imperfectly. Unfortunately, it often fails to furnish full employment. "Full employment" has come to be a euphemism for an economy that functions satisfactorily. Many refer to "the goal of full employment" as an ideal to be reached and maintained; in the expression lurks the admission that this condition is not the normal one. This amounts to the severest indictment of the efficiency of the economy.

Prior to Keynes most economists contended that the only way to reduce unemployment is to reduce real wages. This will reduce cost of production, output will be increased, and, at the lower prices of goods prevailing, demand will revive. The unemployed will have been absorbed, and all set right.

Not so, said Keynes. When money wages are cut, workers must cut their consumption. Since workers comprise the bulk of the community and have the highest propensity to consume, aggregate demand will fall off. The increase in supply of goods will not be bought, even at lower prices, for the workers' money wages have been cut proportionately. Indeed, in all probability money wages have been cut by more than, or before, prices have been reduced. At best, real wages have not been improved. Workers (practically the community as a whole) can buy no more than before. Output shrinks, unemployment persists. The only change is that the economy staggers along at a lower level of wages and prices.

Economists holding to the classical expedient (cut real wages) sought for an answer to Keynes, who had discredited their analysis. One reply was that of Pigou, Keynes's friend, teacher, and colleague. When wages, and consequently prices, fall, persons with assets of fixed money value (bonds, annuities, savings deposits, cash on hand) find themselves better off, vis-à-vis prices of goods and services. They increase their consumption, demand and employment rise, and so the original wage reduction has had the effect of improving employment. This result is doubtful. The holders of assets of fixed value, or even of income the purchasing power of which has increased, constitute a relatively small proportion of consumers; their propensity to consume is comparatively low; instead of loosening their purse strings, they may prefer to wait for still lower prices.

Keynes found that, contrary to classical *laissez faire* doctrine, equilibrium might be reached at less than full employment. How get the machine going, move the driving wheels off of dead center? For him the only means was to increase aggregate demand. In the short run, at least, this would not be generated by any force within the private economy. Government intervention (collective and planned) is required. Public resources must give a blood transfusion to the anaemic capitalist economy. To change the figure, the hand of government, the organized community, must wind the spring of the clock which threatens to run down.

Little can be done to stimulate private investment directly, and by this avenue employment and consumer demand. President Hoover in the United States near the onset of the Great Depression of the 'thirties summoned representatives of principal industrial corporations to the White House and exhorted them to expand their operations, particularly by constructing new facilities, such as factories and power plants. Some promised to try, but this "pep talk" was a waste of breath. Generous lending by banks cannot persuade business men to borrow because, while demand for goods is languid, they see no prospect of gain. Keynes thought that lowering the rate of interest invited little investment so long as consumers remained numb.

If investors will not produce and consumers will not or

cannot spend, then government must substitute for both groups. How will government get the means of emergency expenditures? If by extra taxation, the tendency will be to reduce spending by those taxed. As a choice of evils, tax the rich, for they consume a smaller proportion of their income than do those receiving less. But taxes from any source will not yield the massive sums which government must suddenly command.

Among his recommendations for exit from depression, Keynes is best known for advocating deficit spending. That is, government must go into debt for public works, huge loans to business men to take the place of private lending that has dried up, and for relief to the unemployed, many of them destitute. The government will do best to borrow from commercial banks, for they create additional media of payment by giving the government the right to draw on deposits in return for government bonds sold to them. This method of obtaining funds is more indirect than the expedient of printing paper money; it is preferable in several respects, though the result is the same. Of course deficit spending, by definition, unbalances the budget; the government is living beyond its (tax) income. In America in the 'thirties this was decried by many who lingered in the old belief that in time of depression government should practice frugality, not largesse. The wickedness of deficit spending was therefore given the name of "pump priming."

The hope, not entirely imaginary, was that by pouring a little water down into the pump it would begin to suck an abundant stream from the well of resources in the private economy. The "multiplier" would come into operation. Those who received the money—investing enterprisers and consumers —would pass on all or most of it to others, who in their turn, according to their propensity to consume, would transfer a large proportion to still others. This process, so far as it extended, was beneficial. But unless the pump itself truly went to work, drawing purchasing power from the well, not simply from the Treasury, the impulse to spending exhausted itself. In practice it was soon proved that besides furnishing the priming, the Treasury must, in fact, for the time being, become the well. Government must create and sustain demand by a prodigious flow of purchasing media not forthcoming from any other source.

Some who urged this policy believed that deficit spending,

enormous as it was in the United States, should have been pursued on a far larger scale. Then, in their view, the stubborn Great Depression would have been earlier ended. Maybe so. The recession, or relapse, of 1937 followed reduction of the flow of public funds, and it was necessary to resume deficit spending. Further, after eight years of deficit financing and other expedients, this country still had some 8,000,000 unemployed. The unemployed were not returned to work until the government was plunged into the uncalculated deficit spending necessitated by entrance into World War II.

We have been able to offer, in quick outline, only the most applicable features of Keynes's thought. As his *Treatise on Money* and *General Theory* were written for specialists, they are in technical language and, as Charles Lamb would say, they are "villainously pranked" with mathematic formulas. Keynes's expositors—several are particularly recommended below—plus government economists who embodied his ideas in one way or another in practical policy, have transmitted his emphasis to many, perhaps millions who would not puzzle out Keynes's original propositions. We have said that not all he arrived at was novel, though he may not have been aware of earlier models. Marx anticipated Keynes in the principal contention that economic depressions follow from a failure of mass purchasing power. The workers are chronically unable to buy back what they have produced, and recurrently this fading of effective demand becomes acute and precipitates collapse of the economy. Marx, as did Keynes later, talked in terms of aggregates, of the whole of capitalist society, rather than of particular units, whether firms or workers and consumers. Disciples of the economic nationalists (especially the American, Patten) held that, as a consequence of the Industrial Revolution and science, advanced countries passed years ago from a deficit to a surplus economy. This made it appropriate to shift concern from saving to spending, from parsimony to robust consumption.

While Keynes's analyses were more detailed, not to say more intricate, than previous ones, he was not the detached inquirer; he aimed to produce serviceable reforms in economic behavior. As Professor Murad has remarked, "His theories were designed to support the economic policies he championed . . ." His purpose was not to supplant capitalism, but to protect capitalism by correcting assumptions and conduct which produce economic instability with its alternating evils of inflation and contraction. His program called for a degree of government guidance, promotion, and rescue—that is, public guarantee and planning—that would almost subvert the premises of capitalism. He did not think so, nor do those who avow his doctrines. Perhaps Keynes's reforms, though stopping short of renovation, will prove to be significant in the long process by which the economies of democratic countries are transformed.

We may not leave Keynes the man with the publication of his chief theoretical works in the nineteen-thirties. As after World War I he prophesied destruction from the Treaty of Versailles, so after World War II he strove to set the continents on an even keel in currencies and commerce. He played a leading role in the Bretton Woods conference (1946) which provided the greatest controls of all in the International Monetary Fund and International Bank for Reconstruction and Development. He was the successful chief pleader for Britain for a postwar loan from the United States. He had been created Baron Keynes of Tilton. He did not live long to enjoy these triumphs, the esteem in which he was held in many lands, and the large fortune he had accumulated, in great part by bold stock speculation. He had long suffered from heart disease, worsened by constant work and worry in the public behalf. He died almost instantly of an attack on April 21, 1946.

For Further Reading

Keynes, John Maynard, *The Economic Consequences of the Peace* (New York: Harcourt, Brace & World, Inc., 1920).

———, *A Treatise on Money* (New York: Harcourt, Brace & World, Inc., 2 vols., 1930).

———, *The General Theory of Employment, Interest and Money* (New York: Harcourt, Brace & World, Inc., 1936).

Murad, Anatol, *What Keynes Means* (New York: Bookman Associates, 1963). Particularly clear in brief compass.

Dillard, Dudley, *The Economics of John Maynard Keynes* (New York: Prentice-Hall, Inc., 1948; London: Crosby Lockwood & Son, 1956).

Hansen, Alvin H., *A Guide to Keynes* (New York: McGraw Hill Book Co., Inc., 1953).

Kurihara, Kenneth K., *Introduction to Keynesian Dynamics* (New York: Columbia University Press, 1956).

Harrod, Roy F., *The Life of John Maynard Keynes* (New York: Harcourt, Brace & World, Inc., 1951).

INDEX